Wesley's Philosophy
of
Education for Socio-Spiritual Change

Christian Heritage Rediscovered - 38

Wesley's Philosophy of Education for Socio-Spiritual Change

H. G. Mithra

CWI
Christian World Imprints™

First Published in 2016 by

Christian World Imprints(TM)
Christian Publishing & Books from India
H-12 Bali Nagar, **New Delhi-110015**
info@christianworldimprints.com
www.ChristianWorldImprints.com
Phone: +91 11 25465925

ISBN: 978-93-5148-131-7 (HB) ISBN: 978-93-5148-132-4 (PB)

Cataloging in Publication Data--DK
Courtesy: D.K. Agencies (P) Ltd. <docinfo@dkagencies.com>

Mithra, H. G., author.
Wesley's philosophy of education for socio-spiritual change / H.G. Mithra.
pages cm. -- (Christian heritage rediscovered ; 38)
ISBN 9789351481317 (HB)
ISBN 9789351481324 (PB)

1. Wesley, John, 1703-1791--Philosophy. 2. Christian education--Philosophy. 3. Methodist Church--Education--India--Karnataka. I. Title. II. Series: Christian heritage rediscovered ; 38.

BX8495.W5M58 2016 DDC 268.87 23

Dedicated to
My family and Student friends.

Foreword

In the ongoing saga of efforts to improve pedagogy - it's philosophy and practice - Prof. H. G. Mithra's comprehensive study of *Wesley's Philosophy of Education for Socio-Spiritual Change* brings together a number of pedagogical elements and educators, among which are two interesting and significant educationalists, John Wesley from 18th century England and Paulo Freire from 20th century Brazil. While Wesley - the founder, with brother Charles and fellow Anglican cleric, George Whitefield, of the Evangelical Movement known as Methodism - was a man of his times, he was also an innovator in his persuasion that Christian education be dialogic in method and about humanization, liberation and justice in substance. In his comparative study of Wesley's pedagogy and purpose, Mithra also sets forth highlights of Paulo Freire, the 20th century Brazilian philosopher and educator, and leading proponent of a critical pedagogy. This reexamination of Wesley's perspective on education in the light of Freire's critical pedagogy exposes striking similarities between the two. Rejecting what Freire calls the traditional "banking" approach which considers students as empty accounts be filled by the teacher, both Wesley and Freire contend that education must be dialogic, rather than monologic, in a creative process wherein teacher and student together recognize their incompleteness and strive to be more fully human. There is here no such thing as a neutral education process. Education either functions as an instrument which is used to facilitate the integration of traditional generations into the logic of the present system and bring about conformity to it, or it becomes the praxis of freedom, the means by which men and women deal critically with reality and discover how to participate in the transformation of their world. With these considerations in mind Mithra has some significant recommendations for the future trajectory of vital education. All in all, this is a book that ought to be read by all who are concerned with critical education, especially Christian education, as it is of significant relevance and vital interest.

Washington D.C. 2016

Revd. Dr. David C. Scott
Professor of Religion and Culture
Leonard Theological College (Jabalpur), and
United Theological College (Banglore)
(Retired and lives in USA)

Acknowledgement

After a long wait the dream of publishing major part of my research is being realized. Courtesy Christian World Imprints and our Friend Sudhanshu Kanda whose motivation did the trick. I was dreaming for some foreign publishers to help me in this endeavour, but things did not go the way I wanted it to be. Finally, I gave up of seeking foreign publishers due to friendly persuasion of Mr. Sudhanshu, I thank God for his major role played in bringing out this book.

I would continue to retain those whom I thanked with gratitude in my thesis. Major portion of this book belongs to my doctoral thesis. I have made some changes and added some more material which was not part of the thesis.

I am happy to acknowledge that through many struggles, stresses and strains I have reached a stage which I never thought of. The Lord's promise was good to me all these years to realize my long cherished dream of doctoral studies and its publication. Glory and honour belongs to the Almighty God for the unforgetable experiences and processes of learning he took me through, at this age. I owe everything to God and His people.

Late Dr. Samson Prabhakar for facilitating my study programme and being my guide at initial stages. Late Rev. Dr. Fr. Paul Puthanangady, the former Rector of Kristu Jyothi and Director of Vishvadeep, who guided my work patiently with a touch of fatherly care and compassion. He provoked my thinking and helped me to shape my flow of thoughts and consistency in writing. He was a real father figure to me. Despite being busy in his work he spared his precious time for me. I am indebted to his guidance, help and support during the research work. I wish he was around to read this publication.

I am extremely grateful to Dr. David C. Scott, for writing a cryptic foreword. He was my teacher, guide and friend who gave his life time service to India and now leading a happy retired life at Washington D.C. USA.

The Serampore College and College Council played very important role in more ways than one. Serampore College administration arranged a brief exposure trip to Regent's Park College, Oxford, United Kingdom; this book is a byproduct of these helps that were rendered to me while I was engaged in research. I am also thankful to the college for allowing me to use a major part of my doctoral thesis in this research work. My sincere thanks to all those who played their helpful role during those years of research.

I am greatly indebted to my friend and sponsor Revd. Dr. Nicholas Wood, the Fellow and Dean of Regent's Park College and the Director of Oxford Centre for Christianity & Culture, University of Oxford, for facilitating and raising funds to cover this brief trip in consultation with Regent Park College authorities. He has been a blessing and a true friend indeed. He and his colleagues took care of me and my needs while finalizing my work at Oxford. I wish to acknowledge with appreciation, the Principal Revd. Dr. Robert Ellis, Executive Secretary to the Principal Ms. Fiona Floate, the Librarians Ms. Sheila Wood, Ms. Emma Walsh and other Staff of the Regents. Dr. Paul Sheppen and Dr. Peter Colyer of Regents were kind to me. I owe them big thanks. The Revd. Gill Crippen, Regional Minister of Baptist Union of Great Britain, for her generosity and friendship. Dr. Wood and Revd. Crippen were gracious people who made my life comfortable and easy in a strange land like Oxford so that I could work on my research comfortably.

I record my sincere thanks to the various libraries and Librarians of Bodleian, Lincoln, Bristol Baptist College, Bristol; Dr. Steven Finamore, the Principal; Revd. Dr. Ernest Lucas senior most staff and Vice-Principal of the Bristol Baptist College; Dr. Michael Brealey, Librarian, Wesley College, Bristol; Mr. David Worthington Manager of Wesley Chapel, New Room in Bristol; Mr. David Brown former archivist of Kingswood School Bath who helped me to visit important places and get information about Wesley and his educational philosophy.

The whole research work would have been impossible had it not been for my dearest friends and sponsors – Dr. Allan Bapty, his wife Patricia Bapty; Ms. Clare Lillington and their Church donors at Chudleigh, Newton; and Devon, UK. They were on a private visit to Serampore College in 2002, and called on us along with Dr. Allan Bapty and his wife. They audited one of my lectures for Bachelor of Divinity students at Serampore. They spent some time with us and went on their way back to Calcutta. It was like any other visitors visiting us during that year, and there I thought the matter has come to an end. In an answer to our request and prayers to God, they wrote to us after a year to say that they have raised funds from two elderly ladies to support our doctoral studies in India. We were stunned and spellbound. It was amazing! (One of the elderly ladies has already gone to be with the Lord). Baptys held on to that money till I got admitted to the doctoral programme in 2005. Such was their earnestness and sincerity in seeing me through doctoral studies. They stood with me like an unshakable rock throughout my studies at Bangalore. We as a family were able to manage our lives because of their sustained and timely support. They were indeed God-sent angels (from unknown quarters on September 6, 2002). We are ever so grateful to these dear souls.

Apart from them we have had many well wishers, prayer partners who were of immense source of strength in more ways than one. Many friends from UK, UAE and US did uphold us in their prayers and with occasional help. A host of them have done something beautiful for us; out of them two families deserve special mention at this point in time; they are the N. E. Soans' and P. Maben's families. They have been such faithful friends since 2007 till 2009. I owe them all my sincere thanks. It is my prayer that God shall reward them for every act of kindness shown to us. I thank Rev. Ernest Victor and Rev. John Weir, Ministers of the Anglican Church at Dubai for doing their bit in 2008-2009.

I am thankful to many of my pastor friends, their congregations in Bangalore and elsewhere. They have been a support to me through their prayers and encouragement. While research was stressful and the Church was a place of relief, I let go my stress and strain while worshiping with them.

I thank the Archivist Mr. David Brown, Principal Mr. Simon Morris, former Principal Gary M. Best of Kingswood School which Wesley started way back in 1748; they were very helpful in providing materials for my research work. I thank Dr. Christopher J. Anderson, Methodist Librarian, Drew University, Madison, New Jersey, USA, for photo copying a rare book and sending it through Mrs. Margaret Shafer. I thank her for locating the book and carrying it for me. She was called to the eternal rest two years ago.

I thank profusely Revd. Arun Kumar Wesley for editing, correcting and even helping me to shape my thinking and thoughts at times. He was more than a mere help. I thank Mrs. Margaret Shafer for her help in reading the manuscripts and making helpful suggestions for improvement.

UTC librarian Mrs. Rita Wesley and her staff were extremely kind and supportive in providing all the material needed for this research. I thank them all for every help rendered to me. My student friends were great help too. I also acknowledge the help and support I received from the librarians of SAIACS, St Peter's Seminary and Dharmaram College and others.

The SATHRI staff, were of great help in times of need. Every little thing they did was a big help and encouragement.

All my work would be impossible without the help of my beloved family. Their constant prayers, patience and understanding when I was going through immense pressure during the studies. My wife Irene did her best in supporting my work by taking the load of daily affairs of the family including children's studies at home, keying in material on the computer and proof reading at times. Disha was a refreshing factor with all her antics during the course of my research. Divya, Deepa, Disha and Irene were supportive of the research work through their daily prayers. Particularly all three of them – Divya, Deepa and Disha helped me while sorting out the questionnaire-answers and in their tabulation too. I owe them all a big hug and thanks.

Also, I thank my mother and other sisters for their moral and prayer support.

My close family friends, especially a dear student Samuel P. Rajan and his family who were generous to me; he went out of his ways to take me to Kristu Jyothi to see my guide beyond Krishanrajpuram. Members of Wesley Church, prayer partners and well wishers deserve a big thank you from me. Apart from these, there are many more who have been sources of encouragement and blessing, I thank them all.

Particularly all the Methodist pastors, principals, hostel superintendents, teachers, youth and members whose co-operation was great during the interviews and questionnaires. I thank all of them for their help and support.

In fact, I must thank the Union Biblical Seminary for compelling me to publish this book. If had the time, I would have done better job of turning this into a text book. I hope to do that whenever I get an opportunity.

List of Abbreviations

CE	=	Christian Education
CEEFI	=	Christian Education Department of Evangelical Fellowship of India
CRE	=	Christian Religious Education
cf. (latin word *confer*),	=	compare one source with another
DS	=	District Superintendent (like Area Chairman in Church of South India)
e.g. (*exempli gratia*),	=	for example
ed., eds	=	editor, editors
et al. (*et alii*),	=	and others refering to other authors
etc. (*et cetera*),	=	and others of the same class
HIV/AIDS	=	Human Immunodeficiency Virus/Acquired Immune Deficiency Syndrome.
IMC	=	Indira Nagar Methodist Church
ISSU	=	India Sunday School Union
ibid. (*ibidem*),	=	same source
i.e. (*id est*),	=	that is to say
KMC	=	Koramangala Methodist Church
MCI	=	Methodist Church in India
MCSA	=	Methodist Church in Southern Asia
MYF	=	Methodist Youth Fellowship
NCCI	=	National Christian Council of India
n.d.	=	no date
NGOs	=	Non-Governamental Organizations
n.p.	=	no page
p., pp	=	page, pages
RE	=	Religious Education
RTMC	=	Richmond Town Methodist Church
[sic]	=	thus (used to indicate that an error in a quoted passage was in the original; placed immediately after thc error)

SCM	=	Student Christian Movement
SCMI	=	Student Christian Movement of India
SIRC	=	South India Region Conference
SPCK	=	Society for Proclamation of Christian Knowledge
SVM	=	Student Voluntary Movement
SS	=	Sunday School
s.v. (*sub verbo, sub voce*)	=	under the word or heading; used for making references to listings in encyclopedias and dictionaries.
TNIV	=	Todays New International Version
VBS	=	Vacation Bible School
Vol., vols	=	volume, volumes, as in "vol. XII"
WSCS	=	Women's Society for Christian Service
YMCA	=	Young Men's Christian Association

Principal Events in John Wesley's Life[1]

1703	17 June, Born at Epworth.
1707	18 December, Charles Wesley was born.
1709	9 February, John Wesley was rescued from Rectory fire.
1714-20	28 January, Admitted to the Charterhouse School London.
1720	Enters Christ's Church, Oxford.
1725	19 September, Ordained Deacon.
1726	17 March, Elected Fellow of Lincoln College, Oxford.
1728	22 September, Ordained Priest.
1729	The "Holy Club," founded at Oxford.
1735	25 April, Death of His father.
	21 October, Sails for Georgia.
1736	5 February, Landed in Georgia.
1737	2 December, Returns to England.
1738	1 February, Landed in England.
	1 May, Fetter Lane Religious Society founded.
	Meets Peter Bohler.
	24 May, Evangelical Conversion at Aldersgate Street.
1739	First open-air preaching in Bristol and Kingswood.
	Building the new room, Bristol (May-June).
	11 First service at the Foundery in London. Begins to publish his *Journal.*
1740	The Methodists separate from the Moravians.
1741	Separation from Whitefield.
1742	Allows lay Preaching. First visit to New Castle upon Tyne.
	Death of his mother, Susannah Wesley.
1743	First visit to Cornwall, the riots at Wednesbury.
1744	25 June, First Methodist Conference in London.
	24 August, His last University sermon.

[1] Dates and events are collected from different sources and certain events mentioned by other authors are not recorded for they were not considered very important. Bonamy Dobree, *John Wesley: Great lives* (London: DuckWorth, 1933), pp. 7-8.

1747	First Visit to Ireland.
1748	24 June, Opens new Kingswood School.
1751	18 February, Marries Mrs. Vazeille. 1 June, Resigns from his Fellowship. His first visit to Scotland.
1755	Conference discusses separation from the Church of England, judged "not expedient."
1769	First Preachers sent to America.
1770	30 September, Death of Whitefield.
1771	His wife leaves him. Definite break with the Calvinists.
1778	1 November, City Road Chapel opened in London. Starts *Arminian Magazine.*
1779	Is Wesley to rule alone? Discussed by conference of preachers at Bath.
1781	8 October, Death of his wife Mary Wesley.
1784	1-2 September, He Ordains Priests for first time. Appoints Thomas Coke and Francis Asbury as Superintendents.
1788	29 March, Death of Charles Wesley.
1790	27 July, Wesley's last conference. 6 October, last open-air sermon.
1791	23 February, His last sermon at Leatherhead. 2 March, Dies at 88th year. 9 March, burial at City Road Chapel, London.

List of Tables

Table One: Respondents, Sex, and Age Group
Table Two: Educational Qualifications of Respondents
Table Three: Urban and Rural Respondents
Table Four: Age of the (Respondents') Church
Table Five: Church has grown in all aspects
Table Six: Church Services
Table Seven: Enjoy Worship Services
Table Eight: Describe your Church Service
Table Nine: Who contributes to the Inspirational Services?
Table Ten: Ministry of the Church is Edifying
Table Eleven: Church Leaders/Pastor – a general opinion of the members/ministers
Table Twelve: John Wesley's Theological and Spiritual Teachings
Table Thirteen: Founders Day Celebration
Table Fourteen: Educational and Boarding Institutions
Table Fifteen: Sunday school Materials used in the Church
Table Sixteen: Sunday school Materials promote Transformation
Table Seventeen: Describe your Sunday school
Table Eighteen: Sunday school Leaders/Teachers
Table Nineteen: Methods of teaching applied in Sunday schools
Table Twenty: Major activities of the Youth
Table Twenty One: Role of the Youth in main Church Services
Table Twenty Two: Fellowships are training ground for Leadership
Table Twenty Three: Activities of Women's Fellowship
Table Twenty Four: John Wesley - his educational thoughts & practices
Table Twenty Five: Meaning of Christian Education
Table Twenty Six: Objectives of Christian Education

Table Twenty Seven: Available Sources for Children to make Moral/Ethical Decision

Table Twenty Eight: Most Cherished Family Values

Table Twenty Nine: Influences on your Character Formation

Table Thirty: General Survey of Educational System in India

Contents

Foreword vii

Acknowledgement ix

List of Abbreviations xiii

Principal Events in John Wesley's Life xv

List of Tables xvii

Introduction 1

Chapter 1: Wesley and the Methodist Movement 15

A. A Brief Survey of the Context 17

B. A Short Biography of John Wesley 28

C. Founding of the Movement 39

Chapter 2: John Wesley- The Educator 45

A. The Formation of his Thoughts on Education with its Philosophical Grounding and its Analysis from a Biblical and Theological Perspective 47

B. Wesley and Christian Education: A Biblical and Theological Perspective 75

C. Distinct Characteristics of Wesley's Educational Theory and Approach 97

D. Limits in John Wesley's Method and Pedagogical Approach to Christian Education 105

Chapter 3: Analysis of the Empirical Data Tracing the Link in the use of Wesley's Educational Method in the Christian Education Ministry of the Methodist Churches in Karnataka 109

A. Biblical and Theological Foundations of Educational Ministry 112

B. Board of Education Ministry of the Methodist Church in Karnataka 113

C. Analysis and Assessment of Christian Education Programmes based on Empirical Study 116

Chapter 4: A Critique of John Wesley's Theory and Practice of Christian Education from the Perspective of Freirean Education Theory of Liberation 153

A. Paulo Freire's Educational Theory and Approach - A Brief Sketch 155

B. Re-reading Wesley's Thoughts on Christian Education, and his Pedagogical Approach from the Perspective of Freirean Liberatory Pedagogical Paradigm 178

Chapter 5: Towards a Relevant Model of Christian Education 197

A. Theological Reflections, Findings and Recommendations 199

B. Relevance of Wesley's Christian Educational thoughts for Contemporary Christian Education, Particularly Methodist Churches in Karnataka 208

Conclusion 215

Bibliography 223

Appendix A 249

Appendix B 253

Appendix C 255

Appendix D 256

Introduction

Many a person in history of thought has rendered yeoman service by serving the society not only by putting forth their thoughts and works, and by their very living but also thinking ahead of their time. Some of their thoughts come in handy as we make our lives and work relevant today. Among the many thoughts and works that these persons propose one of the areas which necessarily needs relevance and implementation is in terms of education – education as in learning and teaching, for transformation and liberation. That is, transformation of lives, in terms of attitudes, outlook and values and in terms of liberation – material, physical and mental bondage, for a transformed society.

Education both formal and informal have had a great influence and impact on people and attitudes, in the proper and normal formation of personalities to uphold values of truth, justice and freedom, for example, for a transformed life and thus towards a transformed society. One thus educated would render the society with leadership, statesmanship and so on to lead the state and the nation at large towards a healthy and a fruitful society.

One of the stalwarts of the Church who has done a remarkable impact on the people at large in terms of inculcating values – Christian values is John Wesley. His leadership in the Church and in the society has had tremendous influence in making education worthwhile – not only inhibiting and strengthening the Gospel values but also in their liberative and thus their transformative aspect.

The history of United Kingdom would have been poorer without the life and story of John Wesley and his immense contributions to transformation of British soci-political and Spiritual life. Wesley stands tall among many leaders of that nation till date. His movement called Methodists spread like wild fire everywhere. It is assumed that it has probably more communicant members than the Anglican Church that disassociated itself from him and his services. He was reformer of a kind in his time.

This study identifies the transformative and liberative factors in John Wesley's thoughts on Christian Education and assesses their relevance to the present day churches in particular Methodist[2] Church in Karnataka.

Christian Education

Christian education teaches its learners to interact with both God and environment resulting in transformation of a person. Christian education is concerned with larger vision for humanity rather than narrow interest of an organization/institution or a denominational church. According to Vimala Paulus, Christian education is to help people attain the knowledge of Christ, that they may consciously make a choice to structure their lives in accordance with what Christ would have them do and be.[3] Wesleyan Christian education could well be defined as biblical theism which is informed by Wesleyan – Arminian [sic] presuppositions which provide a foundation for structuring and communicating a view of God, man and the universe.[4] Paul H. Vieth, a Methodist defines Christian education as the process by which persons are confronted and guided by the Christian gospel.[5] According to many Religious Educators, Christian education is a reflective process – *information for transformation*[6] or faith formation through lifelong learning. In other words, Christian Education is a lifelong journey of learning about oneself, family, the church, society, universe, environment and God in broader sense. Christian Education is not indoctrination of Christian doctrines and dogmas, but teaching people how to practice what it means to be a Christian in word, work and walk. According to Donald Campbell Wyckoff as quoted by author - Christian education is "interested in re-creating personality, restructuring personality, and transforming personality.... Personality configurations ... must be taken as indicative of ways in which the individual can develop abundant Christian living". [7] It is a ministry of education carried out by both language of words and language of relationships, must be personal and divine – human encounter should be responsible for the transmission of the subject matter resulting in credible transformation.

---

[2] There are 300 Churches with 6,00,000 membership in Karnataka. 200 educational institutions; 205 A category Pastors, 250 Preachers and Evangelists according to the Methodist Church Statistician's report of 2006.

[3] Vimala Paulus, *Introducing Christian Education* (Madras: Christian Literature Service, 1986), p.1.

[4] J. Duane Beals, "Doing Christian education in a Wesleyan Mode: A Response to Wesley Tracy," in *Wesleyan Theological Journal*, Vol. 17, No.1, (Spring 1982), p. 54.

[5] Paul H. Vieth, *The Church and Christian Education* (St. Louis: The Bethany Press, 1960), n.p.

[6] Emphasis is mine.

[7] H. G. Mithra, "Analytical Survey of Christian Religious Education and its relationship with other fields of studies" Assessment paper submitted to South Asia Theological Research Institute (SATHRI), Bangalore on 28.10.2005 (unpublished), p. 8.

John Wesley and the Church

John Wesley was an ardent member of the Church of England till his death even though his inclination and support gravitated towards the reformed form of the Church in terms of the Methodist Church which he engineered to project and that which eventually became a separate entity.

As an ordained clergy of the Church of England, John served the Church in all earnestness and commitment, but was struggling in his ministry to make the Gospel relevant to the times and context – one of poverty, unemployment, illiteracy, profligacy and so on, which the Church at that time was unable or unwilling to do. In response to these challenges, John attempted in his own way to resolve these issues with a concern for the people to have a personal relationship with God and thus enabling it forward towards transformed lives. One of the ways in which John tried was through education, providing children and adults towards literacy, inculcating Christian values and outlook that would steer them away from vagrancy, profligacy, alcoholism, etc., so that these transformed people thus have a better chance to get jobs, gain dignity in life, in the Church, family and society.

Having embarked on this vein, John set forth in his own way and within the limitations of resources, facilities and venues for inculcating Christian values through education by setting up schools and Sunday schools besides his preaching in and outside the Church precincts.

Christian Education and John Wesley

Wesleyan Christian educational thinking is based on the three-fold understanding of human beings: Firstly, humanity is graced (prevenient grace), secondly, human beings can hear and understand the gospel, and thirdly, a person is free to receive or reject the whole or part of what one learns. This three-fold understanding of human being, coupled with Wesleyan epistemology called the Quadrilateral[8] truth i.e. Scripture[9], reason, experience and tradition provides a minimal formula for developing a liberative and transformative approach to Christian education.

Wesley's educational thoughts and pedagogy are based on his theological convictions and personal experiences which helped him to formulate an approach to mitigate the existing socio-economic, religio-cultural, political system and a kind of reaction to his contemporaries in the field of education.[10] The nature and

---

[8] J. Duane Beals, "Doing Christian education in a Wesleyan Mode: A Response to Wesley Tracy," in *Wesleyan Theological Journal*, Vol. 17, No. 1, (Spring 1982), p. 54.

[9] Scripture refers to the inspired and sufficient written word of God, the 66 canonical books of the Bible. Upon this foundation church traditions are adopted which agree with the biblical text, and those which are inconsistent are discarded. Next, reason is received as a gift intrinsic to the image of God. Finally, with Scripture, tradition and reason in place, human beings are prepared to *experience* the reality of God's love. *www.theopedia.com/Wesleyan_Quadrilateral - 21k*

[10] James Riley Estep Jr. "John Wesley's Philosophy of formal Childhood Education" in *Christian Education Journal*, Vol. INS, No. 2, (Fall 1997), p. 44.

content of his educational thoughts were centred on Scripture with an objective to liberate humanity and to reform the ritualistic trend in the Church of England as well as the society of his time. Wesley's approach to education was different from the then existing system of learning. Therefore, it is an interesting area to discover by reading and researching his approach to Christian education and derive its relevance for pedagogical excellence today.

Disciplined

John Wesley's Christian education programmes and approaches seem to be harsh for modern Christian educators in more ways than one. Wesley had no room for play in his curriculum. His daily schedule seems to have been heavily packed with subjects and spiritual activities; he did not let the children visit parents until they graduated from the course, they were kept away from the people's environment. Corporal punishment was allowed as part of the discipline. He seems to have had a narrow educational objective – to save souls as against the popular holistic transformation and liberation of the learner/educand. With this kind of theology and thoughts on Christian education, how he was able to impress the world of his time and reform both the educational system as well as the ritualistic Church of England was an interesting discovery of this research.

John Wesley is in fact regarded as a pioneer of popular education in the eighteenth century England. He conducted educational enterprises continuously for over fifty years.[11] He seems to have picked and chosen educational and pedagogical ideas from different schools of thought. Therefore, he is best called a "synthesizer" of educational theories.[12]

Wesley as an astute theologian and an educational theorist was influenced by John Locke, John Milton and a gifted mother who produced one of the best-educated English families of the era. John Wesley learned the potency of education quite literally at his mother's knee. The other major influence upon Wesley's philosophy of Christian education was the Moravians (a German pietistic group), whom he admired and at some points emulated. John Wesley found the work of John Amos Comenius and Nicholas Ludwig Zinzendorf most instructive, and from them he learned several basic principles which guided his educational efforts.[13]

---

[11] Elmer L.Towns, "John Wesley" in *A History of Religious Educators*, edited by Elmer L.Towns, (Grand Rapids: Baker Book House, 1975), p. 212. It is on record that by 1834 the British Wesleyan Methodist conference had more than a third of a million children enrolled in its schools and these children were served by some 60,000 voluntary teachers. By 1904 British Methodist Sunday school enrolment exceeded a million. Quoted in *World-Changers: Karl Marx and John Wesley*, by John Wilkins Sigsworth, Ontario: Easingwold Pulications, 1982), p. 234.

[12] *Ibid.*, p. 44.

[13] Gayle Carlton Felton, "John Wesley and the Teaching Ministry: Ramifications for education in the Church Today", in *Religious Education*, Vol. 92, Issue 1 (Winter, 1997), p. 3.

He understood the potential of education as an instrument of both spiritual and social reform. He also sought to use education for the benefit of the disadvantaged socio-economic class of the society. Some experts contend that he was the only leader of importance who raised his voice in the eighteenth century England for educational reform.

John Wesley on the other hand, seemed to have adapted some extreme views on education. For instance, his view on children's discipline explains his rejection of play as being detrimental, both educationally and spiritually. "As we have no play days, so neither do we allow any time for play on any day; for he that plays as a child will play as a man."[14] Wesley's attitude toward play differed from both his predecessors and successors. A century later, Horace Bushnell advocated play as the symbol and interpreter of Christian liberty.[15] However, he advocated the home/family as the primary source of Christian education.

One of Wesley's main focuses appears to have been to fight sin, ignorance and poverty by Christian education, discipline and the Gospel of grace.[16] In the light of this view, he developed two preliminary convictions regarding the role of education and discipline for students. First, sin in a child's life must be corrected through education. Second, "the child's will must be curbed so that the soul may be saved."[17] In furtherance of this conviction, Wesley did not hesitate to suggest corporal punishment to bring the child's will under submission but with a rider that it should be the last resort.

Scriptural

Wesley conceptualized the purpose of religious education to be: "the design of Christian education, by forming their minds, through the help of God, to wisdom and holiness, by instilling the principles of true religion, speculative and practical, and training them up in the ancient way, that they might be rational, Scriptural Christians."[18] However, he asserted that the "goal of all work with children whether based on the family, church or academic institution were designed to make children pious, to lead to personal religion and to insure salvation."[19] He further stated that the "purpose of religious education is to instil in children true

---

[14] James Riley Estep Jr. "John Wesley's Philosophy of Formal Childhood Education" in *Christian Education Journal*, Vol. INS, No. 2, Fall 1997, p. 49.

[15] J. E. Reed and R. Prevost, *A History of Christian Education* (Nashville: Broadman and Holman, 1993), p. 319.

[16] Wesley Tracy, "Christian Education in the Wesleyan Mode," in *Wesleyan Theological Journal*, Vol. 17, No.1, (Spring 1982), p. 40.

[17] Elmer L. Towns, "John Wesley" in *A History of Religious Educators*, edited by Elmer L. Towns (Grand Rapids: Baker Book House, 1975), pp. 220-221.

[18] Gayle Carlton Felton, "John Wesley and the Teaching Ministry: Ramifications for Education in the Church Today", in *Religious Education*, Vol. 92, Issue 1 (Winter, 1997), p. 2.

[19] John Wesley Prince, *John Wesley on Religious Education* (New York: Methodist Book Concern, 1926), p. 87.

religion, holiness and the love of God and mankind (sic) and to train them in the image of God."[20]

Wesley seems to have recognised the fact that persons of all ages need to be taught what they as Christians believe and how Christians ought to live. He believed that such teaching was a cognitive process of didactic learning and a formative process of spiritual nurturing.[21] During his long career, John Wesley wrote 371 books on enormous range of subjects,[22] much about educational theory and was involved in a variety of educational endeavours. As in the 20th century, what Paulo Freire did with education in Latin America, John Wesley seems to have understood the potential for education and used it as an instrument for social and spiritual reform and sought to use it for the benefit of the disadvantaged socio-economical classes. He prepared an important document for the education and spiritual nurture of children entitled *Lessons for Children,* a series of 200 Bible studies. In addition to this he edited a French document and called it *Instruction for Children.*[23] Experts contend that he was the only leader of importance in the eighteenth century England who sounded a voice for educational reform. He says, "I preached on the Education of Children, wherein we are so shamefully wanting."[24] Some believed that Wesley's thoughts on education were far advanced for his time.[25]

Further, Wesley appears to have had a negative attitude towards secular education. For him, purely secular education was equivalent to "sending them to the devil" and he regarded "large public schools as nurseries of all matter of wickedness."[26] He was even critical of Rousseau's *Emile* to be the "most empty, silly, injudicious that ever a self-conceited infidel wrote", suggesting that if Rousseau's educational principles were used at Kingswood [27] school, we would be *continually*

---

[20] John Wesley Prince, *John Wesley on Religious Education*, p. 96.

[21] Gayle Carlton Felton, "John Wesley and the Teaching Ministry: Ramifications for Education in the Church Today", in *Religious Education,*Vol. 92, Issue 1 (Winter 1997), p. 1.

[22] Elmer L.Towns, "John Wesley" in *A History of Religious Educators*, edited by Elmer L.Towns (Grand Rapids: Baker Book House, 1975), p. 225.

[23] Wesley Tracy, "Christian Education in the Wesleyan Mode", in *Wesleyan Theological Journal,* Vol. 17, No. 1, (Spring 1982), p. 34.

[24] *John Wesley Journal,* January 30, 1767.

[25] J. O. Gross, *John Wesley: Christian Educator* (Nashville: Board of education, Methodist Church, 1954), p. 9.

[26] James Riley Estep Jr. "John Wesley's Philosophy of formal Childhood Education" in *Christian Education Journal,* Vol. INS, No. 2, (Fall 1997), p. 48.

[27] Note Kingswood and Cokesbury are educational Institutions prominent in early Methodist History, near Bristol, UK. Kingswood is a small village near Bristol predominately occupied by miners, formers and Dock workers then. To educate the deprived people Wesley established a residential school for children of those miners and the economically poor class of the society. Unfortunately, the School is relocated to Bath a Roman town about fifteen miles away from Bristol and does not serve the poor anymore. It continues as one of a famous educational institution with 1000 students.

ruining fifty children at a time.[28] Wesley said that Rousseau, Voltaire and David Hume had removed revelation from religion and God from His creation.[29] He seems to have had strong views and objectives about education. How he arrived at such conclusions is to be studied. His impact seems to be immense in the area of education. How was he able to inspire people with his evangelical theory and approach to education? How did he evolve his thoughts on education is to be researched to uncover their relevance to educational ministry of the church of Christ at large and in particular Methodist Church which claims the legacy of Wesleyan theology and philosophy of education in India.

Contextual

During Wesley's day the nation was ravaged with crimes of the most violent sort but it was commonly ignored. Gambling and gin-drinking became the national pastimes. Only one child in every 25 attended any school of any kind. Into this revolution-ripe context John Wesley came stressing antidotes for diseases of the times calling for– discipline, education, evangelism, religion and love. To reach the goals of saving his society required a thorough multifaceted scheme of Christian education.[30] Education was in no way secondary to evangelism for Wesley. Education and evangelism were bound together with education coming first.

The Foundry was the first school which Mr. Wesley started on his own. The Foundry was a dilapidated building in Windmill Street near Funsbury Square, London, which had previously been used as a factory for casting of cannons. Wesley obtained a long lease on this building and erected on the site a preaching house with a classroom. The northern end of the building served as a schoolroom and was used later for the sale of Wesley's publications.[31] It was located in a poor part of London where he noted that the teeming offspring of the poor were given no schooling at all and so grew up "like the wild ass's colt."[32] Therefore, this kind of a ground reality seems to have forced him to establish schools first as a place of Christian character formation. He seems to have adapted a military type of discipline to achieve the stated purpose. The children were to come to

---

[28] John Wesley, *A Thought on the Manner of Educating Children* (1783), p. 2.

[29] John Wesley, "The unity of the Divine Being', in *The Works of John Wesley*, Vol. 7, A bicentennial edition, edited by Reginald W. Ward and Richard P. Heitzenrater (Nashville: Abingdon press, 1988), 271.

[30] Wesley Tracy, "Christian Education in the Wesleyan Mode," in *Wesleyan Theological Journal*, Vol. 17, No.1 (Spring 1982), p. 32.

[31] Ralph Waller, *John Wesley - A Personal Portrait* (London: SPCK, 2003), p. 52.

[32] Wesley Tracy, "Christian Education in the Wesleyan Mode," in *Wesleyan Theological Journal*, Vol. 17, No.1 (Spring 1982), p. 35.

Kingswood[33] school established in village near Bristol and not to see their parents at home again until they finished the course of study.[34]

His thoughts on Christian education are based on Scripture in place of the speculative system of the ancient society and he thought Scriptural education must be rational and more effective for transforming humanity. His ultimate focus seems to have been to fight against sin, ignorance and poverty which existed among the communities of his time through education and discipline. This method raises many questions today. Have the Methodists in Karnataka deviated from his vision and focus today? How did he seek to have his educational objectives fulfilled through the ministry of teaching in the early Methodist movement? Can his model be an ideal model for the Methodist Church today? How and to what extent is the Wesleyan model of education liberative? To what extent can a particular approach to education bring socio-economic changes? These are some of the queries that the author wishes to investigate in order to understand the complex issues and challenges of Christian education that are faced in Methodist churches today. Also this research is an effort to find out to what extent John Wesley's approaches are applied in the boarding schools and churches of Methodists in Karnataka and how far they are successful.

Therefore, the author wishes to critique/analyse Wesley's thoughts and approaches to Christian education and study the relevance of his approach to Christian education ministry of the Methodist Churches in Karnataka. Thereby to suggest a relevant model/approach to improve the present day ministry based on the outcome of both research and empirical studies with select Methodist churches in Karnataka.

Literature Resources

There are a couple of books which deal specifically with John Wesley's views on Christian education namely, *John Wesley: Christian Educator;* by John Owen Gross; *John Wesley on Religious Education* by John Wesley Prince; *John Wesley and Education;* by Alfred H. Body; *Pity my simplicity: The Evangelical Revival and Religious Education of Children 1738-1800* by Paul Sangster and there are quite a few articles on his views concerning Christian education such as "Wesley and Education," "John Wesley and A Christian Education," "Susanna Wesley's Views on Education" by Gary Michael Best, the Principal of Kingswood School; "Christian Education in the Wesleyan Mode" by Wesley Tracy; "Doing Christian Education in the Wesleyan Mode: A Response to Wesley Tracy," by J. Duane

[33] Kingswood is a small village near Bristol, where John Wesley started school named after that in descript village, where labour class, minors and slaves stayed. Now it is developed into a modest town. History of Wesleyan movement takes off from this small place and makes a big imprint on the world map. There is also a place maintained with a write up that says from here, Wesley and his friend Whitefield held public preaching.

[34] Wesley Tracy, "Christian Education in the Wesleyan Mode", in *Wesleyan Theological Journal*, Vol. 17, No.1, (Spring 1982), p. 39.

Beals; "John Wesley and the Teaching Ministry: Ramifications for education in the Church today" by Gayle Carlton Felton; "John Wesley and The Education of Children" by Donald Tranter; "John Wesley's Scientific Education" by J. C. English; "John Wesley's Philosophy of Formal Childhood Education" by James Riley Estep Jr. and others.

The Collection of his sermons by Thomas Jackson Nos, 94, 95 and 96 deal with children's education, children's obedience to parents and family education etc.

The major thrust of these books and articles is to show how John Wesley used education to bring about revival in England and the response to his traditional education theory. He seems to have used every occasion be it pulpit, street, public preaching etc to educate people to liberate them from the ills of the society and the Church of England. For him, education was the key to bring about socio-cultural, economic, religio-political liberation and transformation. The main content of his educational programme was the Bible. His views are based on the Bible. For him sin, ignorance and poverty of the people are the subjects to deal with. His main objective seems to be liberating people from those ills, and thereby usher in revival/transformation both inside and outside the church.

Apart from these focused materials, there are umpteen numbers of books and articles authored by Wesley himself as well as several other scholars.

Author's Objective

The author's objective in this work is to discuss analytically Wesley's educational thoughts, theory and approach and to draw lessons for educational ministry of various churches especially the Methodist Churches in Karnataka. In this vein the author wishes to assess Wesley's pedagogical methodology, and present its unique pedagogical approach to Christian Education, reconstructing where necessary Wesley's educational theory to make it more effective for the use of Church's ministry today offering relevant alternative approaches to contemporary Christian education programmes for the Methodist Church in Karnataka.The value of this research will depend upon its applicability in the life of the Christian Church particularly the Methodist Church today.

As such there has been no study done from this perspective, neither an analysis/critique of Wesley's educational thoughts has been done by an Indian thus far; therefore, I have endeavoured painstakingly to follow his philosophy in this research work.

Wesley has strong views about educating a child which not many Christian educators of 20th century support. However, he has strong evangelical thoughts on Education which are worthy of research and for inspiration to recharge the Methodist churches in Karnataka.

The findings are a motivating factor to stir up the Methodist Churches in Karnataka to hear Wesley's clarion call afresh.[35] For Wesley, nothing else mattered more in life than that of making every individual a good Christian.

An evaluation of the existing Christian education programmes to enable the Christian Education ministry to be effective in the Methodist Churches in Karnataka in the light of the findings of this study will be helpful to reconstruct the present Ministry of the Churches.

As with the Church of England then as followers of Christ, Methodists seem to have deviated from the vision and the teaching objectives of Wesley which were the basis of its existence. Presumably deviations have been caused by socio-cultural, spiritual, structural and leadership crises for the last couple of decades. Reacting to the then decadence in society, Wesley embarked on a programme with a strong emphasis on Biblical teaching, Preaching and Christian education. Will the Scripture-Centred education programmes help modern education activities or is it a necessity of the time, needs to be clarified. Now as it appears the Methodist Church in Karnataka has gone through a sea change over the years and a seeming deviation from Wesley's thoughts on Christian education, Spirituality, and Teaching. A fresh look at his educational thoughts, theory and approach may impact the present conditions as it did in his times to bring about an effective form of Christian education programme.

Limitations of this work

This book is limited to the analysis of John Wesley's thoughts on Christian education. It will not venture into the ocean of materials written on Wesley and his theology. This research covers his life story briefly, and the focus will be on his educational thoughts, theory, approach and methodology of teaching. The empirical study will cover select central Methodist churches in Karnataka, particularly their Christian education activities through Sunday schools, Youth fellowships, Men's fellowships and Women's fellowships which Wesley termed those groups as "societies, bands and clubs". It is limited to proposing guidelines for the existing ministry of the Methodist Church in Karnataka.

This research is not a final answer to the concerns raised in this work but is a humble effort to re-read John Wesley's eighteenth century educational thoughts into the post-colonial and post-modern world today.

Framework

The author has researched into Methodist history and has gathered material from various libraries besides a survey of select schools.

[35] "Make Christians, my dear sister, make Christian!" as John Wesley wrote to Mary Bishop, who operated schools for girls in Bath. Quoted in, "John Wesley and the Teaching Ministry: Ramifications for Education in the Church Today", Gayle Carlton Felton, in *Religious Education* (Winter 1997), p. 1.

The author has adapted Paulo Freire's framework to analyse Wesley's thoughts and approach to Christian Education. Wesley seems to have used a multifaceted approach. His is a content and teacher-centred approach whereas Freire's is a learner's-centred approach. For Wesley, Scripture and human sin sets the agenda for Christian education, for Freire context in which education takes place sets the agenda, and social analysis provides the perspective for Christian education programmes of the Church. Freire strongly advocated participatory and dialogical education. An important concept in his pedagogy is the participation of the people in learning. He used education as liberating and conscientization process of change, to bring about social justice, cultural freedom, equality, humanization, respect and dignity to human life. The concept of Wesley's pedagogy is transmission, leading to transformation of the learner and the society in which one lives. Therefore, the researcher has preferred Paulo Freire's approach as the framework to appraise Wesley's thoughts on Christian education over against the other educators' approaches.

The use of Paulo Freire's framework in this research work does not advocate the wholesale adoption of the Freire's revolutionary theory of education; instead its intention is to serve as a framework to analyse the Wesleyan Christian education thoughts. The present context of the Methodists today seems to be no better than that of people's condition during Wesleyan era and Freire's people in Latin America. Therefore, this book endeavours to assess the educational thoughts of Wesley and Methodists from the perspective of Freirean liberative approach to education and to propose a relevant model to Christian education whose aims and contents must be rooted in praxis. It is assumed that such an approach will have the capacity to be truly liberating and transforming.

Glimpses of Content of the Research Work

The book has five chapters besides the introductory chapter. Chapter one highlights the major events in the formative years of John Wesley. It describes the contextual setting in which he was born, reared and shaped his views. The state of socio-religio-cultural and political conditions, the pitiable situation of public education and Wesley's reactions to the existing education system are discussed. The next section of the chapter sketches his life history and his personality formation. The last section highlights the founding and the growth of Methodism.

Chapter two forms the central piece of the research work as it were. The focus here is on Wesley - the educator. It runs through all the aspects of his educational endeavour as much as possible. His passion for Christian education and children, formation of educational thoughts, various influences that contributed to his educational thought formations are discussed. The purpose of Christian education, its theory and methodology, the theological convictions of Wesley, distinct characteristics of Wesleyan theory and method are analysed.

Finally, limitations of his theory and approach to Christian religious education are discussed.

Chapter three analyses the empirical data and interprets its content to infer the use of Wesleyan education thoughts in the ministry of Methodists in Karnataka. It has thirty tables to assess the ground-reality of the Methodist educational work in Karnataka. The views and opinions of select number of respondents and interviewees are considered in this chapter for inferences. Empirical findings are listed in the conclusion of the chapter.

Chapter four, deals with the re-framing John Wesley's thoughts, pedagogy and practice of Christian education in the light of Paulo Freire, a modern educator. The first Section will discuss briefly the educational theory and approach of Freire. It highlights his formative years in life; it explores his educational concepts, theory and methodology of education. His suggestions for an alternate approach such as the participatory and dialogical methods will be briefly considered. Freire in fact revolutionized the educational system in a radical way, as a liberative praxis (a concrete or performative action) which in a way parallels John Wesley's Christian education programme as transformative and personality formation. Freire's contributions are briefly sketched in this section. He is a well known educator; however, this section concludes with the critical views from some of the modern educators about his theory and approach to education.

Section two of the chapter discusses Wesley's thoughts on Christian education and pedagogical approach from the perspective of Freirean liberation pedagogical paradigm. Here, Freirean educational views will help analyse and reconstruct Wesleyan thoughts on education. It also will help in framing and proposing a relevant model of Christian education for the Methodists education ministry in Karnataka.

Chapter five reflects on the theological and biblical bases of Wesley's educational convictions, findings of the research and viable recommendation/ proposals made for the improvement of the existing educational ministry of the Methodists. The second section discusses the relevance of Wesley's Christian education thoughts for contemporary Christian education particularly the Methodists education ministry in Karnataka. An attempt is made to state the implications and proposals as part of the findings and recommendations towards a relevant Christian education for today drawing insights from Freire and Wesley's educational legacy. To summarize one of his greatest passion [education] is to quote Russell Richey, professor of church history at Duke University, USA wrote in an article to commemorate the 250th anniversary of Wesley's creation of Kingswood School: Wesley's investment in education was pervasive, and personal. Wesley was a teacher for Methodism. *There was a teaching purpose to almost everything he did, and he was willing to teach almost anyone he met who proved in any way open and responsive.* Certainly, he taught his preachers, in conference and out; and he held them accountable to educate themselves using the resources that he provided.... **He created systems that clearly served educational purposes.**

His correspondence, tracts, re-publications, sermons, his classes and societies... indeed the entire structure of Methodism – exhibit a remarkable drive to educate people.[36]

[36] This was quoted by Gary M. Best former Principal of Kingswood School at Bath, UK in his paper presented at Lincoln College, Oxford on 14th May 2003, p. 4.

Chapter 1

Wesley and the Methodist Movement

Introduction 17

A. A Brief Survey of the Context 17

1. Socio-Religious, Cultural and Political Context of Wesley 17

a. Socio-Religio-Cultural Scene of Wesley Days 17

b. Political Scene of the Eighteenth Century 23

2. A Brief Account of the Educational Context in the Eighteenth Century England 25

a. Condition of United Kingdom during John Wesley's time 25

b. John Wesley's Assessment of the state of Public Education 27

B. A Short Biography of John Wesley 28

1. His Family, Birth and Boyhood 29

2. His Formal Education 30

3. His Personality and Character 31

4. His Christian Experience 34

5. His scholarship 37

C. Founding of the Movement 39

1. Origin 40

2. Purpose 41

3. Growth 42

Chapter 1

Wesley and the Methodist Movement

Introduction

The Methodist Movement is noted for its radical and revolutionary paradigm in the history of the eighteenth century England. Thus, it was no mean revolution as far as its impact on the socio-religious, politico-economic and educational life of the people was concerned. A brief background study of the setting and the context in which John Wesley stirred up the nation using education as a tool, the Bible as its content and salvation or eternal life as the final destiny will help in understanding his thoughts on education as they propelled the Movement.

A. A Brief Survey of the Context

1. Socio-Religious, Cultural and Political Context of Wesley

a. Socio-Religio-Cultural Scene of Wesley Days

In the eighteenth century Britain, most of the people earned their living by cultivating the land. Conditions of life and labour varied with each small difference of configuration, sub-soil and climate.[37] Although it was called the age of Enlightenment, yet to a great extent that century in which Wesley appeared was dissolute, irreligious, and corrupt. Carlyle rated it "a bankrupt century."[38] Lord Acton called it a period of "dim ideals and expiring hopes."[39] Thus, the evidences of decadence were overwhelming during Wesley's time.

---

[37] T. S. Ashton, *The Industrial Revolution, 1760-1830* (New York: A Galaxy Book, Oxford University Press, 1964), p.18.

[38] John Wilkins Sigsworth, *World-Changers: Karl Marx and John Wesley* (Ontario, Canada: Easingwold Publications, 1982), p. 39.

[39] Lord Acton, *Cambridge Modern History*, quoted in *World-Changers: Karl Marx and John Wesley* (Ontario, Canada: Easingwold Publications, 1982), p. 39.

England was in the grip of the Industrial revolution[40]. It revolutionized the living and working conditions of the people to such an extent that housing conditions were outrageous, where ten persons per unfurnished room was a common sight.[41] Streets were littered and piled up with horses' manure polluting the residential areas. Diseases like typhoid, smallpox, dysentery, and cholera ravaged the city almost unchecked.[42] One fourth of the babies born died in the first week of their lives. The whirlwind of industrialization brought in death, diseases, crime, and malnutrition[43] as well as the provision of jobs, ways of earning easy money etc.

Crimes of the most violent sort were so common that they were commonly ignored.[44] Highway robbery was so common that many travellers were afraid to travel after dark. It was a century of almost continuous disorder.[45] Gambling was almost a national disease and gin-drinking became the national pastime. For children, there were the streets or sweat-shops to while away the time. Only one child in every 25 attended any school of any kind.[46] Into this revolution-ripe setting, John Wesley came stressing as antidotes for the diseases of the times – discipline, education, evangelism, religion and love. John Wesley preferred to use the term 'disease' for all kinds of sin and evils of his time. He sought to help those sorrowful victims of squalor to see their essential dignity before God. John Wesley thought of beginning this with the children, and through their education. However, according to him, to reach the goals of saving the society of his time required a thorough, multifaceted scheme, including that of Christian education. Education was in no way secondary to evangelism for John Wesley. He once said that he had spent more time on a single educational project at Kingswood[47] than on any other project in his life.[48]

As a minister of the church, and one who was concerned about the people and intent on their reform, John Wesley expressed his goal succinctly thus: "To reform the continent and spread scriptural holiness over these lands."[49] But his preaching

---

[40] Wesley Tracy, "Christian Education in the Wesleyan Mode" in *Wesleyan Theological Journal,* Vol. 17, No.1, (Spring 1982), p. 31.

[41] Wesley Tracy, "Christian Education in the Wesleyan Mode" in *Wesleyan Theological Journal,* Vol. 17, No.1, (Spring 1982), p. 31.

[42] Wesley Tracy, "Christian Education in the Wesleyan Mode", p. 32.

[43] *Ibid.*

[44] *Ibid.*

[45] John Wilkins Sigsworth, *World-Changers: Karl Marx and John Wesley*, p. 41.

[46] Wesley Tracy, "Christian Education in the Wesleyan Mode" in *Wesleyan Theological Journal,* Vol. 17, No.1, (Spring 1982), p. 32.

[47] Kingswood and Cokesbury were educational Institutions prominent in early Methodist history, near Bristol, UK. Kingswood was established as a residential school for children of miners and the economically poor class of the society. It continues to serve as an educational institution even today.

[48] Wesley Tracy, "Christian Education in the Wesleyan Mode" in *Wesleyan Theological Journal,* Vol. 17, No.1, (Spring 1982), p. 32.

[49] John Wilkins Sigsworth, *World-Changers: Karl Marx and John Wesley*, p. 138.

and the consolidation of his conversions into Methodist Societies[50] produced a mammoth moral and spiritual reform in the British Isles in the improvement of sordid social conditions. Let us consider first the ones against which he was vocal. They include political bribery, press gang tactics, smuggling, (Smuggling in sea port areas was widespread, while the 'importing, selling or buying of … goods … which have not paid the duty' - was inexcusable, necessitating the collection of extra taxes. "A smuggler … is a thief of the first order" Wesley wrote in 1756 in a book called *The Doctrine of Original Sin*. Eleven years later, his clarifying pamphlet, *A Word to a Smuggler* appeared. His preachers were required to mention the evil frequently to Societies near the Coast and expel any members who persisted in the practice. Gin and rum were probably the most commonly smuggled goods, but tea was another popular item. Plundering wrecked vessels off the coast of Cornwall was a common racket in John Wesley's day, especially by the non-Methodist tin miners. It was alleged that some Cornwallians used to plant decoy lights to lure nearby ships to plunder them by deceit)[51], plundering wrecked vessels, liquor trafficking, shameful prison conditions, gambling, slavery and the slave trade. Concerning bribery he had this emphatic word in a letter to the Bristol societies: "Give, not sell, your vote."[52]

John Wesley insisted that the evil could be stamped out if the gentry there strictly enforced existing laws and agreed to discharge from work and advertise the names of those guilty. At any rate, Wesley's reform efforts are believed to have produced a measure of success.

Drinking[53]: Consumption of distilled liquors especially gin, up to almost the middle of the century was enormous. Wesley who regarded it as destructive to

---

[50] John Wesley never called his groups of followers as a denomination but rather he called them as a Society. It was a company of men having the form and seeking the power of godliness, united in order to pray together, to receive the word of exhortation, and to watch over one another in love that they may help each other to work out their salvation. These *societies* were subdivided into *Classes* of about 12 persons each. Each class had a *leader* whose duties included seeing each person in his class once a week at least, in order to inquire how their souls prosper; to advise, reprove, comfort, or exhort as occasion may require. The *bands* were small groups whose sharing, intimacy and achievement excelled the best of the cell group explosion of modern times.

[51] John Wilkins Sigsworth, *World-Changers: Karl Marx and John Wesley*, pp. 39, 139.

[52] Ibid., p. 139.

[53] John Wesley regarded the drinking of distilled liquors (those with high alcohol concentration as whiskey, brandy, gin, rum) as destructive both of body and soul and opposed it as well for contributing to the misery of the poor. He even wrote privately to Prime Minister William Pitt urging him to work towards classifying the industry as a felony. Naturally he incorporated into Methodism's "General Rules" a clause against buying or selling such liquors, as well as drinking them "unless in cases of extreme necessity." Consumption, especially of gin, up to almost the middle of the century, was enormous - as much as 11,000,000 gallons in a year – and "threatened … to destroy the whole of the working classes of London," wrote Besant in his *London in the Eighteenth Century*. Government acts designed to restrict the distilleries curtailed the trade little because of weak popular support. But John Wesley's wide forceful appeals to the enslaved worker, the manufacturer and seller, and the English citizen in general eventually stirred the national conscience. And this stirring

both the body and soul incorporated into Methodism's "General Rules" a clause against buying or selling of such liquors. His forceful appeals to the English citizen in general coupled with changed appetites of Methodist converts contributed to the reduction of consumption.

Prisons[54]: Wesley was studying at Christ Church College when he learnt about the wretched conditions in which prisoners were living. That is when he sort his father Samuel Wesley's and the bishop of Oxford's permission and blessings to visit prisoners. The miserable state of affairs of prisoners had moved his heart of compassion to win them for Christ. Wesley continued his service of preaching to the prisoners, visiting prisons till his old age. He compared the degrading conditions of filth, stench, disease, misery and immorality found in most prisons especially at Newgate, with that of the improved Bristol jail where a Methodist was in charge. What Wesley is implying here is that where-ever a Methodist served, they did it whole heartedly to bring about Christian transformation in lives of people and their work place.

Slavery: For John Wesley, the greatest evil of all was **slavery** and the trade that went with it. The latter with its barbarities he characterized in 1772 as "that execrable sum of all the villainies."[55]

After further research he released in 1774 his own booklet *Thoughts upon Slavery* which sold three editions in the first year. Bready suspects that it proved to be the most effective treatise against slavery ever written. It exploded the myth that Negroes were taken for their own good, exposed the deaths occurring enroute and during training, lamented the shame of enforced nakedness at times of branding and buying, and pictured the grief of family separations before settling for a life of treatment comparable to that of beasts of burden. Wesley was by no means convinced that abolition would result in less prosperity, as some argued, but insisted that of the two, wealth was of less important to the nation than its moral and spiritual integrity. Captains, merchants and buyers were called on to give up their business. In 1780 the Methodist Conference formally condemned the trade and the Methodists freely supported and involved in anti-slavery campaigns. Much of Wesley's vocal protest/attack against various vices of the time began before his evangelical conversion in 1738.[56] According to Bready, Wesley's *Thoughts about*

---

coupled with the changed appetites of thousands of Methodist converts doubtless contributed to the reduction in consumption which Harkness (*The Methodist Church in Social Thought and Action*) tells it did occur around the mid-century. John Wesley's highly popular book called *Primitive Physic* was partly designed to show there were other medicines besides alcohol. Cf. *World – Changers*, p. 139.

[54] Once, in a nine-month period he visited prisons at least 67 times. Many prisoners received his message too and found peace. Most prisoners appreciated his kindness. In 1761 in the *London Chronicle* John Wesley criticized Newgate's degrading features and compared it with an improved Bristol jail where a Methodist was in charge. About that London prison he wrote: "Of all the seats of woe on this side hell, few, I suppose, exceed or even equal Newgate." Cf. *World-Changers*, p. 140.

[55] Cf. John Wilkins Sigsworth, *World-Changers: Karl Marx and John Wesley*, p. 140.

[56] *Ibid.*

Slavery was the most effective treatise ever written to expose many myths. Wesley believed that the nation's spiritual and moral integrity was more important than wealth and prosperity. Slaves by the thousands were being brought to England and sold by auction to work on the estates there. The cruelties associated with these transportations are almost unbelievable. Yet the Bishop of London approved the slave trade.[57]

John Wesley's last letter written only four days before his death in early 1791 to Wilberforce who led the Parliamentary drive to abolish the slave trade shows his concern. He wrote: "Go on in the name of God, and in the power of His might, till even American slavery, the vilest that ever saw the sun, shall vanish away before it."[58]

Child Labour: Rapidly expanding population meant an explosion of children. The children of the poor had always worked as soon as they could walk, but now their work was exceptionally valuable to factory owners. Children were tractable and easy to discipline; for simple repetitive operations they were ideal, and they were cheap. Naturally they had none of the ingrained antipathy to factory work common among adult workers. So, the factories and the mines absorbed them; and child labour was more deliberately exploited than ever before. One of the most visible and appalling exploitations of child labour in the eighteenth century was the chimney sweep.[59] Rapid growth of population was one of the major features of the social history of Industrial revolution period leading to a number of problems. The children of the poor were used as labourers in industries and other sectors.[60] Worse conditions, long hours, irregular payments, gross exploitation of women and child labour were to be found in small-scale and domestic industry. Discipline in factories - especially with children – was harsh, frequently cruel. Living conditions were desolate and drab. And for most there was nothing to hope for. For the poor who worked in factories life was bitter and hard. It was a bitter life they lived. All houses and cellars were desperately overcrowded and ten to a room was common in Manchester. Most of the cellars were inhabited, not only by people but also by their pigs, fowls sometimes even by their horses and cattle.

People were faced with the wearisome and endless repetition of simple processes, haunted by the fear of unemployment and starvation. Diseases, poverty fear, malnutrition, were the common lot of eighteenth century people in UK. Mondays and Tuesdays were often given up to drink, cockfights, bear-baiting and other tough and brutal amusements of the poor and the week's work was done in a blind rush, in four sixteen or seventeen- hour days to compensate for two-days reckless living. Violence, born of despair and greed, belonged to the poor alone.

[57] John Wilkins Sigsworth, *World-Changers: Karl Marx and John Wesley*, p. 39.

[58] *Ibid.*, p. 140.

[59] J. H. Plumb, *England in the Eighteenth Century* (Baltimore-Maryland: Penguin Books, 1969), p. 87.

[60] *Ibid.*

There were no law enforcing agencies in villages and small towns except for two parish constables.[61] Children, many of them only seven years of age, had to work twelve, or even fifteen hours a day, for six days a week. According to, one of the parents: "Their young lives were spent, at best in monotonous toil, at worst in a hell of human cruelty."[62]

Condition of Women: Women in the eighteenth century did not have many rights and were financially dependent on their husbands or families. An average wife spent some 15 years either in a state of pregnancy or in nursing a child for the first year of its life.[63] Women and children were hired to spin on the jenny in their own homes because they were unable to come to the factory for work since they had a large number of children to look after.[64]

Morality and Religion: 18th century England, was characterized by a decay of religious licentiousness of morals, public corruption and profaneness of language.[65] In other words, corrupt behaviours in public life and foul language seemed common in Wesley's days. Loose living, rioting and lawlessness were normal/common sights during 1740-60. Christianity had no bearing for the people. Class distinction existed and, moral standards among aristocracy had reached an all time low. Some leading fathers had even felt that it was their duty to instruct their sons in the art of seduction to round out their education. A Woman encouraging her husband to be unfaithful seems to have been usual during this century.[66] Court life was corrupt. Bribery was rampant especially in the affairs of the government. Bribery was so common to the extent that Prime Minister Walpole's government was kept in power by bribing the then Parliamentarians/ law makers.[67] In the first half of the 18th century nearly half of the land was uncultivated. Large tracts were forests; people lived in hamlets, villages and small towns. But in the latter half of the century population of England and Wales had increased by 40% to six and a half million.[68] This rapid growth of population led to a number of administrative and religious problems and becoming a major feature of the social history of Industrial revolution.

---

[61] Plumb, *England in the Eighteenth Century* pp. 12, 87-89.

[62] T. S. Ashton, *The Industrial Revolution, 1760-1830* (New York: Oxford University Press, 1965), p. 78.

[63] Internet reading of eighteenth century England, www.google – search of 18th century.

[64] T. S. Ashton, *The Industrial Revolution 1760-1830*, p. 80.

[65] Matt Pattison, *Religious Thoughts in England* noted the period from 1714 to 1744 to be characterized by a decay of religion, licentiousness of morals, public corruption, and profaneness of language: It was an age whose poetry was without romance, whose philosophy was without insight, and whose public men were without character; an age of light without love, whose very merits were of the earth, earthly. Cf. George Eayrs, *John Wesley: Christian Philosopher and Church Founder*, p. 20.

[66] John Wilkins Sigsworth, *World-Changers: Karl Marx and John Wesley*, p. 39.

[67] *Ibid.*

[68] T. S. Ashton, *The Industrial Revolution, 1760-1830*, p. 4.

John Wesley in his *Appeals to Men of Reason and Religion* dealt with the issues of ignorance, immorality, and irreligion of all classes. He affirmed that at least during the first half of the century, these were not seriously challenged. In 1745, he declared:

> Our nation stands on the very brink of destruction. And why are we thus, but because the cry of our wickedness is gone up to heaven? Because we have so exceedingly, abundantly, beyond measure, corrupted our ways before the Lord.[69]

While describing Bristol city he says:

> A few people in each of those centres were intellectual, inquisitive, witty and brilliant. With exceptions, they were ignorant of the sources of spiritual light and power. Gay and fashionable people were more numerous. Their plight was worse in these respects. Around the intellectual and fashionable there were multitudes of neglected people for whom none seemed to care; they were without God and without hope in the world. Gross superstitions swayed all classes. Few people could read. *I offered them books, but they could not read.*[70]

The French political philosopher Montesquieu observed that among the English society he visited "If one speaks of religion, everyone begins to laugh."[71] Situation was such that anyone who spoke of religion was considered a person being out of his/her mind. Christianity for many had become meaningless. John Wesley's own blunt mid-century estimate was that nine-tenths of the English people had no more religion than horses.[72]

b. Political Scene of the Eighteenth Century

The Industrial Revolution led to a rapid increase in national prosperity. The birth-rate rose slowly because killer diseases such as smallpox, dysentery, consumption, and typhus were widespread. Shortage of food, inadequate housing conditions and also excessive drinking of cheap gin had disastrous effects on the poorer classes. The rich were exposed to disease due to a general disregard of hygiene. However, throughout the 18th century important improvements in living conditions were made, and by the early 19th century the population of England and Wales had almost doubled. This was mainly due to increased production of food, including potatoes, cheese, and fresh meat. Thanks to the availability of coal, homes could be warmer in winter. In general clothing and soap were cheaper

---

[69] George Eayrs, *John Wesley: Christian Philosopher and Church Founder,* (London: The Epworth Press, 1926), p. 21.

[70] *Ibid.,* p. 31.

[71] John Wilkins Sigsworth, *World-Changers: Karl Marx and John Wesley*, p. 40.

[72] *Ibid.*

than previously. Nevertheless, about 80 per cent of the population remained poor. A majority of the people still lived in the countryside and their main occupations were agriculture and rural crafts. Most farmers were smallholders renting up to 8 hectares of land. Freeholders owned their land and were socially superior to smallholders. At the bottom of the social structure were the landless labourers who worked on large farms, especially in summer; in winter they were often out of work. At the top of the social hierarchy were the nobility, who held the highest offices and accumulated the greatest wealth, and the gentry, who included the major landowners in a county but were not necessarily of noble birth. The chief landowner in a village was called the squire. He was usually the local Justice of the Peace. Another important person in the district was the parson who looked after the religious needs of his parishioners. In the late 18th century there were the beginnings of a movement of population away from the countryside into the towns, partly as a result of enclosures. This meant that the old common land used by peasants for grazing was taken over by private landowners for more intensive agriculture and enclosed by hedgerows. This seems to have led to the rich and the poor divide, discontentment in the country which in turn affecting human relations and social harmony in the community. [73]

Eighteenth century Britain was free from the revolutionary atmosphere that prevailed in the 17th century. The country became wealthier through trade; the middle-class and landowners lived in a mood of complacency. The power of the king continued to decline. For the first time the king's ministers became real policy-makers. In 1707 the Act of Union formally united England and Scotland. In 1714, when Queen Anne, the last of the Stuarts died, Parliament chose the German-speaking elector of Hanover who was crowned as George I. He was succeeded by his son, George II, who, like his father, had little interest in British internal affairs.[74] The most outstanding political leader of this time was Sir Robert Walpole (1676-1745), the first Prime Minister, who developed the idea of the Cabinet, i.e. a group of ministers who took the actual control of administration from the Crown. In Parliament a two-party system began to evolve. Those who chiefly represented the financial and mercantile interests of the cities and towns, and the progressive element in the aristocracy opposed to any interference in politics by the monarchy were called Whigs. *Those who were strongly attached to tradition and the monarchy were called* Tories. The Tories were supported by the gentry, the landed aristocracy, and the Anglican Church.[75] At the end of the 18th century Britain entered the period known as the Industrial Revolution, brought about by the use of machinery and steam power for the manufacture of goods

[73] J. H. Plumb, *England in the Eighteenth Century* (Maryland: Penguin Books, 1969), pp. 11-20, 47-51.

[74] www.google search – titled "Political condition during eighteenth century Britain". Contributed by J. H. Plumb.

[75] J. H. Plumb, *England in Eighteenth Century* (Maryland: Penguin Books, 1969), pp. 47-51.

as a result of the invention of the steam engine by James Watt in 1769.[76] At the end of the 18th century Britain entered the Industrial revolution which led to a rapid increase in national prosperity and the population of England and Wales had doubled. But there was a general disregard to hygiene and killer diseases were widespread.[77] These appalling socio-political conditions deprived many of their right to education. The next section highlights the state of public education during Wesley's time.

2. A Brief Account of the Educational Context in the Eighteenth Century England

a. Condition of United Kingdom during John Wesley's time

Eighteenth-century England was marked by distrust and division between classes and the masses," and a lack of educational opportunities added to make this division complete.[78] Conditions during John Wesley's times are painted grim and gloomy by the historians as well as by other writers when they deal with educational institutions. In this situation, assessing the value of a moral directive and a religious motif was crucial. In alleviating the problem John Wesley therefore realized the intricate connection between the success of the Great Awakening and establishing Christian education. Hence, his primary criticism of the state of public education was "a total lack of religion and religious motive, and it is this which gives us at once the clue to his chief educational idea: religion and education must go together."[79]

Robert Southey says, "There never was less religious feeling, either within the establishment or without, than when John Wesley blew his trumpet and awakened those who slept."[80] The state schools of John Wesley's days admitted only the children of the upper classes, and these institutions fell far below his expectations.[81] In 1732, the weekly Newspaper stated that zeal for godliness looked as old upon a man as the dress of his great-grandfather. While many free thinkers' clubs flourished, candidates for ordination were scandalously ignorant of the Bible.[82] Religion and its adherence were at low ebb.

With this in the background, John ventured to put into action his radical concept of establishing schools on the basis of moral principles. Thus, John Wesley's perception of education was made available to the public, as he established schools

---

[76] www.google search – titled "Political condition during eighteenth century Britain". Contributed by J. H. Plumb.

[77] Ibid.

[78] Martin Schmidt, *John Wesley: A Theological Biography, Vol. II – John Wesley's Life Mission*, Part II, translated by Denis Inman, {New York: Abingdon Press, 1973), p. 175.

[79] Alfred H. Body, *John Wesley and Education* (London: The Epworth Press, 1936), p. 47.

[80] John Telford, *The Life of John Wesley* (London: Hodder and Stoughton, 1886), p. 114.

[81] Elmer L. Towns, (ed), *A History of Religious Educators* (Grand Rapids, Michigan: Baker Book House, 1975), p. 212.

[82] *Ibid.*

such as Kingswood[83] as an alternative to public educational institutions. In 1781, John Wesley published his 'A Plain Account of Kingswood School,' restating his motivation for the creation of an educational institution near Bristol in accordance with his educational philosophy. He made several comments and points about the educational situation in this short write up which is already mentioned in the preceding discussion. The third point through to the seventh point in the 'Plain Account' denote John Wesley's five[84] criticisms of public education in England, to which he regarded Kingswood as the solution. Some of his criticisms were:

1. Most schools were located in "great towns" wherein children could be distracted from their studies by the activities of the community
2. Most schools admitted students indiscriminately, with the worse corrupting the better.
3. Defective religious education, and hence the aim of education, in Wesley's opinion, was misguided.
4. Basic study skills, such as reading and writing, were neglected for more formal educational pursuits, such as classical languages.
5. Finally, when classical education was provided, the order of instruction and flow of curriculum was arbitrarily arranged.
6. John Wesley was, through his brothers closely connected with Westminister. Both were educated there; his elder brother Samuel had become an usher, and it was with him at his house in Dean's yard that he lodged during the vacations from Charterhouse.He was thus well posted about what really went on at Westminister, and an illuminating piece of evidence, which seems to relate to conditions around 1690, has recently come to light which is only too consistent with the charges levelled by Wesley at the public schools. The theme of the indictment is lack of supervision: too few masters, big boys tyrannizing over younger ones, making them fetch what their elder's "greedy stomachs craved"; if they resisted, beating them with ropes' ends and sometimes with sticks and cudgels; boys seen both by day and by night out of the college and without their growns, dressed up with swords,laced cravats (scarf) and cravat strings, handing about younger women in the streets and fields; and "some of them have lain out of college whole nights, and come in again early in the morning, having always command of the door". Lock and key were not able to confine them "without some particular eye to watch them besides". Perhaps things were not always as bad as

[83] Kingswood is located in Bath, near Bristol, UK, where Wesley started a residential school in 1748 as a model school to counter the existing state schools. See appendices for pictures Appendix C.

[84] James Riley Estep Jr., "John Wesley's Philosophy of formal Childhood Education" in *Christian Education Journal*, Vol. INS, No. 2, (Fall 1997), p. 51. Cf. John Wesley, *Plain Account of Kingswood School, The Works*, Vol. XIII, pp. 289-301. Elmer L. Towns, "John Wesley," pp. 213-214, John Wesley Prince, *Wesley on Religious Education*, pp. 137-138.

they seem to have been around 1690; but Lord Chesterfield, writing to his son in 1750, remarked casually that Westminister School was undoubtedly the seat of illiberal manners and brutal behaviour. If, as we shall soon see inwhat follows, Wesley's regime seems altogether too restrictive, at least the faults of which he complained, especially the placing of schools in large towns and almost total lack of supervision out of school, were not imaginary. His criticisms were directed, he said, to the schools in or near London.[85]

b. John Wesley's Assessment of the state of Public Education

The essence of John Wesley's indictment of the public schools of his time was that religion and education should go hand in hand;[86] because John Wesley seemed to have believed that the Christian religion and education are like the two faces of the same coin.

John Wesley was not only concerned about children's education but adult education as well. Early Methodists, including the first itinerant preachers, came largely from the underprivileged class which was deprived of an opportunity for education. John Wesley knew that helping these people involved educating them. He sincerely believed that although Methodists were poor, they need not be ignorant, and he realized that the **results of his revival would be permanent only if the revival was united with education.**[87] John Wesley wanted his preachers to have a broad, general knowledge, insisting that they spend five hours daily in hard study. Interestingly John Wesley provided materials for their study and he knew what he wanted them to study. In 1745, he published a list of books covering such areas as practical and doctrinal divinity, philosophy, astronomy, poetry, and history to guide the preachers in their self-education. He went so far as to say that their success in preaching would be in proportion to their appeal to the hearers' minds. In other words he did not wish his preachers to be ignorant of biblical, socio-intellectual and historical worldview of their days, instead that they should be informed of various issues as preachers.

In Alfred H. Body's judgement, credit must be given to John Wesley for supplying a course of higher education. He says, "John Wesley may be regarded as the true successor to Erasmus by providing great provincial universities of our day, which have spread knowledge and culture throughout the land, breaking down the barriers of privilege and creed, and making learning accessible to all."[88] The next section discusses the life and growth of John Wesley as a leader and reformer.

---

[85] A. G. Ives, *Kingswood School in Wesley's Day and Since* (London: Epworth Press, 1970), pp. 7-8.

[86] Elmer L. Towns (ed), *A History of Religious Educators*, p. 213.

[87] *Ibid.*

[88] Alfred H. Body, *John Wesley and Education*, p. 142.

B. A Short Biography of John Wesley

John Wesley's[89] life has amazing and surprising antecedents. John Wesley's great-grandfather, Bartholomew, was born about 1595 and died about 1680. His only child John after a course at Oxford became the minister of Winterborn Whitchurch in Dorset by invitation of the parishioners. After securing the approval of his appointment May 1658, he seems to have offended certain local people by discarding the Liturgy and was summoned by the then Bristol Bishop Dr. Gilbert Ironside for questioning his deviation from the set orders of worship. After that he challenged the Bishop and went about preaching "Christ the Crucified" as itinerant preacher. According to the available information about the family of John Wesley (grandfather of John Wesley, founder of Methodism), had two sons: Mathew who was physician in London and Samuel who became the Rector of Epworth. Samuel Wesley got married in 1688 to Susanna, the youngest (25th Child) daughter of Dr. Samuel Annesley, one of the best known, most highly honoured and erudite nonconformist divines of his day.[90] It dates back to a period as early as A.D. 938. His ancestry included monks, priests, at least one abbot of a monastery, and a Crusader; at a later date a Chaplain to King Edward the IV and others in holy orders. These may be mere names until one comes to the immediate ancestors of John Wesley who have been described as respectable for learning, conspicuous for piety and firmly attached to those virtues of Christianity.[91]

John Wesley's parents Samuel and Susanna Wesley were both people of strong character and convictions. Samuel Wesley's father and grandfather had been puritan-minded clergymen who had lost their position in the Church of England because of their refusal in 1662 to abide by the English Prayer Book.[92] Samuel however returned to the faith of his forefathers, growing up as an almost loyal royalist and an ardent high churchman. Samuel and Susanna had 19 children; John Wesley was one among the 19 of which only ten survived. John's mother Susanna herself was the 25th child of her father Dr. Samuel Annesley. Large families seem to be common in those days. A history of the Wesley family amply makes it clear that the preaching legacy and adventurous nature did run in John Wesley's blood since his forefathers, who stood their ground based on their scriptural faith and convictions.[93] All this background vivifies that hereditary forces helped in shaping the personality and preaching career of John Wesley.

---

[89] Dr. Adam Clarke in his edited book entitled – *The Wesley Family,1836,* actually traces the name back to Arabic language, in a root meaning *union* and *conjunction,* quoted in *John Wesley – Preacher,* by W. L. Doughty, p.1.

[90] W. L. Doughty, *John Wesley – Preacher,* (London: The Epworth Press, 1955), pp. 1-2, 5.

[91] Adam Clarke, edited, *The Wesley Family, 1836,* Chapter I, page 21, quoted in *John Wesley – Preacher,* by W. L. Doughty, p. 1.

[92] V. H. H. Green, *John Wesley,* (London: Thomas Nelson and Sons Ltd, 1964), p. 9.

[93] W. L. Doughty, *John Wesley – Preacher,* p. 3.

1. His Family, Birth and Boyhood

John Wesley was born on June 17, 1703[94] to Samuel and Susanna Wesley. He was the fifteenth child in a family of nineteen.[95] On February 9, 1709 five year old "Jackie"[96] (John Wesley was fondly addressed as Jackie by family members) was dramatically rescued. A fire broke out at the rectory shortly before the mid-night. Everybody escaped down the staircase, others by the windows. Young John Wesley was left asleep in bed. When he woke up, he saw the house on fire. He tried his best to get out but it was too hard for a five year old. When he appeared through the window, a light man was set on another man's shoulders and just before the roof fell in, little John Wesley was lifted safely out.[97] His thankful parents considered it a sign of special providence for John Wesley. The miraculous escape from the burning rectory made them regard Wesley as a child of destiny.[98] When an adult, John often referred to himself as "a brand plucked from the burning."[99]

John's father Samuel was studious and courageous but an unpopular rector of the not too cultured Anglican parish church in Epworth town of eastern England's Lincoln County. His mother was both a matriarch and a saint. She was a brilliant well-read pious and dutiful rectory lady, who presided with equal grace and firmness over the affairs of a large, impoverished family – mother, teacher, and lodestar.[100] Both the parents of John Wesley had come from the Puritan Non-conformist stock. However, both in their youth had chosen Anglicanism.

Early schooling for each of the Wesley household was provided at home by their mother who, herself a model of discipline, imparted this virtue to her children. She spent quality time with each of her children during the week. Jackie's weekly hour was on Thursday nights.[101] For John, in particular, Susanna was a major influence in shaping his life. He was very close to his mother and carefully adhered to her advice as long as she lived. He also shared a strong bond with his father. Though the household had high-born connections, poverty persisted and sometimes bread was the only food. Once it is said that his father was imprisoned three months for the debt he could not pay.[102] Financing Wesley's higher education had been a struggle for the family, because his father with a large family and a small parish income was in no position to help him much. But with a studentship from Charterhouse, an annual gift from his older brother Samuel, ill-afforded crumbs from his father and loans from his friends he made it to the

---

[94] J. Telford, *The Popular Life of John Wesley* (London: Charles H. Kelly, 1900), p. 12.

[95] John Wilkins Sigsworth, *World-Changers: Karl Marx and John Wesley,* p. 5.

[96] Albert C. Outler, (ed), *John Wesley* (New York: Oxford University Press, 1964), p. 6.

[97] J. Telford, *The Popular life of John Wesley* (London: Charles H. Kelly, 1900), p. 14.

[98] John Wilkins Sigsworth, *World-Changers: Karl Marx and John Wesley,* p. 5.

[99] John Wesley, *The Journal of the Rev. John Wesley A.M., Vol. IV,* (London: Wesleyan Conference Office, 1895), p. 90.

[100] Albert C. Outler, (ed), *John Wesley*, (New York: Oxford University Press, 1964), p. 6.

[101] John Wilkins Sigsworth, *World-Changers: Karl Marx and John Wesley,* p. 5.

[102] Ibid.

higher education. The Lincoln Fellowship[103] would have provided money towards the Master's studies.[104]

2. His Formal Education

In 1714 at about 11 years of age, John was sent to the Charterhouse School in London on a scholarship provided by the Duke of Buckingham an old patron of his father.[105] While at Charterhouse, he was the Gown-boy from 1714-1720. His father had instructed him to run 3 times round the garden every morning and this helped him greatly to preserve his health. Six years training under Dr. Thomas Walker and his usher and successor Andrew Tooke, firmly laid the foundations for John Wesley's future Scholarship.[106] Six years later he was matriculated as a Charterhouse scholar in Christ Church, Oxford. Being one of the smaller lads in structure he often had some of his food stolen and as a result sometimes suffered hunger. As an adult he wondered if these experiences had stunted his growth, for his mature height was only five foot six and his weight about 120 pounds. With all these hardships he earned distinction as a scholar while at Charterhouse.[107] Despite the fact that Oxford was in the doldrums during Wesley's time there, it was still a splendid repository of books and learning where he could lay claim to a great cultural heritage. With good tutors and a compulsive disposition, the young John acquired an excellent education which served him well for the rest of his life and ministry.[108]

At 17, John enrolled at Christ Church, one of Oxford's largest and most distinguished colleges. This was the natural place to pursue his study since his father, both paternal and maternal grandfathers and a great grandfather were all Christ Church students. He earned his B.A degree before reaching 21 years and his M.A. some three years later in 1727.[109] By 24, John Wesley had completed his post graduation. In 1726 during his M.A. studies he was elected Fellow of Lincoln College. This established his academic status in the university and assured him of financial security so long as he remained celibate.[110] This exemption from economic burden seems to have done a great deal of good for John to develop himself as a preacher and revivalist. He was a serious and disciplined

[103] Lincoln Fellowship was scholarship for the scholarly and deserving students in Lincoln College one of the many colleges at Oxford.

[104] John Wilkins Sigsworth, *World-Changers: Karl Marx and John Wesley,* p. 6.

[105] Albert C. Outler, (ed), *John Wesley* (New York: Oxford University Press, 1964), p. 6.

[106] J. Telford, *The Popular Life of John Wesley*, (London: Charles H. Kelly, 1900), p. 16.

[107] John Wilkins Sigsworth, *World-Changers: Karl Marx and John Wesley,* p. 6.

[108] Albert C. Outler, (ed), *John Wesley*, p. 6.

[109] John Wilkins Sigsworth, *World-Changers: Karl Marx and John Wesley,* p. 6.

[110]However, in February 1751 John married, and on June 1 he submitted his resignation to the rector and fellows of Lincoln; this note is found in *Journal, III*, 513-516, note, 527. It is also quoted by Albert C. Outler, (ed), *John Wesley*, p. 8. In any case he did not have a happy married life.

student. [111] John Wesley's Oxford studies were broad including not only divinity but metaphysics, ethics, logic, natural philosophy and various languages. This qualified him to be the moderator of classes, and a Greek lecturer.[112] John Wesley was too frail to excel in sports; therefore, he played tennis and rowed. He was law abiding and a disciplined student.[113]

3. His Personality and Character

John Wesley's stature:[114] Though small in stature, John Wesley was impressive in appearance. He had piercing hazel eyes and an aquiline nose. However, he was alert and vigorous. He was frail throughout his life with frequent sicknesses. Despite all of this he had an apostolic look. John parted his black hair which eventually became white giving him an apostolic look. He had long flowing curly hair over his shoulders. Some critics had opined that John grew his hair to avoid expensive barber's fee. At 72, he had little hair and therefore he wore a wig. His clerical clothes were neat and immaculate- "wondrous clean" as Horace Walpole expressed it but his dressing was plain and simple. He avoided expensive dressing such as buckles, silk, and velvet. His movements were agile and dignified. Though he lived 88 (1703-1791) years, he was generally frail and his health was irregular. His journals mention some 69 different attack of sickness, some serious and some common sicknesses.

Alexander Knox an Irishman who had known Wesley for many years wrote, despite his frail body, Wesley's countenance was both cheerful and serene, "in truth the most perfect specimen of moral happiness which I ever saw." Yet being human he had the moments of depression as one reads in his journal.[115]

John Wesley was fond of children. When he entered a house where he was known, children would run to meet him and pluck his gown. And he reciprocated by displaying genuine affection for them - a benediction, a handshake, or a kiss. John Wesley had a special place and recognition for children – place and time did not matter. A Papist who went to hear him in Dublin was more impressed by his kissing of a child on the pulpit stairs than anything else he did. Robert Southey, 70 years younger to John, recalls a time when John Wesley picked up his own

---

[111] While studying at Oxford, John Wesley had written in a letter to his mother regarding use of time, "Leisure and I have taken leave of each other." John Wilkins Sigsworth, *World-Changers: Karl Marx and John Wesley*, p. 10.

[112] V. H. H. Green, *The Young Mr. Wesley* (London: Edward Arnold Ltd, 1961), p. 125.

[113] V. H. H. Green tells us that his only recorded breach of university regulations was his failure on one occasion to wear his required square cap on the campus. For this failure he had to pay a fine. John Wilkins Sigsworth, *World-Changers: Karl Marx and John Wesley*, p. 6.

[114] His rivals called him "little John", for he was only five foot six inches in height and weighing some 120 pounds. John Wilkins Sigsworth, *World-Changers: Karl Marx and John Wesley*, p. 25.

[115] John Wilkins Sigsworth, *World-Changers: Karl Marx and John Wesley*, pp. 25-26.

little sister in his arm and kissed her. After which "he put his hand on my head and blessed me."[116]

Though John Wesley was a serious type of man yet he did use wit and humour in his conversation with people around. He had light-hearted comments about, old age, celibacy, and host of other life situations.

With regard to his family life, W. H. Fitchett, who devotes a whole chapter to the topic, condenses it thus: "All of John Wesley's love affairs were disasters but his marriage was a tragedy."[117] May be he had failed to sustain his romance and relationship because his deep respect for womanhood which Brailsford points out in his book entitled -*A Tale of Two Brothers*, considers that his repeated hesitation in romance related to the high ideal of womanhood he derived from his mother.[118]

According to the records, John Wesley's personal and emotional life was a mess.[119] Wesley did not plan on personal marriage. The lady who was know as Grace Murray heard him preach in the open –air at London's Moorfields and had accepted Christ as her personal saviour, seeing her new faith, her husband Mr. Murray ship's captain went to sea again and died during the voyage. Wesley was getting closer to this lady by appointing her as a class leader, visitor to the sick, eventually as housekeeper of Methodist Children home at Newcastle. In time he decided she was for him and arranged an agreement of sorts. The Clever Wesley had drawn up an impressive list of reasons why he needed a wife now (this episode was after three years of his mother Susanna's death) and why Grace Murray was an ideal one. Charles Wesley learnt of the situation and her low background thwarted the plan and got her married away to John Bennet, a fellow preacher who too was interested in this lady. This incident broke JohnWesley's heart and wrote 27 stanza lament committing the whole experience to God's providence, as he worked on his personal grief. Thus, he had very disturbed personal love affairs in life.[120]

---

[116] John Wesley's founding of schools and holding of services for children are both further evidences of this affection. Another is his publishing of a children's hymn book tells of his love toward the children. John Wilkins Sigsworth, *World-Changers: Karl Marx and John Wesley*, p. 26.

[117] W. H. Fitchett, *Wesley and His Century*, (Cincinnati: Jennings and Graham, 1966), p. 95.

[118] Mabel Richmond Brailsford, *A Tale of Two Brothers* (New York: Oxford University Press, 1954), pp. 217f.

[119] As early as 1729-30, when British Methodism lay spawning in the club room of Lincoln College, Oxford, Wesley's correspondence reveals the machinery of a naïve, complicated and almost mysterious romantic net-work, complete with code names: Varnase for sally Kirkham, Selima for Ann Granville, Aspasia for Mrs. Mary Pendarves, Sappho for Sarah Chapone, Araspes for Charles Wesley and Cyrus or primitive Christianity was coded name for Wesley himself. The short-term affair with Sophia Hopkey in Georgia, prior to that, Wesley had developed a secret tenderness for a vivacious young lady, one of the three daughters of a rector near Oxford. He used to visit in this home of an Oxford fellow-student. In his Diary Wesley called her Varanese. Investigation ultimately revealed she had other intentions. John Wilkins Sigsworth, *World-Changers Karl Marx and John Wesley*, pp. 26-27.

[120] John Wilkins Sigsworth, *World-Changers Karl Marx and John Wesley*, p. 27.

John Wesley at 57 resigned his Oxford Fellowship of many years and, without consulting others he did marry in February 1751, Mrs.Vazeille, the widow of a London merchant.[121] Before the marriage John Wesley had her to "settle" her resources on herself and her family of four grown up children. This was to negate any charge that he was marrying her for her money. This pair did not prove companionable either.

John Wesley undoubtedly lacked the conjugal virtues, especially at the age when he married. But, he made it clear in advance that he would not slacken his preaching or travelling. He did not wish to betray his religious vocation. And Bishop McConnell in rating John Wesley's wife "at least half-crazy"[122] may not have been far from the truth. Or Southey who said of her: "She deserves to be classed as one of the three typical bad wives of the world"[123] - the other two in his mind belonged to Socrates and Job.

Apart from certain pitfalls in life particularly with reference to his married life, John Wesley was without doubt an extremely disciplined person. He could be called workaholic looking at his working hours and his passion for travel to visit societies at different places.[124]

His simplicity in food habits did not change though he had enough to indulge but continued to practice frugality of Oxford days. His love for both God and people are reflected in many of his sermons. His fondness for aesthetic values is noted in his writings.[125]

John Wesley's psychological character was well known. Even a stranger like John Smith recognized the fact that Wesley's:

> strong –mindedness was something of a family trait; that caution and aintheartedness had been bred out of him; that he was constitutionally incapable of doing anything half. John had a psychological pattern in life: hard-driving, yet also sensitive; intense, yet also patient; detached, yet also charming; self-disciplined, yet also intensely emotional; opinionated, yet also curious; open to counsel, yet impervious to pressure; brusque with bad faith, yet also tolerant of contrary opinions.[126]

---

[121] John Telford, *Popular Life of John Wesley* (London: Charles H. Kelly, 1900), p. 51.

[122] John Wilkins Sigsworth, *World-Changers Karl Marx and John Wesley,* p. 27.

[123] *Ibid.*, p. 28.

[124] For many years, he rose at 4.00 a.m. after discovering it took that early an hour to ensure he did not lie awake needlessly during the night. With bedtime being 10.00 p.m., this gave him an 18-hour day, except for day-time naps he took when he grew old. A young preacher who once wanted to continue talking after the pair went to bed (a young preacher) got this rebuke: "Joshua, when I go to bed, I go to bed to sleep." John Wilkins Sigsworth, *World-Changers Karl Marx and John Wesley*, p. 28.

[125] John Wilkins Sigsworth, *World-Changers Karl Marx and John Wesley*, p. 28.

[126] Albert C. Outler (ed), *John Wesley*, (New York: Oxford University Press, 1964), p. 5.

This character, once identified, is discernable in every aspect and context of John Wesley's entire career.

4. His Christian Experience

In the Wesley household religious training began early. Children had to be quiet at prayer time and to ask a blessing by sign without making noise. They learned the Lord's prayer, to which by degrees, other prayers were added. Profane and rude words were never allowed to be uttered or spoken.[127] Despite coming from a puritan's family, John Wesley says that he was not sure of his personal experience with the Lord. He was religious, sincere and hard working but he did not seem to have had the salvation experience as his personal testimony reveal.

His boyhood home was one of piety and his mother's spiritual nurture was considerable. John Wesley's evaluation of Charterhouse school days indicates that he rated himself somewhat sinful at times; by his own admission his undergraduate Oxford days were on the frivolous side.[128]

> In 1725 just prior to his "taking holy orders", an unmistakeable seriousness becomes discernable. It dates from a serious reading of some of the so-called mystics, especially A'Kempis (*Imitation of Christ*), Taylor's (*Holy Living and Holy Dying*) and Law's (*Serious Call to a Devout and Holy Life and On Christian Perfection*). These books led to an intensification of his devotional life, I resolved to dedicate all my life to God, and a more rigorous disciplining of himself in the use of time. Leisure and I have taken leave of each other, he wrote in a letter to his mother.[129]

John Wesley took his Master's degree in the year 1726-27, then assisted in his father's parish till late 1729, at which time he was called back to Oxford, for standards were low and his scholarship was needed. Activities there included Bible study (using the Greek New Testament), prayer, communion, self-examination, planning, visiting the sick and imprisoned, teaching poor children and dispensing charity.[130] John Wesley seems to have had the Nazareth manifesto in view as he went about with his ministry: "...he has anointed me to proclaim good news to the poor...freedom for the prisoners...." Luke 4:18 and Jesus' saying "Truly I tell you, whatever you did for one of the least of these brothers and sisters of mine, you did for me" (Matt.25:40). Keeping this in mind John and his company were engaging themselves with above mentioned social services.

Turner (*The More Excellent Way*) thinks that Oxford's general irreligion at that time had a part in Wesley's move towards piety. George Whitefield, who was

---

[127] John Telford, *Popular Life of John Wesley*, p. 16.

[128] John Wilkins Sigsworth, *World-Changers Karl Marx and John Wesley*, pp. 9-10.

[129] *Ibid.*

[130] *Ibid.*, pp. 10 & 158.

to become the outstanding preacher of his generation, was a member of the club. During his Oxford years John Wesley produced two sermons on the Holy Spirit which were to become classics. And yet he was uncertain of himself, not knowing whether he was a Christian. The seclusion of the university had not produced the personal holiness he craved.

John Wesley's ill-fated Georgia jaunt of 1736-38 is an epoch in itself and is written in details by many of John Wesley's biographers. However, John Wesley returned from the New World realizing himself a failure, but the experience helped him to make two important discoveries. The first was that he himself still had an incredible spiritual lack. Of this he lamented in his Journal while returning: "I went to America to convert the *Indians,*[131] but oh! Who shall convert me?" It would appear he had hoped this good work would somehow produce the assurance he craved. The other discovery was that his deficiency could be supplied. He made this discovery through observing and talking with some of his fellow passengers during a fierce Atlantic storm on the way out. They were Moravians from Germany. While John Wesley and most of the other passengers were terrified by the storm, these Moravians calmly sang a psalm of joy in a worship service they were holding. After the gale subsided, Wesley conversed with one of them and received the impressive assurance that they were not afraid to die.

When the Moravians asked, 'Do you know yourself? Have you the witness within yourself? Does the Spirit of God bear witness with your Spirit that you are a child of God? Do you know that he has saved you?' John Wesley records that he was surprised and knew not what to answer. With embarrassment he muttered an affirmative reply – I do. But *I fear they were vain Words.*[132] On his deathbed a little earlier, John Wesley's father had insisted, "The inner witness, my son, that is the strongest proof of Christianity."[133]

In spite of his godly home, his university education, his devotional reading, his baptism, his ordination, his disciplined lifestyle and his years of preaching and administering the sacrament, John Wesley had not arrived spiritually. Back in England John Wesley conferred for nine weeks with another Moravian named Peter Boehler. Boehler's contention that salvation was by faith alone was hard for one who had sought to grasp it by works and the disciplined life. Boehler even introduced him to three other Englishmen who professed to have "saving faith" and promised to bring eight more, if numbers were needed to dispel John's disbelief. By March 5, 1738, John Wesley was convinced of his absence of faith, and was thinking to give up preaching. John Wesley seemed to have enquired, how can one preach to others who has no faith himself? Boehler asked him to continue preaching. John Wesley's query was what can I preach? Boehler seemed

---

[131] This term refers to Red Indians and not to those belonging to the Republic of India.

[132] J. Ernest Rattenbury in his book, *The Conversion of the Wesley's* (London: The Epworth Press [Edgar C. Barton], 1938), pp. 63-64. Also quoted in *John Wesley His Way of Knowing God* by Robert O. Reddish, Jr. (Colorado:The Rorge Publishing Company, 1972), p. 11.

[133] John Wilkins Sigsworth, *World-Changers Karl Marx and John Wesley*, p. 10.

to have said, "Preach faith *till* you have it; and then, because you have it, you *will* preach faith."[134]

Despite his personal struggle with salvation experience, he records in his Journal how he prayed with a condemned prisoner and brought the man assurance of sins forgiven. Many seem to believe that the encounter with Peter Boehler from March 5-7, 1738 probably was John's **intellectual** conversion to Protestant truth, or rather a process leading him to personal experience.[135]

The unique experience came to John on a Wednesday night, the May 24. Twice during that day he had opened his New Testament at random, a practice he later discouraged. Each time the words he first read heightened his expectations (One passage read: "Thou art not far from the kingdom of God.") In the afternoon with a friend he attended a service at St. Paul's Cathedral. Even the anthem played and sung held a promise for the little still-groping 35-year-old cleric-don.[136]

According to Leslie Newman (*The Philosophical Thought of John Wesley*), he never made his experience a norm for others. Actually he waited 28 months to publish the account. However, this is what John Wesley wrote:

> In the evening I went very unwillingly to a society in Aldersgate Street where one was reading Luther's preface to the Epistle to the Romans. About a quarter before nine while he was describing the change that God works in the heart through faith in Christ, **I felt my heart strangely warmed**. I felt I did trust Christ. Christ alone, for salvation; and an assurance was given me that He had taken away my sins, even mine, and saved me from the law of sin and death.[137]

After his **heart warming** experience, John Wesley seem to have had a dramatic change in his attitude towards other people. He records in his journal saying: "I began to pray with all my might for those who had in a more special manner despitefully used me and persecuted me."[138]

According to Fitchett (*Wesley and His Century*) John Wesley "spent thirteen sad blundering years in solving the problem of religion for himself." Now for him the "faith barrier" was at last broken. What the famous Anglican bishop and philosopher Joseph Butler did not experience till his deathbed and what even the saintly Susanna Wesley did not know experimentally until a short time before her passing, John Wesley had received at 35 and would confess across 53 more fruitful years. That Aldersgate Street building where John Wesley with the little group

---

[134] J. Ernest Rattenbury in his book, *The Conversion of the Wesley's* (London: The Epworth Press [Edgar C. Barton], 1938), p. 70.

[135] *Ibid.*

[136] John Wilkins Sigsworth, *World-Changers Karl Marx and John Wesley*, p. 11.

[137] John Wesley's Journal I, 475: "May 1738" quoted by J. Ernest Rattenbury in his book, *The Conversion of the Wesley's* (London: The Epworth Press [Edgar C. Barton], 1938), p. 81.

[138] *Ibid.*

of worshippers met under an unnamed lay leader – some think he was William Holland – has been demolished. Until the late 1960s a branch of Barclay's Bank stood in its place and the experience of a heart-warming that was destined to shake England and the world. On May 24, 1981, a new huge bronze memorial bearing John Wesley's diary entry was erected near the conversion spot.[139]

William Lecky, a leading historian of eighteenth-century England, rated that humble Aldersgate meeting and the religious revolution it precipitated of greater historic importance than all Pitt's[140] victories of war by land and sea.

So different was John Wesley's life afterwards that George Grant Cell author of *The Rediscovery of John Wesley* has suggested that if no Journal account of his conversion experience existed, "The facts would compel us to invent one."[141] After that, God was for Wesley the great reality.

Some of John Wesley's biographers with a limited appreciation for such matters have tried to minimize the Aldersgate experience. True, John Wesley referred to himself as an "almost Christian" from that early date on, and is even alleged to have had some later second thought on his famous denial of being a Christian when he went to Georgia. But he never printed the statement in his lifetime, and he may or may not be its author, says Cell. It would seem that the best that can be said for 1725 is to call it the year of his intellectual conversion, as is quoted earlier, terming 1738 as his evangelical conversion which, psychologist Mavis notes, a contributor to *Aldersgate Heritage*, released him from guilt, freed him from hostility and delivered him from anxiety. Obviously such an experience was something deeper than the "psychological re-assurance" that another student of John Wesley had settled for.[142] When John Wesley found God, he found himself. Very soon he also found his place in the history of a needy world.[143]

5. His Scholarship

His prowess in winning both a Studentship from Charterhouse to Oxford and a fellowship to Lincoln after taking his first degree have been mentioned earlier. Christ Church College where he took that first degree was renowned for its library. They tell that the Wesley brothers, as they made the 75-mile trek on foot between

---

[139] John Wilkins Sigsworth, *World-Changers Karl Marx and John Wesley*, p. 11.

[140] William Pitt was the Prime Minister of the then England.

[141] Elmer T. Clark, in What Happened at Aldersgate, had identified at least 24 references in Wesley's writings to this time as the beginning of his 'vital faith." It seems, as Schofield has suggested in the same compilation, that John Wesley's centre of gravity had shifted from himself to God. John Wilkins Sigsworth, *World-Changers Karl Marx and John Wesley*, p. 12.

[142] John Wilkins Sigsworth, *World-Changers Karl Marx and John Wesley*, p. 12

[143] *Ibid*. There is a book entitled: *The Conversion of the Wesley's*: *A Critical Study* by J. Ernest Rattenbury in 1938, which looks at different aspects of John's and Charles' conversion. It is therefore, not necessary to discuss the same in details here. A summary of different views about John's conversion are recorded here to serve the purpose of this research.

Epworth and Oxford, used to improve their time by reading to each other, one reading while the other watched the path to keep him from stumbling.[144]

Apart from English, his mother tongue, John eventually knew ten languages including continental languages – Arabic, Latin and, of course, Hebrew and Greek which enabled him to read the Scriptures of the Old and New Testaments in the original. He read all kinds of books including those on Church history, Church fathers, theologians of the reformation period and other classics. Wesley called himself "a man of one book" yet as Haddal (*John Wesley*) makes clear, he "read books of all ages and by all sorts of authors." He was steeped in church history, drank deeply from the writings of the early church fathers – Ignatius, Polycarp, etc. – and mastered the literature of medieval mysticism, a Roman Catholic school of religious experience that focussed on union with God. He also studied Protestant theologians from the Reformation on, including the Puritans. He was thoroughly familiar with the teachings of the so-called Deists of his day who believed in God as creator but little more. Yet John's reading was in no sense limited to religious themes. He devoured the ancient classics, the dramas – especially tragedies – of Shakespeare, the scientific writings of both earlier and his own days (these included the works of Newton, Bacon, Franklin, Huyghens and Priestley), volumes of history, novels of men like Swift, whose style he greatly admired and the political theory of Machiavelli. The major poets and philosophers of all ages he knew well. Like Cowper he regarded Milton's *Paradise Lost* the world's finest poem. Voltaire's views disgusted Wesley so much that he wrote a pamphlet denouncing certain of that scoffer's (Voltaire's) teachings. John called Voltaire, the French Philosopher, "a creature", certainly, never was a more consummate coxcomb.[145]

John Wesley's long-term study of medicine is an interesting aspect of his career. No wonder, many Methodist pastors in Karnataka know First-Aid, a basic knowledge to treat common diseases. This legacy probably traces its history to John Wesley's interest in medicine and his followers.

While it cannot be argued that he was a distinguished specialist in any field of knowledge, yet his contemporary Dr. Samuel Johnson who was the dominant literary figure of his age and a man not extravagant with compliments, testified that Wesley could talk on any subject, adding "I could converse with him all night," terming John Wesley the "contemporary Plato." The Monthly Review in 1768 acknowledged him as a profound scholar and Cambridge's Glover grouped John Wesley, Luther, Augustine and the Apostle Paul as four "Intellectuals" whom God greatly used. Like a true scholar John Wesley confessed that he kept his mind ever open on subjects so he might 'be better informed in future than in the past." Though John Wesley was skilled in logic, he seems to have given little time to mathematics, even though it excited him. That one as physically active as John

[144] John Wilkins Sigsworth, *World-Changers Karl Marx and John Wesley*, p. 18.
[145] *Ibid.*, 19.

Wesley was, and so immersed in administrative tasks as he became in mature years, should continue as a scholar is almost unbelievable. But as he confessed, he often read poetry, history and philosophy while riding his horse, or later travelling in his carriage. His "other employment at other times" dictated that he do it then or not at all. The monument at Bristol of the typically mounted John Wesley portrays him with a book in his hand. Someone has counted comments in his Journal regarding almost 300 volumes and these in six different languages. Evidently the books were mostly, if not all, read as he travelled in one way or another. Knowing John Wesley's accomplishments and personal study pattern will help us understand better his expectations for Methodist preachers, as disclosed in his thoughts on Education further.[146]

John Wesley was widely recognised as a leader, administrator and a scholar. Here are some of the statements about his leadership and scholarship. Agnostic Leslie Stephen called him the greatest captain of men of his century; Lord Macaulay rated him as having as great genius for government as Cardinal Richelieu; Roman Catholic Piette compared him with Ignatius for his genius as an organizer; Catholic Dallinger considered him one of the two most significant protestant figures since reformation; and Anglican Bishop Warburton was opposed to Wesley's views and his stand against the Church of England, still admitted that "John Wesley was formed of the best stuff nature ever put into a fanatic to make him the successful head and a leader of a sect."[147] Finally, one might add to these testimonials the words of British Premier Lloyd George: "... Undoubtedly the greatest religious leader the Anglo-Saxon race ever produced."[148] Though, he was a younger member of his family, his brothers and sisters often consulted him for advice. Such was the scholarship that the Creator had implanted in frail and small looking John Wesley.

C. Founding of the Movement

This Movement was in response to the people as they went about preaching. Who said we want you likewise to talk with us often to direct and quicken us. The rise of Methodism was in November, 1729, when four of us met together at Oxford; the second was in Savannah (USA) in April, 1736, when twenty or thirty persons met at Wesley's house; the last was in London on this day May 1, 1738, when forty or fifty of us agreed to meet together every Wednesday evening in order to have free conversation, begun and ended with singing and prayer. [149]

As is discussed above the socio-political and religious conditions were degenerating and appalling. Spirituality was a foreign element to many religious

[146] John Wilkins Sigsworth, *World-Changers Karl Marx and John Wesley*, p. 19.

[147] *Ibid.*, p. 157.

[148] *Ibid.*

[149] Cf. John Wesley, *A Concise Ecclesiastical History* (London: 1781, IV), p. 175, quoted by Maximin Piette, in *John Wesley in the Evolution of Protestantism* (London: Sheed and Ward, 1938), pp. 455-456.

leaders.[150] In this context the Wesley brothers John & Charles and their friends thought it best to keep themselves away from such contamination by meeting for prayer and Bible study at Oxford regularly. This spiritual fellowship inspired them to share the gospel truth with others such as prisoners and sick people around Oxford. Gradually this fellowship grew up to be a movement in course of time despite the Church of England's opposition. It spread to different parts gathering people and momentum. As a Movement becoming a Church, it is perceived by Methodists today as the second largest protestant Church in the world.

1. Origin: In November, 1729, four young gentlemen of Oxford – John Wesley, Fellow of Lincoln College, Charles Wesley, Student of Christ Church College, William Morgan, Commoner of Christ Church, and Robert Kirkham, John's great friend from the Gloucestershire parsonage,[151] and a member of Merton College began to spend some evenings in a week together, in reading, chiefly Greek New Testament. Gradually some of Wesley's students sought permission to join them; afterwards one of Charles' pupils too joined the group.[152]

Because of the exact regularity of their life, discipline and studies a young gentleman of Christ Church made a casual comment – "Here is a new set of Methodists sprung up;"[153] alluding to some ancient physicians who were so called. The name was new and quaint, so it spread quickly and soon the Methodists were known all over the University. Other thoughtless young men around them made fun of them, and invented all sorts of nicknames. Their little meeting was called in ridicule – the 'Holy Club'; because of their reverence for the Bible led to their being spoken of as 'Bible moths' and 'Bible Bigots' etc.[154] But the only name that has lasted to date is Methodists.

Intially the four members of the Holy Club had agreed to spend three or four evenings each week together reading the classics on week days and reading a work on divinity on Sundays. When William Morgan had suggested they visit prisoners and those who were ill. Wesley wrote to his father who himself was an Anglican minister to consult and sought permission of the Bishop of Oxford through the good offices of his chaplain. Both gave their blessing to these activities which were suggested by Morgan. With this supportthe members of the Holy Club continued to meet together; they partook in Lord's supper once a week and did all the good they could for their known people, for prisoners and for few poor

[150] John Wilkins Sigsworth, *World-Changers Karl Marx and John Wesley*, p. 40.

[151] W. B. Fitzgerald, *John Wesley on Horseback* (London: The Epworth Press, n.d.), p. 53.

[152] It was 1732, Ingham, of the Queen's College and Broughton, of Exeter College, were added to their number. In April of the same year Clayton along with his pupils were added to the group. About the same time, James Harvey was permitted to meet with them too. In 1735, George Whitefield a famous preacher joined the group which was meeting daily at Oxford. *The Works of John Wesley*, Vol. VIII, 3rd edition (Grand Rapids, Michigan: Baker Books, 1998), p. 348.

[153] *The Works of John Wesley*, Vol. VIII, 3rd edition (Grand Rapids, Michigan: Baker Books, 1998), p. 348.

[154] W. B. Fitzgerald, *John Wesley on Horseback* (London: The Epworth Press, n.d.), pp. 51-52.

families in Oxford. Wesley then set out a series of questions about doing good that he believed encapsulated the spirit of the Holy Club. These questions covered four distinct areas[155]:

- Whether all people should imitate Christ who went about doing.
- Whether we should do good to our acquaintances.
- Whether we should do good to those in need.
- Whether we should do good to those who are in prison.

Wesley indicated that he did not approve of any person who answered these questions negatively. With this clarion call of Wesley, many people enrolled into Holy Club and membership got enlarged by day.

They were zealous members of the Church of England and they knew all her doctrines and discipline thoroughly. They were not just religious minded but socially responsible members as well. They were zealous observers of the University rules for their conscience sake not because somebody kept an eye on them. They did not do this to please anyone in the University. But their one desire and design was to be downright Bible-Christians taking the Bible as the whole and sole rule for their behaviour and conduct.[156]

2. Purpose: In the event of the evolution of the Methodist movement the Church of England was experiencing doctrinal, disciplinary and ceremonial life's utter disorganization.[157] The powerlessness of life of the Church to counter moral and spiritual decay was a serious concern. The irreligious attitude of the people and Wesley's new found faith in Christ was a motivating factor to speak out with conviction to bring about change. Therefore, he organised small groups and societies to teach them the biblical truth and to challenge the religio-political systems of his time.

Thus, by mid 1732, John Wesley had gathered around him a group of friends who shared his commitment to a disciplined Christian living. However, there were many obstacles to their gathering and coming together, for e.g., when William Morgan one of the original members of John Wesley's group died, word spread around the university that he died as a result of extreme ascetic practices encouraged by John Wesley.[158] This pushed John Wesley into public eye not only in Oxford and Dublin (Morgan's hometown), but also in London and throughout the British Isles. Such attacks forced John Wesley to explain his beliefs, convictions

---

155 Ralph Waller, *John Wesley – A Personal Portrait* (London: SPCK, 2003), p. 28.

156 *The Works of John Wesley*, Vol. VIII, 3rd edition, p. 348.

157 Maximin Piette, in *John Wesley in the Evolution of Protestantism* (London: Sheed and Ward, 1938), p. 119.

158 Richard P. Heitzenrater, *The Elusive Mr. Wesley*, 2nd edition (Nashville: Abingdon Press, 2003), p. 63.

and activities to the public which in turn did some good service to the spread of the Movement.

Therefore, the group was charged as extreme righteous and scrupulous people, because they insisted too much on observing both Church and university rules and regulations. It was alleged that they took the Scriptures in too strict and literal sense. Meanwhile, they began to be convinced, that "by grace we are saved through faith," that justification by faith was the doctrine of the Church as well as of the Bible. As soon as they believed, they spoke, salvation by faith being their standard topic. Of course, they emphasised this fact vociferously day and night. In a short time they eventually became popular preachers. They attracted a large congregation wherever they preached. The name – Methodists, that was to be a mockery of their life style, was revived; all these gentlemen were entitled Methodists.[159] Soon, those who called themselves Bible Christians were included in the general name of Methodists. However, many of them separated themselves from John Wesley later in years due to doctrinal differences; one such was Whitefield who strongly advocated Calvinism. But those who remained with Wesley, endeavoured to live according to what they preached, to be plain Bible – Christians. And they met together at convenient times to encourage one another. They tenderly loved many, though not their opinions and they did not react to people's hatred and accusations. It was their constant endeavour to please all men [women] for their good and edification. But they knew that it cannot be done, because they knew the words of Apostle Paul, "If I yet please men, I am not the servant of Christ." However, they continued on. "Through honour and dishonour, through evil report and good report;" desiring only that their Master may say in that day, Servants of God, well done!"[160]

3. Growth: It is to be asserted however that, John Wesley never detached himself from the mother Church till his death. However, the Church of England did not respond positively to his activities. Though he did not desire to start a denomination it became a movement based on biblical teaching and discipline. To serve its cause better he organised his followers into Societies and Bands giving them a list of rules and regulations to maintain Methodists' basic principles. John Wesley never called his groups of followers as a church/denomination but rather he called them as the Societies. This term was common concept in the UK at Wesley's time. Society was a company of men having the form and seeking the power of godliness, united in order to pray together, to receive the word of exhortation, and to watch over one another in love that they may help each other to work out their salvation. These *societies* were subdivided into *Classes* of about 12 persons each. Each class had a *leader* whose duties included seeing each person in his class once a week at least, in order to inquire how their souls prosper; to

[159] *The Works of John Wesley*, Vol. VIII, 3rd edition (Grand Rapids, Michigan: Baker Books, 1998), p. 349.

[160] *Ibid.*, p. 351.

advise, reprove, comfort, or exhort as occasion may require. The *bands* were a small group who's sharing, intimacy and achievement rivals the best of the small group explosion of modern times

The Methodist Movement produced a mammoth moral and spiritual reform in the British Isles. This movement spread far and wide in no time beyond Britain triggering missionary movements around the World. All figures and facts related to his movement are noted in Chapter two under "Mission".

Summary

This Chapter has highlighted some of the salient features in the life and background of John Wesley. His passion for the marginalized and their liberation was his main concern of his movement – Methodism. The following Chapter will discuss his major tool – Education, in bringing about reformation in his Church and Country. Specifically the Chapter will look at Wesley as an educator and his methodology in using education as a tool for transformation. His theological understanding of issues related to humanity and God in brief enrich the foregoing discussion.

Chapter 2

John Wesley - The Educator

A. The Formation of his Thoughts on Education with its Philosophical Grounding and its Analysis from a Biblical and Theological Perspective 47

1. Influences: On Educational and Philosophical Thought Formation 49
   - a. Susanna Wesley 49
   - b. John Amos Comenius 51
   - c. John Locke 53
   - d. German Pietism 55
2. Role of Christian Education 56
   - a. His views on the Role of Teachers 58
   - b. Wesley's Admonition to Schoolteachers 60
3. Wesley's Thoughts on Education: Methodology and Approach 61
   - a. His Educational Thoughts (Philosophy) 61
   - b. His Educational Methodology 66
4. Reactions to Educational Theorists and General Education of his time 67
5. Implications for Contemporary Christian Education 70

B. Wesley and Christian Education: A Biblical and Theological Perspective 75

1. Views on God, Man, Sin and Salvation 76
2. Understanding Humanity 82
3. Community and Society 83
4. Church and Mission 86
5. Family and Education 91

C. Distinct Characteristics of Wesley's Educational Theory and Approach 97
1. Learning Theory 97
a. Personologism 97
b. Situationalism 97
c. Interactionism 97
2. Practice of Christian Education 97
a. Objectives of Christian Education 98
b. John Wesley's Theory and Method 98
c. Pedagogy of Liberation 100
d. The Preachers as Teachers 100
e. The Parents as Teachers 101
3. Christian Education for Humanization, Liberation and Justice 103
a. Education for Humanization 103
b. Education is Liberation and for Justice 104
D. Limits in John Wesley's Method and Pedagogical Approach to Christian Education 105

Chapter 2

John Wesley - The Educator

A. The Formation of his Thoughts on Education with its Philosophical Grounding and its Analysis from a Biblical and Theological Perspective

In the previous chapter, the context in which Wesley emerged as a noted personality in the history of United Kingdom was briefly sketched. The present chapter will focus on Wesley as an educator - his educational and philosophical formation and analysis of his Christian educational thoughts from a Biblical and Theological perspective. This research does not commit itself to dealing with John Wesley as mere educational philosopher but as a practitioner of education. Though many educational philosophers do not count him as one among them. Wesley used the pulpit as tool to impart education, which in itself was liberation. He was an interesting personality, as one would notice in the following sentence. Specialized studies have looked at him as a philanthropist, sociologist, philosopher, theologian, church founder, scientist, physician, electrotherapist[161], educator, and even letter writer.[162] This is evident in number of books and more than 200 biographies authored by different scholars about his life and work.[163] Above all, John Wesley was an educator; he and his followers established numerous day schools and boarding schools, of which Kingswood is the best known. Wesley as an educator and his passion for education have been insightfully discussed by scholars such as Alfred H. Body, John W. Prince, John Owen Gross, Joseph William Seaborn,

---

[161] A person who treats diseases by the use of electricity, example to generate heat or stimulate muscular activity in tissues. *The New Penguin English Dictionary*, s.v. "electrotherapy".

[162] John Wilkins Sigsworth, *World-Changers: Karl Marx and John Wesley* (Ontario: Easingwold Pulications, 1982), p. 240.

[163] *Ibid.*

Jr. and a host scholars.[164] This research is limited to analysing and examining Wesley's views or thoughts on education, particularly Christian Education, and its relevance for today with special reference to Methodists' Christian education programmes and activities in Karnataka.

It is acknowledged that John Wesley was a pioneer of popular education.[165] He conducted educational enterprises continuously for over fifty years, and some experts contend that he was the only leader of importance in eighteenth-century England who had a real and practical interest in educating children of all classes.[166] The movement for popular education which Wesley helped inaugurate grew so rapidly that by the middle of the nineteenth century, a stigma was associated with illiteracy.[167] Prior to this, illiteracy was part of the common people's life.

It is on record that by 1834 the British Wesleyan Methodist conference had more than a third of a million children enrolled in its schools; some 60,000 voluntary teachers served these children.... By 1904, British Methodist Sunday school enrolment exceeded a million.[168] Wesley seems to have recognised that persons of all ages had to be taught the Christian faith and practice. He believed that such teaching needed to be a cognitive process of didactic learning and a formative process of spiritual nurturing.[169]

John Wesley was a legend in his own way. He had a heroic public image and the traditional statistics speak for themselves: "250,000 miles travelled on horseback, over 40,000[170] sermons preached during the span of sixty-six years, more than 400 publications on nearly every conceivable topic"[171] till his death in his 88th year. Much of this has about his educational theory and he was involved in a variety of educational endeavours. As the modern radical educator, Paulo Freire, a Brazilian philosopher revolutionized the educational system in Latin America and elsewhere by using pedagogical theory; so too John Wesley used education and preaching to reform the eighteenth century England. He understood the

[164] Gayle Carlton Felton, "John Wesley and the Teaching Ministry: Ramification for the Church Today" in *Religious Education*, Vol. 92, Issue I, (Winter 1997), p. 102.

[165] Elmer L. Towns, (ed), *A History of Religious Educators* (Grand Rapids: Baker Book House, 1975), p. 212.

[166] Alfred H. Body, *John Wesley and Education* (London: The Epworth Press, 1936), p. 42. cf. Elmer L. Towns, (ed), *A History of Religious Educators* (Grand Rapids: Baker Book House, 1975), p. 212.

[167] John Owen Gross, *John Wesley: Christian Educator* (Nashville: Board of education, the Methodist Church, 1954), p. 14.

[168] John Wilkins Sigsworth, *World-Changers: Karl Marx and John Wesley* (Ontario: Easingwold Publications, 1982), p. 234.

[169] Gayle Carlton Felton, "John Wesley and the Teaching Ministry: Ramifications for Education in the Church Today," in *Religious Education*, Vol. 92, Issue 1 (Winter 1997), p. 99.

[170] Gary M. Best, The present Principal of Kingswood School, who has held this position for more than twenty years records as 45,000 sermons in his unpublished paper presented at Lincoln College Oxford 2003.

[171] Richard P. Heitzenrater, *The Elusive Mr. Wesley*, 2nd edition (Nashville: Abingdon Press, 2003), p. 27.

potential for education to function as an instrument of social and spiritual reform and sought to use it for the benefit of the disadvantaged socio-economical classes.[172] Historians and biographers such as W. E. H. Lecky, Robert Southey, J. H. Plumb, J. W. Bready, Elmer Towns, Albert C. Outler, William Cannon, and others contend that he was the only leader of importance in the eighteenth century England who sounded a voice for educational transformation. "His educational philosophy was a compilation of his theological convictions, personal experience and the reaction to his contemporaries in the field of education"[173]. He notes in his *Journal:* "I preached on the Education of children, wherein we are so shamefully wanting."[174] "It is the opinion of some of the Methodist scholars that John Wesley's philosophy of education was far more advanced for his time."[175] Yet one does not customarily revere John Wesley as an educator[176]. A probable reason for not considering him as an educator could be that he seemed to have chosen educational and pedagogical ideas at random from different schools of thought. He is called by many a "synthesizer" of educational theories.[177]

It is worthwhile, to discover, how John Wesley, an Anglican preacher plunged into the educational arena?

The following section on educational and thought formation will discuss various influences on John Wesley. It highlights his educational thoughts, in developing his own educational theory, method and approach.

1. Influences: On Educational and Philosophical Thought Formation

Recognizing his enormous educational contributions, this section examines those individuals and events that influenced the formation of John Wesley's educational thoughts or philosophy.

a. Susanna Wesley[178]: One of the chief sources of John Wesley's detailed programme of training for children was his mother. Ten of the nineteen children born to the Epworth rector's wife survived infancy, and Susanna Wesley was almost exclusively responsible for their training. She refused to send them to the local schoolmaster, John Hollan, because she felt he was notoriously incompetent and wicked. Susanna was a skilled educator. Her servants did the housework while

[172] Gayle Carlton Felton, "John Wesley and the teaching ministry: Ramification for the church today" in *Religious Education*, Vol. 92, Issue I (Winter 1997), p. 100.

[173] James Riley Estep Jr. "John Wesley's Philosophy of Formal Childhood Education" in *Christian Education Journal*, Vol. INS, No. 2 (Fall 1997), p. 44.

[174] *John Wesley Journal,* January 30, 1767.

[175] John Owen Gross, *John Wesley: Christian Educator* (Nashville: Board of Education, Methodist Church, 1954), p. 9.

[176] James Riley Estep Jr. "John Wesley's Philosophy of Formal Childhood Education" *in Christian Education Journal*, Vol. INS, No. 2, Fall 1997, p. 43.

[177] *Ibid.* p. 44.

[178] See Appendix A, for her views on education and her imprint on John Wesley's educational philosophy. John Wesley was very close his mother and she had an extraordinary influence on his life.

she taught the ten children on regular school day schedule.[179] She looked upon all her children as talents entrusted to her by God, and she desired to impart to them useful knowledge and, even more basic, to save their souls.[180] She made it her habit to converse one evening a week with each child separately. Thursday evenings were devoted to John, and so deeply was the boy impressed with these one-to-one teaching sessions that many years later when the care of all the churches weighed heavily upon him he requested his mother to spend part of each Thursday evening praying for him.[181] Observing John at the age of eight his father judged him fit to receive Holy Communion.

Susanna found no textbooks that met her severe requirements; therefore, she wrote and edited her own books. Such as: *An Exposition of the Apostles' Creed; An Exposition of the Ten Commandments, and Religious Conference Written for the Use of My Children.*[182]

Susanna wrote to her son John in later years: "I insist upon conquering the will of children betimes because this is the only strong and rational foundation of a religious education, without which both precept and example will be ineffectual."[183] She ran a strict school, largely by the principles of essentialism, [Essentialism: The aim of essentialism is to transmit knowledge, to master the facts. Its curriculum is content-centered. Its symbol is the lecture room and the library. Its methodology is lecture and research. The teacher skill required is lecturing. Principal weaknesses include: tendency to be dull: knowledge about replaces knowledge of; can become authoritarian indoctrination. Strengths include: perpetuation of the good traditions of civilization, the wisdom of the ages, and provision of the student with an encounter with greatness. Exponents: Aristotle, Aquinas, John Locke, Maria Montessori, John Milton, Bertrand Russell].[184] but her education was laced with parental love, saturated with tears and prayers for salvation, and highlighted by individualized instruction.[185] She did not believe in conquering their wills only by severe punishment.

---

[179] Wesley Tracy, "Christian Education in the Wesleyan Mode", in *Wesleyan Theological Journal*, Vol. 17, No. 1, (Spring 1982), p. 44.

[180] Elmer L. Towns (ed). *A History of Religious Educators* (Grand Rapids: Baker Book House, 1975), p. 214.

[181] John Wesley, *The Works of John Wesley*, 3rd edition, 14 Vol. (Kansas City, Missouri: Beacon Hill Press of Kansas city, 1978, Vol. VI), p. 593. Quoted by Wesley Tracy, "Christian Education in the Wesleyan Mode", in *Wesleyan Theological Journal*, Vol. 17, No. 1, (Spring 1982), p. 44.

[182] Elmer L. Towns, (ed)., *A History of Religious Educators*, p. 214.

[183] John Wesley, *The Journal of the Rev. John Wesley, A.M. Vol. IV* (London: Wesleyan Conference office, 1895), p. 34. Cf. John Telford, The Popular life of John Wesley, (London: Charles and Kelly, 1900), p. 12.

[184] Wesley Tracy, "Christian Education in the Wesleyan Mode", in *Wesleyan Theological Journal*, Vol. 17, No. 1, (Spring 1982), p. 44. see Wayne R. Rood, *Understanding Christian Education* (Nashville: Abingdon Press, 1970), pp. 338ff.

[185] Wesley Tracy, "Christian Education in the Wesleyan Mode", in *Wesleyan Theological Journal*, Vol. 17, No. 1, (Spring 1982), p. 44.

In another letter to John, Susanna articulated her 8 principles of child rearing; the main points are summarized as follows:

i. Because cowardice and fear of punishment often encourage a child to lie, anyone charged with a fault, which (sic) would confess it and promise to amend, would not be beaten.
ii. No sinful action such as lying, pilfering, playing at Church, playing on the Lord's Day, disobedience, or quarreling ever went unpunished.
iii. No child was beaten twice for the same fault.
iv. Every single act of obedience was commended and rewarded.
v. Anything done out of obedience or an intent to please, but not done well, should be accepted with kindness, and the child patiently shown how to do better in the future.
vi. Personal property was inviolable and no one was permitted to invade the property of another to the smallest extent.
vii. Promises were observed strictly. Once a gift was bestowed, thegiver relinquished all rights to the gift.
viii. No girl was taught to work until she could read well, and then she was taught to work with the same application and for the sametime that she was held to reading.[186]

There is little doubt that Susanna Wesley, profoundly influenced John's educational endeavour. Her puritanical ideas toward behaviour and child rearing are present in Wesley's educational theory and practice.[187] Such an upbringing helped John Wesley focus on the human element of his educational work.

b. John Amos Comenius (1592-1670): Jan Amos Komensky was born in Nivnitz, a village near western Moravia. He later latinized his name, as was the fashion in those days, to Comenius. After his studies in different parts of Europe he returned to Moravia where he wrote books, taught in school, and served as bishop of Moravian brethren.[188] Comenius has an outstanding place in the history of general education such that secular educators have called him the "father of modern education."[189] But he was a Christian educator par excellence. He has written more than a hundred treatises and textbooks. Those were summed

---

[186] John Wesley, *The Journal of the Rev. John Wesley, A.M. Vol. IV, August 1, 1742* (London: Wesleyan Conference office, 1895), pp. 34-39. For detailed information on this subject refer J. W. Prince, *Wesley on Religious Education* (New York: The Methodist Book Concern, 1926), pp. 103-105; Also referred in *History of Religious Educators*, edited by Elmer L. Towns, pp. 214-215.

[187] R. C. Monk, *John Wesley: His Puritan Heritage* (Nashville: Abingdon Press, 1966), pp. 185, 190. Also referred by James Riley Estep Jr. "John Wesley's Philosophy of formal Childhood education" in *Christian Education Journal*, Vol. INS, No. 2, (Fall 1997), p. 44.

[188] Elmer L. Towns (ed). *A History of Religious Educators*, p. 177.

[189] C. B. Eavey, *History of Christian Education* (Chicago: Moody Press, 1964), p. 169.

up in his theoretical work; *The Great Didactic,* a truly remarkable educational treatise.[190]

John Wesley visited Jena and Herrnhut in Germany and saw the Moravian schools in action. It is possible that at Herrnhut he discovered the practical application of the principles of John Amos Comenius for whom education was not merely a means to eradicate natural sin but a way to build moral control. One of Comenius' principles was that no subject is to be left until the students thoroughly understood it,[191] and John Wesley echoed this:

> Above all, let them not read or say one line without understanding what they say. Try them over and over; stop them short almost at every sentence and ask them what you mean by that; read it again. So that, if it be possible they must pass nothing until it has taken hold upon them.[192]

Another of Comenius' principles was that the child's will is to be completely surrendered to the teacher's, and Wesley agreed completely.

> A wise parent should begin to break . . . [his child's] will the first moment it appears. In the whole act of Christian education . . . there is nothing more important than this . . . the will of the parent is to a little child in the place of the will of God. But in order to carry this point, you will need incredible firmness and resolution; for after you have once begun, you must never give way.[193]

The influence of Comenius' principles on Wesley is difficult to measure because Mrs. Susanna Wesley's independently formulated philosophy or 8 by-laws paralleled those promoted by John Amos Comenius. Hence, when John Wesley observed and studied Comenius' principles and practices while visiting with the Pietists in Germany, Comenius' principles certainly reinforced what Wesley had learned from his mother.[194]

Here are those *The Great Didactic*[195] principles that John Wesley borrowed from John Amos Comenius which helped humanize his education. They include:

---

[190] C. B. Eavey, *History of Christian Education* (Chicago: Moody Press, 1964), p. 169.

[191] Alfred H. Body, *John Wesley and Education* (London: The Epworth Press, 1936), pp. 49-51. Also referred by Elmer L. towns, in *History of Religious Educators,* p. 215.

[192] *Ibid.*

[193] Elmer L. Towns, (ed)., *A History of Religious Educators*, p. 215, quoted in Alfred H. Body, *John Wesley and Education,* pp. 49-50.

[194] James Riley Estep Jr. "John Wesley's Philosophy of Formal Childhood Education" in *Christian Education Journal,* Vol. INS, No. 2, (Fall 1997), p. 44.

[195] Wesley Tracy, "Christian Education in the Wesleyan Mode", in *Wesleyan Theological Journal,* Vol. 17, No. 1, (Spring 1982), pp. 44-45.

i. Developmental Concerns. John Wesley echoed Comenius' principle of teaching orderly progression from the known to unknown. Teachers must grasp the right occasion to make learning effective. Use teachable moment to effect education. John Wesley was insistent that the content be adapted to child's level of thinking.

ii. Understanding versus memorizing. Comenius termed the practice of recitation which plagued European schools as the "slaughter house of the mind," and insisted on understanding rather than memorization. John Wesley gave same advice to parents and teachers repeatedly to stop while learning and let the child explain meanings in his [her] own words.

iii. Knowledge, virtue, piety, in this order, as without knowledge neither virtue nor piety could happen. John Wesley strongly advocated this process.

iv. Education must begin in pre-school years. Both Comenius and John Wesley were keen about teaching children at the very first sign of understanding.

v. "Amending" the will was Comenius' concept but Wesley went one step further and developed a concept called *will-breaking* theory.

vi. Love in education. Comenius came out of this philosophy-love in education, out of his own schooling experience where he had been thrashed through; therefore, he established a school based on love. John Wesley's love for children has been well documented. He speaks of it in word and deed.

vii. Education of the poor was a keynote of both Comenius and Wesley. In fact the humanitarian tone of the Methodist revival gave somewhat of a humane flavor to Methodist education.

viii. The education is pleasurable. John Wesley seems to have rejected this revolutionary idea of Comenius that the most effective learning occurs in an atmosphere of pleasant environment. John Wesley believed that education must be *painful to be profitable;* probably this is because of two different experiences at two differing contexts. John Wesley thought that that is the way the children would learn best. This is the way he devised his educational programme that was primarily based on essentialism, tempered with personal concern.

c. John Locke (1632-1704): He was an English Philosopher and educator who influenced Wesley.[196] He represented materialistic rationalism. His description of education was "a sound mind in a sound body."[197] However, he did not neglect morals and religion; instead he maintained that individual's consciousness is both

[196] James Riley Estep Jr. "John Wesley's Philosophy of formal Childhood education" in *Christian Education Journal*, Vol. INS, No. 2, (Fall 1997), p. 46.

[197] C. B. Eavey, *History of Christian Education* (Chicago: Moody Press, 1964), p. 167.

the source and the criterion of all truth.[198] Perhaps the most influential English educator of the eighteenth century for John Wesley was John Locke. Wesley seemed to have been familiar with Locke's *Essay on the Human Understanding and Thoughts on Education*, and Wesley was so impressed by this *Essay*, that, he made it a point to include it to be read in the fourth year of study at Kingswood school.[199] Locke's influence is particularly evident in the "disciplinary concept of Education" practiced by Wesley.[200] Wesley, then, combined sound religious training with perfect control of the children. He had lots in common to agree with the works of John Locke, and he did not hesitate to adopt it. A number of passages from John Wesley's works show not only a striking similarity in thought to Locke's thoughts concerning education, but also a marked similarity in expression. Wesley wrote that "the bias of nature is set the wrong way: education is designed to set it right." Wesley's use of the term **bias** in this context is hardly natural, and the whole sentence is, according to Alfred Body (*John Wesley and education*, p. 59) a typical Wesleyan abridgment. Body concluded that "in spite of the manifest differences between the schemes of education proposed by each man," such parallel passages as this leave one with the "strong feeling that Wesley was really indebted to Locke for much of his educational theory.[201]

Locke was not the only English educator who influenced Wesley. His attitude toward home-visits and family visitations at boarding schools can be attributed to

---

[198] C. B. Eavey, *History of Christian Education*, (Chicago: Moody Press, 1964), p. 167.

[199] John Wesley Prince, *Wesley on Religious Education*, (New York: Methodist Book Concern, 1926), p. 103 quoted by Alfred Body, *John Wesley and Education*, p. 61, referred by James Riley Estep Jr. "John Wesley's Philosophy of formal Childhood education" in *Christian Education Journal*, Vol. INS, No. 2, (Fall 1997), p. 45.

[200] James Riley Estep Jr. "John Wesley's Philosophy of formal Childhood Education" *in Christian Education Journal*, Vol. INS, No. 2, (Fall 1997), p. 45. Quoted from, *John Wesley and Education*, by Alfred Body, p. 33.

[201] Locke, for example, wrote that most children are born with "some bias in their natural temper, which it is the business of education to take off or counter balance."

Some other striking similarity between John Locke and John Wesley are cited below.

> Locke: This ought to be observed as an inviolable maxim, that whatever once is denied them [i.e., children], they are certainly not to obtain by crying or importunity, unless one has a mind to teach them to be impatient and troublesome by rewarding them for it when they are so.
>
> Wesley: Let him have nothing he cries for; absolutely nothing, great or small: else you undo your own work.
>
> Locke: Most children's constitutions are either spoiled or at least harmed by cockering and tenderness . . . Let his bed be hard, and rather quilts than feathers. Hard lodging strengthens the Parts; whereas being buried every night in Feathers melt and dissolves the Body.
>
> Wesley: All their beds have mattresses upon them, not featherbeds, both because they are most healthy, and because we would keep them at the utmost distance from softness and effeminacy.

John Milton's[202] *Treaties on Education.*[203] In fact, Milton and Wesley both express the same view - the true aim of education, that is, 'restoration of humanity from the fall.'[204]

John Wesley being a voracious reader of varied subjects and personalities seems to have been influenced by many eminent scholars other than the ones mentioned above. John Wesley's idea of liberation/restoration of humanity from the fall also held in common with William Law[205] as is evident if one reads his sermon no. 45 and *A short account of the school in Kingswood* near Bristol, will have clear idea about it. Likewise, it has been suggested that John Norris had profound influence on Wesley's concept of Knowledge. Probably it is true because Wesley published an abridgement of Norris' book – *Reflections*. However, Wesley did not fully agree with its content, as he identified and explained in the abridgement.[206]

As an eclectic reader John Wesley no doubt had many other factors to influence his life and ministry but the above mentioned persons and their lasting influence is specific to his educational thought formation.

d. German Pietism: John Wesley was exposed to the theological influence of German Pietism both in America and later in Germany that salvation is by grace through faith not by good works. However, Wesley being a high Anglican was not swayed by their philosophical influence as much as one would imagine. As W. T. Smith notes, "Wesley was as English as 4:00 tea, as Yorkshire pudding. Attempts to make him a disciple of Lutheran tradition leave much to be desired. Wesley was of Oxford, not Wittenberg."[207] Though his theological views were transformed as result of Moravians' influence however; that did not change his Church affiliation/denomination until his death.

It refers to Wesley's strong convictions about his theological and Spiritual foundations that were laid by both his family heritage and his parents. No doubt, that his association with the Oxford community deepened his convictions as an Anglican Christian further. However, the Moravians did influence Wesley's education theory as was noted in the above discussion. Particularly, Count

---

[202] He is the author of *Paradise lost* a famous book.

[203] John Wesley, "A Plain Account of Kingswood school", *Works,* Vol. XIII, p. 296, point 16. Refer Wesley Tracy, "Christian education in Wesleyan Mode," *Wesleyan Journal of Theology* (Spring 1982), p. 36. J. W. Prince, *Wesley on Religious Education*, p. 103.

[204] Alfred H. Body, *John Wesley and Education*, p. 34. Also refer, James Riley Estep Jr. "John Wesley's Philosophy of Formal Childhood Education" in *Christian Education Journal,* Vol. INS, No. 2, (Fall 1997), p. 46.

[205] James Riley Estep Jr. "John Wesley's Philosophy of Formal Childhood Education" in *Christian Education Journal,* Vol. INS, No. 2, (Fall 1997), p. 46.

[206] J. C. English, "John Wesley's Indebtedness to John Norris," *Church History* (March 1991), p. 67, quoted in James Riley Estep Jr. "John Wesley's Philosophy of Formal Childhood Education" in *Christian Education Journal,* Vol. INS, No. 2, (Fall 1997), p. 46.

[207] Warren Thomas Smith, "Eighteenth Century Encounters: Methodist-Moravians," *Methodist History*, Vol. XXIV, No. 3, (April 1986), p. 156. Also referred in *Christian Education Journal,* Vol. INS, No. 2, (Fall 1997), p. 44.

Zinzendorf, a Moravian, impressed on John Wesley's educational theory. A paradigm for the Moravian ideal, of which at Halle the Orphan house was a marvel.[208] The Kingswood school near Bristol was indeed a product of this model.

2. Role of Christian Education

In *The Radical Wesley*, Snyder notes, "the story of John Wesley's life and ministry is the story of creating and adapting structures to serve the burgeoning revival movement.[209] Wesley "realized that the result of his revival would be permanent only if the revival was united with education."[210] John Wesley's educational endeavours through out his life were whether based on the Church, family, or academic institutions were designed "to make them pious, to lead to personal religion, and to insure salvation."[211]

Hence, two preliminary thoughts or convictions about the role of education were developed regarding children. First, sin in a child's life must be countered through education. John Wesley had strong views about receiving a purely secular education; for him receiving purely secular education was equivalent to "sending them [children] to the devil" and he regarded "large public schools (as) nurseries of all matter of wickedness."[212] His views were probably based on the context in which the secular school of his time was imparting education. It is noted in the history of eighteenth century England that the secular schools did not have religious teaching as part of their curriculum, and the discipline of those children who attended those schools was a matter of concern.

Second, the child's 'will must' be curbed so that the soul may be saved.[213] This is not to suggest that he advocated a totalitarian or unrestrained form of child discipline. In "A Thought on the Manner of Educating Children," first published in 1783 by *The Arminian Magazine*, Wesley stated:

> Even religious masters may not have the spirit of government to which some even good men are strangers. They may habitually lean to this or that extreme, of remissness or of severity. And if they give children too much of their own will, or needlessly and churlishly restrain them, if they either use no punishment at all, or more than are necessary,

---

[208] Warren Thomas Smith, "Eighteenth Century Encounters: Methodist-Moravians," *Methodist History*, Vol. XXIV, No. 3, (April 1986), p. 150. Referred in *Christian Education Journal*, Vol. INS, No. 2, (Fall 1997), pp. 44-45.

[209] H. A. Snyder, *The Radical Wesley and Patterns for Church Renewal* (Downers Grove: Inter-Varsity Press, 1980), p. 53.

[210] Elmer L. Towns, (ed). *A History of Religious Educators*, p. 213.

[211] James Riley Estep Jr. "John Wesley's Philosophy of Formal Childhood Education" in *Christian Education Journal*, Vol. INS, No. 2, (Fall 1997), p. 48, quoted from J. W. Prince, *Wesley on Religious Education*, p. 87.

[212] Elmer L. Towns, (ed). *A History of Religious Educators*, p. 220.

[213] *Ibid.*, p. 221.

the leaning either to one extreme or the other, may frustrate their endeavours.[214]

In other words, what John Wesley felt was that no extreme actions are useful; instead one must strike a balance between what is said and done.

John Wesley's view on childhood discipline explains the severity of his rejection of play as being detrimental, both educationally and spiritually. "As we have no play days at Kingswood School, so neither do we allow any time for play on any day; for he that plays as a child will play as a man."[215] John Wesley's attitude toward play differed from both his predecessors and successors. For example, a century later Horace Bushnell advocated play "as the symbol and interpreter of Christian liberty."[216] This statement is repeated here to reinforce his views on 'play' which was stated under the elaboration of the research problem in introductory section.

While John Wesley was an earnest advocate of religious education, he maintained that not all contemporary forms of religious education were beneficial. In fact, he considered some of it to do "more harm than good"[217] citing instances of false religions, poor instruction, and undisciplined teachers. Hence, he argued that the family and professional instructors must provide sound education that insures them of receiving not just a religious education, but also a Christian one.

John Wesley's convictions regarding childhood education were based on his perception of the nature of children. On the other hand, critics alleged that Wesley lacked imagination; as a result, he had little in understanding the young children.[218] However, John Wesley held to three basic beliefs regarding children, which centred on their relationship to God, saving-faith, and religious instruction. This was his basic perception about children and their innate nature.

First, he believed strongly that the *Children are a Focus of God's Plan for Salvation.*

John Owen Gross commented that to John Wesley never considered the child as a child, but rather as a unit for salvation, "bred in sin, apt to evil and altogether

---

[214] Elmer L. Towns, (ed). *A History of Religious Educators,* p. 222.

[215] James Riley Estep Jr. "John Wesley's Philosophy of formal Childhood education" *in Christian Education Journal,* Vol. INS, No. 2, (Fall 1997), p. 49, quoted from Wesley's, *A Short Account of the Kingswood School,* p. 5.

[216] J. E. Reed and R. Prevost, *A History of Christian Education* (Nashville: Broadman and Holman, 1993), p. 319. Cf. James Riley Estep Jr. "John Wesley's Philosophy of Formal Childhood Education" in *Christian Education Journal,* Vol. INS, No. 2, (Fall 1997), p. 49.

[217] John Wesley, "A Thought on the manner of Educating Children", in *The Works of John Wesley,* Vol. XIII, Edited by Thomas Jackson (Grand Rapid, Michigan: Baker Book House, 1998), pp. 474-475. Cf. *Christian Education Journal,* Vol. INS, No. 2, (Fall 1997), p. 49.

[218] Gerald. R. Cragg, *The Church in the Age of Reason, 1648-1789* (New York: Penguin Books, 1970), p. 149, quoted in *Christian Education Journal,* Vol. INS, No. 2, (Fall 1997), p. 43.

as a **brand to be plucked out of the burning.**"[219] This is a favourite phrase that he often used to explain his childhood tragic experience when he was caught in a blazing fire in the Epworth Rectory from where he was rescued by fire fighters in 1709. In John Wesley's view, children were equal with adults concerning their need of grace and God's liberative work in Christ. Also, knowledge of God was not restricted to the adult believer, but open to everyone including the child.

Secondly, Wesley believed that *children are Capable of Genuine Faith and Religious Experience* "John Wesley's view that even young children are capable of mature religious consciousness was grounded in his doctrine of grace. When the Spirit is the teacher, there is no delay in learning."[220] This conclusion was not only based on his theological convictions, but his pastoral experience in dealing with children. For example, on several occasions John Wesley noted in his *Journal* that, children as young as two and a half years old made confessions of faith during extreme illness or even on their deathbeds.[221] These *Journal* notations "show that John Wesley believed it was possible for very young children to be religious."[222]

Finally, John Wesley believed that *children Must Receive Instruction in Early Childhood.*

John Wesley maintained, "That every stage in religious experience is possible in childhood," and hence considered religious education essential for early faith development.[223] He stressed that the child must understand the truth, not simply memorize it. He warned those involved in teaching, "Beware of that common, and accursed, way of making children parrots, instead of Christians."[224] In other words, he was against making children recite some liturgies and lessons without any understanding. Learning by rote was discouraged in John Wesley's scheme of education. Hence, it was Wesley's opinion that a child was never too young to receive religious instruction.

a. His views on the Role of Teachers

In John Wesley's estimation, the most important element of an academic institution was its faculty; and the most important quality of the instructor was his spirituality. "The human aspect of the teacher's role was rated higher than his

[219] John Owen Gross, *John Wesley: Christian Educator* (Nashville: Board of Education, the Methodist Church, 1954), p. 9. Also quoted in *Christian Education Journal*, Vol. INS, No. 2, (Fall 1997), p. 47.

[220] Elmer L. Towns, (ed)., *A History of Religious Educators*, p. 219. Cf. *Wesley on Religious Education*, p. 85.

[221] Cf. Wesley, Journal, 16th September, 1744, 28th June, 1746 and 8th April 1755. Also Towns, *A History of Religious Educators*, p. 219.

[222] John Wesley Prince, *Wesley on Religious Education*, p. 85.

[223] *Ibid.*, p. 87.

[224] James Riley Estep Jr. "John Wesley's Philosophy of Formal Childhood Education" in *Christian Education Journal*, Vol. INS, No. 2, (Fall 1997), p. 48.

technical task."[225] John Wesley was not merely looking for qualified (technically/degree wise) teachers in his school but committed for the task and spiritually sound persons. In explaining how he would "procure Masters" to teach at Kingswood School, John Wesley wrote:

> I was not satisfied that they (masters) had learning sufficient for their several departments, unless they had likewise the fear of God, producing an unblamable conversation. I saw none would answer my intention, but men who were truly devoted to God; who sought nothing on earth, neither pleasure, nor ease, nor profit, nor the praise of men; but simply to glorify God, with their bodies and spirits, in the best manner they were capable of.[226]

In plain words, John Wesley was not looking for teachers by their degree qualifications *per se*, but men and women who were intently dedicated to honour God both with their bodies and with spirits through their teaching wholeheartedly. In this context, similar sentiments were expressed when writing to Thomas McGeary, a young man of twenty-two, about his appointment as Headmaster of Kingswood School. Wesley wrote:

> You seem to be the man I want. As to salary, you will have 30 pounds a year; board, etc. will be 30 more. Nevertheless, do not come for money.
>
> i. Do not come at all unless purely to raise a Christian school.
> ii. Anybody behaving ill, I will turn away immediately.
> iii. I expect you to be in the school eight hours a day.
> iv. In all things, I expect you should be circumspect.
>
> However, you will judge better by considering the printed rules. The sooner you come the better.[227]

After Thomas McGeary, took over the school, a year later the school experienced a gracious outpouring of God's Spirit. On *Friday* the 21st July, 1786 Wesley visited the school and found it in excellent order. He remarked:

> It is now one of the pleasantest spots in England. I found all things just according to my desire; the rules being well observed and the

---

[225] Martin Schmidt., *John Wesley: A Theological Biography*, Vol. II, Part 2, translated by Denis Inman (Nashville: Abingdon Press, 1973), p. 180.

[226] John Wesley, "A Plain account of Kingswood School", *The Works of John Wesley*, 3rd edition, Vol.13 (letters) (Michigan, Grand Rapids: Baker Books, 1998), p. 292.

[227] Elmer L. Towns, (ed)., *A History of Religious Educators*, p. 222, quoted from John Wesley, *Methodist Magazine* (1876), p. 324.

whole behaviour of the children showing that they were now managed with the wisdom that cometh from above.[228]

After more than three years later Wesley records in his Journal on *Friday*, the 11th September 1789:

> I went over to Kingswood: sweet recess! Where everything now is just as I wish . . . again on *Saturday, 12th Sept.* I spent some time with the children; all of whom behaved well: several are much awakened, and a few are rejoicing in the favour of God.[229]

Thus, John Wesley's belief in selecting the right teacher and importance of the good teacher was confirmed with the kind of report he witnessed on his visit in September 1789.

John Wesley regarded teachers as very important persons who could shape the life and the destiny of those children who study under their care. For him it was not a mean responsibility to be entrusted with: therefore, he was extremely cautious in selecting his teaching faculty. Wesley had probably learnt this the hard way when two of his teachers cheated him and walked away with money meant for the schoolchildren.

The good teachers must play the role of parents too while handling different levels of students. They must teach not as a duty but to see that the learner understands what is being taught. Parental role and patience are vital in teaching vocation. The good teacher, then, must be capable of governing and leading students.

The teacher must also have within him [her] the spirit of true religion. As for those pretenders among the ranks of religious instructors, John Wesley held that their thinking they have religion when they have none at all, add pride to their vices.[230]

John Wesley considered good teachers so crucial to the success of religious training that he did not hesitate to change teachers in the Kingswood school when things were not going well at the school.

b. Wesley's Admonition to Schoolteachers

John Wesley was not merely critical of public education, but sought to reform it as well by supplying materials and texts to be used for instruction by teachers or parents. In July 1743, John Wesley published *Instructions for Children* with

[228] Thomas Jackson (ed)., *The Works of John Wesley, Vol. IV, (Journal)* (Grand Rapids, Michigan: Baker Books House, 1998), p. 343. Cf. Elmer L. Towns, *A History of Religious Educators*, p. 223.

[229] John Wesley, *The Works of John Wesley, Vol. IV, (Journal) Sept 13, 1773-Oct. 24, 1790,* p. 471. Cf. Elmer L. Towns (ed). *A History of Religious Educators*, p. 223.

[230] Elmer L. Towns (ed). *A History of Religious Educators*, p. 222.

a prefix entitled "To All Parents and Schoolmasters."[231] There, he states the following admonitions:

i. Establish a paradigm of Christian education as being both religious instructions and academic study. E.g., "Why may they not be taught the knowledge of God? and the knowledge of letters, at the same time?"
ii. Truth is applicable to all, "worthy of deepest consideration both of the oldest and youngest of men."
iii. Personal application of truth is necessary before teaching truth. "By this means they will learn to think, as they learn to read."

Similarly, in the preface to his lesson books for children, he penned another letter, "To all Parents and Schoolmasters," describing how to make the most effective use of the material:

- Create paraphrases of the Scriptures for children so they may easily learn them.
- Learning means understanding, not mere memorization of facts. Hence, one should engage the student with more than simple, factual questions about the text.[232]

By this, John Wesley sought to improve the quality of education. These prefaces reflect his concern over the condition of public education, and the desire to change it at a fundamental level. Therefore, he held both parents and teachers in high esteem to bring about transformation in educational system of his time. Thus, John Wesley's voice need not be silenced by the passage of time, and though his practices may be outdated, his principles do offer a relevant direction for Christian education today.

3. Wesley's Thoughts on Education: Methodology and Approach

a. His Educational Thoughts (Philosophy)

To ascertain the relationship between John Wesley's thoughts on education and his theology, one must turn primarily to study the available documents such as: "A Treatise on Baptism," "On the Education of Children . . . On Family Religion," and "On Obedience to Parents." Also of help in this are several articles and tracts such as: "A Thought on the Manner of Educating Children" (originally published

---

[231] John Wesley, *The Works of John Wesley*, A bicentennial edition, Vol.14, edited by Reginald W. Ward and Richard P. Heitzenrater (Nashville: Abingdon Press, 1988), pp. 217-218. Refered by James Riley Estep Jr. "John Wesley's Philosophy of Formal Childhood Education" in *Christian Education Journal*, Vol. INS, No. 2, (Fall 1997), p. 51.

[232] John Wesley, *The Works of John Wesley*, A bicentennial edition, Vol. 14, edited by Reginald W. Ward and Richard P. Heitzenrater (Nashville: Abingdon Press, 1988), pp. 216-217. Refered by James Riley Estep Jr. "John Wesley's Philosophy of Formal Childhood Education" in *Christian Education Journal*, Vol. INS, No. 2, (Fall 1997), pp. 51-52.

in 1783 in *The Arminian Magazine)*, "A Short Account of the School Near Bristol," "A Plain Account of the Kingswood School," "Remarks on the State of Kingswood School," and "Serious Thoughts Concerning Godfathers and Godmothers."[233] Apart from these documents, what other scholars have commented on his educational endeavours will help assess his educational thoughts and theological convictions reasonably.

John Wesley believed that the entire human race, including its youngest members, is depraved; that both young and old are by nature entirely lacking in God's natural and moral image, and thus are entirely alienated from God. Liberation from sin is the main purpose of life, and transformation begins in repentance, which is the knowledge and conviction of person's despicable condition. When converted, the human is born again and regenerated; when justified, the human's relationship to God is restored. The outward consequences in the individual are holiness, or piety, which is communion with God which increases as one uses the means of grace.

The first step in the redemption of a child, according to John Wesley, is baptism. Adults must first repent and believe the gospel before being baptized, but children need not meet this condition because they cannot. Infants are in a state of original sin, and ordinarily this must be washed away by baptism for them to be saved. They are included in the covenant with God and are capable of being solemnly consecrated to Him. They can be consecrated only by baptism. They have the right to come to Christ, to be engrafted into Him. Baptism regenerates, justifies, and gives the infant all the privileges of Christian religion. The baptism of children is not only proper, it is a sacred duty. John Wesley being an Anglican was faithful to the teaching of his mother Church though it could be contested by other schools of theologians.

John Wesley taught that through baptism "a principle of grace is infused" into children and that the work accomplished is so far effectual, that if they die before they commit intentional sin, they will be eternally safe.[234]

The only way to conserve a child's innocence is to guard them completely against contamination during their helpless years and to build their character. As a result they may resist evil by their own strength when he/she comes of age. This task of guarding and character-building is the task of education.[235]

Therefore, John Wesley believed - **The grand end of education is to cure the diseases of human nature.**[236] The bias of nature leads away from God; education

[233] Elmer L. Towns, (ed). *A History of Religious Educators*, p. 217.

[234] John Wesley, *The Works of John Wesley*, A bicentennial edition, Vol. VI, edited by Reginald W. Ward and Richard P. Heitzenrater (Nashville: Abingdon Press, 1988), p. 14. Also quoted in Elmer L. Towns (ed), *A History of Religious Educators*, p. 217.

[235] John Wesley Prince, *Wesley on Religious Education*, p. 95. Also quoted by Elmer L. Towns, (ed). *A History of Religious Educators*, p. 218.

[236] John Wesley, *The Works of John Wesley*, A bicentennial edition, Vol. II, edited by Reginald W. Ward and Richard P. Heitzenrater (Nashville: Abingdon Press, 1988), p. 310. Also quoted in Elmer

is designed to set it right. This, by the grace of God, is to turn the bias from self-will, pride, anger, revenge and the love of the world, to resignation, lowliness, meekness and the love of God. The work begun by parents is to be continued in the schools by instructors, and this is the reason John Wesley felt that the parents' choice of schools is so important. Granted John Wesley's views on the salvation of children, why did he employ revival methods in working with them? He held, as was noted earlier, that if a child dies before committing actual sin, he is eternally safe. But John Wesley also held that it is natural for the child who survives to commit sin because the principle of nature is still working in him.

And anyone who sins after their baptism has denied that rite and therefore must be born again if he/she is to be saved. . . any willful sin, such as lying, profaning the Lord's day or the Lord's name is a denial of baptism as much as sinful affections, and necessitates a new birth.[237] It could be concluded, then, that John Wesley considered conversion universally necessary for children as well as for adults. In J. W. Prince's words, "John Wesley did not hold that religious education makes conversion unnecessary, but that religious education and conversion supplement each other." John Wesley's position in "On the Education of Children" was, in fact, that religious education should both cure the diseases of nature and train the child in religion. Prince wrote further that:

> The goal of all work with children at home, in the schools, in the Methodist society is to make them pious, to lead to personal religion, and to insure salvation. It is not merely to bring them up so that they do no harm and abstain from outward sin, nor to get them accustomed to use of grace, saying their prayers, reading their books, and the like, nor is it to train them in right opinions. The purpose of religious education is to instill in children true religion, holiness and the love of God and mankind and to train them in the image of God.[238]

John Wesley's educational thoughts can be summarized in several principles.

The child is a unit for salvation. John O. Gross wrote that John Wesley never considered a child as a child, but rather as a unit for salvation, bred in sin, apt to evil, and altogether as a 'brand to be plucked out of the burning.'[239]

The child is capable of genuine religious life. It is difficult to say at what age John Wesley expected to see holiness manifest in children. He frequently failed to

---

L. Towns, (ed), *A History of Religious Educators*, p. 218.

[237] Elmer L. Towns, (ed). *A History of Religious Educators*, p. 218.

[238] John Wesley Prince, *Wesley on Religious Education*, p. 96. Also quoted by Elmer L. Towns, (ed). *A History of Religious Educators*, pp. 218-219.

[239] John Owen Gross, *John Wesley: Christian Educator*, (Nashville: Board of Education, the Methodist Church, 1954), p. 9. Also quoted by Elmer L. Towns, (ed). *A History of Religious Educators*, p. 219.

record the ages of children to whom he referred in his journal as having undergone religious experiences, but there are some exceptions. On 8 April, 1755, John Wesley described a girl who died at two-and-a-half.

> Such a child . . . is scarce heard of in a century . . . If the brother or sister spoke angrily to each other, or behaved [meanly], she either sharply reproved or tenderly entreated them to give over. If she had spoken too sharply to anyone, she would humble herself to them and not rest till they had forgiven her. After her health declined, she was particularly pleased when that hymn was sung, "Abba Father," and would frequently sing that line herself: "Abba Father, hear my cry"![240]

On 28 June 1746 John Wesley wrote of a three-year-old who refused to be comforted when she thought she had displeased God. She held daily prayers and was teaching other children the rudiments of Christianity. And on 16 September 1744 John Wesley described the deathbed conversion of a four-year old that went "to God in the full assurance of faith.[241]

Such excerpts from Wesley's *Journal* show that he;

> believed it was possible for very young children to be religious, and they also give some idea of the nature of the religion which, though striking him as unusual in children so young, he would cultivate as early as possible.[242]

John Wesley's view that children so young are capable of mature religious consciousness was grounded in his doctrine of grace. When the Spirit is the Teacher, there is no delay of learning. If you or anyone say no, they cannot understand when they are so young, I answer, No; if they do not understand at this age they may not when they are fifty years old too, unless God opens their understanding. And can a person not do this at any age?[243]

John Wesley's Kingswood school was swept by recurring revivals, and most of the students saved were between the ages of six and fourteen. John Wesley believed that he himself had been ripe for spiritual change approximately at age ten, for this was when he thought he had sinned away the "washing of the Holy Ghost" he had received at baptism.[244]

---

[240] John Wesley, *The Works of John Wesley*, A bicentennial edition, Vol. IV, edited by Reginald W. Ward and Richard P. Heitzenrater (Nashville: Abingdon Press, 1988), p. 110-111. Also quoted in Elmer L. Towns, (ed), *A History of Religious Educators*, p. 219.

[241] John Wesley has quoted in his *Journal* of 1744 and 1746 on date mentioned above.

[242] Prince, *Wesley on Religious Education*, p. 85. Also quoted in Elmer L. Towns, (ed). *A History of Religious Educators*, p. 219.

[243] Elmer L. Towns, (ed). *A History of Religious Educators*, pp. 219-220

[244] *Ibid.*, p. 220.

The child must receive religious instruction as soon as the child can reason. Conscious religious instruction should begin with the dawn of reason.

> Scripture, reason, and experience jointly testify that, inasmuch as the corruption of nature is earlier than our instruction can be, we should take all pains and care to counteract this corruption as early as possible.[245]

The child must be cured of the disease of sin through education. To praise children for other than religious worth teaches them to value what is unworthy. They, who teach children to love praise, train them up for the devil. John Wesley was not in favour of uncalled for and unrealistic praise of a child or children. Instead he believed that children should be commended exceedingly sparingly and then only if with it they are taught that God alone is praiseworthy and the source of all that God's children possess for which they are commended.[246]

> To strike at the root of their pride, teach your children as soon as possible that they are fallen spirits; that they are fallen short of that glorious image of God wherein they were first created; that they are not now as they once were, incorrupt pictures of the God of glory; bearing the express likeness of the . . . Holy Father's Spirit, but more ignorant, more foolish, and wicked than they can possibly conceive. Show them that, in pride, passion, and revenge, they are now like the devil. And that in foolish desires and groveling appetites they are like beasts of the field.[247]

This practical application of Wesley's doctrine of original sin may seem severe but it was basic to his concept of Christian education and his thoughts on education were developed in that background.

The child's will must be broken. John Wesley's view of discipline was harsh, but his reason for breaking a child's will was to save his/her soul. Even before the child can speak, their parents should:

> Make him do as he is bid, if you whip him ten times running to affect it. Let none persuade you it is cruelty to do this; it is cruel not to do it. Break his will now and his soul will live and he will probably bless you through all eternity.[248]

---

[245] John Wesley, *The Works of John Wesley*, Vol. VII, p. 459. Also quoted in Elmer L. Towns, (ed). *A History of Religious Educators*, p.220.

[246] Elmer L. Towns, (ed). *A History of Religious Educators*, p. 220.

[247] John Wesley, *The Works of John Wesley*, Vol. VII, p. 459. Also quoted in Elmer L. Towns, (ed), *A History of Religious Educators*, p. 220.

[248] Body, *John Wesley and Education,* p. 49. Also quoted in Elmer L. Towns, (ed), *A History of Religious Educators*, p. 221.

However, John Wesley balanced admonitions such as these with others that urged discipline "by mildness, softness and gentleness . . . by advice, persuasion and reproof." He even warned that if teachers exercise needless severity, "it will not be strange if religion stinks in the nostrils" of their students.[249]

John Wesley's letters and sermons are full of suggestions regarding the importance of educating children; he wrote several essays on the 'right upbringing of youth' and insisted on daily self-examination, for which he gave elaborate rules.[250] For John Wesley, the aim of education is **Christian perfection.**[251] This concept is central to Wesleyan theology[252]. The next section briefly discusses Wesley's methodology.

b. His Educational Methodology

In his explorations for a suitable foundation in education, John Wesley the synthesist, the eclectic, studied the schools, scholars and educational literature available to him and critically selected what he considered to be the strengths of each.[253] Moravians had two sessions of walking in the woods to "learn from nature." Taking a cue from them, John Wesley decided that his students could use that time to get acquainted with nature even better through work – so pulling weeds, cutting fire wood, and hoeing in the garden were prescribed. Personalized **love for the pupil** was the bed-rock of the Port Royal discipline and teaching. Port Royal educators' severity and love were admirably combined which John Wesley copied without hesitation and practiced at Kingswood school.[254] Based on this available information, he devised his own educational methodology, and approach. This subject is discussed in details under Section: C. Educational theory and approach – sub-heading John Wesley's theory and Method.

---

[249] John Wesley, *The Works of John Wesley*, Vol. II. p. 305.

[250] Robert Ulich, *A History of Religious Education* (London: University of London Press Ltd., 1968), p. 193.

[251] Emphasis is mine.

[252] According to Wesley, *Perfection* means – the humble, gentle, patient love of God and our neighbour, ruling our tempers, words and actions. This does not mean an infallibility of perfect soul. It does not indicate sinlessness too. Perfection is always wrought in the soul by simple act of faith. Cf. Maximin Piette, John Wesley in the Evolution of Protestantism, (London: Sheed and Ward, 1938), p. 565.

[253] Wesley Tracy, "Christian Education in the Wesleyan Mode", in *Wesleyan Theological Journal*, Vol. 17, No. 1 (Spring 1982), p. 45.

[254] John W. Prince, *Wesley on Religious Education* (New York: The Methodist Concern, 1926), 121. Cf. Wesley Tracy, "Christian Education in the Wesleyan Mode", in *Wesleyan Theological Journal*, Vol. 17, No. 1, (Spring 1982), p. 44.

4. Reactions to Educational Theorists and General Education of his time

John Wesley did not always accept or even respond favorably to his contemporaries. In these instances, the "influence" is in reaction to philosophical or educational ideals which were contrary to John Wesley's own. In fact, his tone even became condemnatory toward some, for example "the great triumvirate, Rousseau, Voltaire and David Hume," who he maintained had removed revelation from religion and God from His creation.[255]

David Hume was criticized by John Wesley to be among the "menders of the Bible" and his adherents "promote the cause of infidelity more effectually than both Hume and Voltaire."[256] In fact, John Wesley's understanding of theology reached its apex when he wrote 'Thoughts upon Necessity,' which debated Hume and his contemporaries' view of human predetermination (i.e., anti-free will), which is fundamental to John Wesley's educational thoughts.[257]

John Wesley read Rousseau on education and dismissed him as useless saying, that he offered no moral emphasis in education. He found Rousseau's *Emile* to be the "most empty, silly, injudicious thing that ever a self-conceited infidel wrote,[258] suggesting that if Rousseau's educational principles were used at Kingswood School we would be "continually ruining fifty children at a time![259] Regardless of how one assesses John Wesley's responses to his contemporaries, one thing is evident: John Wesley was not ignorant of the prevailing educational theories or theorists and education philosophies of his time.[260]

Regarding Kingswood school John Wesley said, just as a hospital is to restore physical health, likewise education at Kingswood school was to restore spiritual health.[261] The need was desperate because everyone born of woman is infected by seven spiritual diseases. Here are those seven which Wesley calls Disease [sin].[262]

a. The Disease of Atheism
b. The Disease of Self-will
c. The Disease of Pride

[255] John Wesley, "The Unity of Divine Being," In *Works,* Vol. VII, p. 271. Cf. James Riley Estep Jr. "John Wesley's Philosophy of Formal Childhood Education" in *Christian Education Journal,* Vol. INS, No. 2, (Fall 1997), p. 47.

[256] John Wesley, *Journal,* August 8, 1773. Cf. James Riley Estep Jr. "John Wesley's Philosophy of Formal Childhood Education" in *Christian Education Journal,* Vol. INS, No. 2, (Fall 1997), p. 47.

[257] Albert C. Outler, *John Wesley,* (Oxford: Oxford University Press, 1964), p. 472-473.

[258] James Riley Estep Jr. "John Wesley's Philosophy of Formal Childhood Education" in *Christian Education Journal,* Vol. INS, No. 2, (Fall 1997), p. 47, quoted from John Wesley, "A Thought on the manner of educating children.

[259] *Ibid.*

[260] *Ibid.*

[261] Wesley Tracy, "Christian Education in the Wesleyan Mode", in *Wesleyan Theological Journal,* Vol. 17, No. 1 (Spring 1982), p. 37.

[262] *Ibid.*

d. The Disease of the Love of the World
e. The Disease of Anger
f. The Disease of Falsehood
g. The Disease of Injustice.

These seven diseases are explained in the following section entitled – "Family and education".

The schools of John Wesley's day admitted only the children of the upper classes, and these institutions fell far below his perceived standards. Wesley's **indictment** of the educational system of his day was **fivefold** as he details in *A Plain account of Kingswood School*:[263] [These points are merely listed under the footnote 83 and here with an explanatory note].

First, most of the schools were located in the great towns of England where the children's peers discouraged study. They were more active with extra curricular activities than serious studies and spent more time wasting away outside the class room than inside.

Second, the schools admitted all sorts of children indiscriminately, with the worse ones tending to corrupt the better. Wesley practiced expulsion in his schools, reporting in his *Journal* that when "one of the boys studiously labored to corrupt the rest," Wesley "would not suffer him to stay any longer under the roof, but sent him home that very hour."

Third, instruction in religion was extremely defective, provoking Wesley to charge that schoolmasters uninstructed in the elements of religion and being ignorant of religious experience themselves; they corrupted the faith of the young children.[264]

Fourth, writing and arithmetic were neglected in favour of the classics and classical languages, including classics which are destructive to religion.

And *Fifth*, the classics were taught in a random order, without grading them according to the difficulty of their subject matter or syntax.

In all this, the essence of Wesley's indictment was that *religion and education* should go hand in hand. The righteous prosper mentally as the green bay tree, while the unrighteous sow the wind of ungodliness and reap a whirlwind of perpetual ignorance.

---

[263] Thomas Jackson (ed), *The Works of John Wesley, Vol. XIII* (Grand Rapids, Michigan: Baker Book House, 1998), pp. 289-291, Cf. Elmer L. Towns, (ed), *A History of Religious Educators*, pp. 212-213.

[264] Masters put authors into the hands of their scholars that "with all the beauty of language, all the sweetness of expression instil into their minds both obscenity and profaneness". He boldly quoated examples of this obscenity – the lewd Epigrams/obscene jokes of Martial, and the shamelss Satires of Juvenal, so earnestly recommending sodomy as well as adultery. A. G. Ives, *Kingswood School in Wesley's Day and Since*, p. 7.

Therefore, John Wesley called the large public schools "nurseries of all manner of wickedness."[265] For this reason boys should not be sent to them. Regarding girls' education he had this to say:

> By no means should girls be sent to large boarding schools. In these seminaries too the children teach one another pride, vanity, affectation, intrigue, artifice, and in short, everything that a Christian woman ought not to learn and will be unable to continue in fear of God and save their souls.[266]

Later John Wesley warned Methodist parents that if they "would send your girls headlong to hell, send them to a fashionable boarding school!"[267]

Early Methodists, including the first itinerant preachers, came largely from the *underprivileged* class which was *deprived* of an opportunity for education. John Wesley knew that helping these people involved educating them. He sincerely believed that although Methodists were poor, they need not be ignorant, and he realized that the results of his revival would be permanent only if the revival was united with education. John Wesley wanted his preachers to have a broad, general knowledge, insisting that they spend five hours daily in hard study. In 1745 he published a list of books covering such areas as practical and doctrinal divinity, philosophy, astronomy, poetry, and history to guide the preachers in their *self-education*. More than two centuries later, Paulo Freire, a Brazilian educator also encouraged people of his country that education is the best way to liberate themselves from their present condition. John Wesley's basic belief was that education is the only way to liberate and transform marginalized farmers and miners of his time. Therefore, he went so far to say to itinerant preachers that their success in preaching would be in proportion to their appeal to the hearers' minds.

In Alfred H. Body's judgment:

> Credit must be given to John Wesley for supplying a course of higher education. John Wesley may be regarded as the true successor to Erasmus by providing great provincial universities in his day, spreading knowledge and culture throughout the land, breaking down the barriers of privilege and creed, and making learning accessible to all.[268]

---

[265] Thomas Jackson, (ed). *The Works of John Wesley, Vol. VII, Sermon 94, Point 13* (Grand Rapids, Michigan: Baker Book House, 1998), p. 83.

[266] *Ibid.*, pp. 83-84.

[267] Elmer L. Towns, (ed). *A History of Religious Educators,* p. 213.

[268] Alfred H. Body, *John Wesley and Education*, (London: The Epworth Press, 1936), p. 142. Cf.. Elmer L. Towns, (ed), *A History of Religious Educators*, p. 213.

John Wesley had several schools operating at Kingswood. There were the schools for boarding students, one for boys and one for girls. There was a day school for the coal miners' children. Further there was a school for adults that operated early in the morning and at night. A little later Kingswood admitted preachers' children free of tuition fee and adults who were called to the ministry, but had no learning.[269] This indeed indicates John Wesley's earnest endeavour to reach out to the deprived classes of the society with his affordable educational programs

5. Implications for Contemporary Christian Education

Having studied the influences on the formation of Wesley's philosophy of education and its chief principles in the previous sections its relevance and practical application of the same remains to be seen in the following discussion.

The Kingswood and charity schools: In order to further the course of education, he started his own schools, choosing carefully the right candidates for teaching. John Wesley did not appreciate the public schools of his day, for they did not have religious education as part of their curriculum ; however, he endorsed private schools of his time which emphasized both religious and secular education. The schools which John Wesley established for the higher education of Methodist boys reflected his belief in the primacy of religious education.

The school at Kingswood was to be a model Christian institution as well as an educational centre superior in many respects to any other school which John Wesley had seen, at home or abroad. He outlined the curriculum and prepared textbooks in English grammar, French, Greek, and Hebrew. There are 1,729 printed pages in the texts John Wesley himself prepared for the use of ordinary school course. In addition to that one must add the 50 volumes of *Christian library* most of which John Wesley wrote at Kingswood between 1749 and 1755, as well as the Compendium of Logic, five grammar books and his four volume *The Concise History of England*, indicating the immense labour involved in John Wesley's quest for excellence.[270] His famous rule forbidding Kingswood students to play games has haunted Methodists from time to time since John Wesley's day: The student shall be indulged with nothing which the world calls play. Let this rule be observed with strictest nicety, for those who play when they are young, will play when they are old. It is a wise German proverb (others called it sour statement), which John Wesley quotes in more occasions than one – 'He that plays when he is a boy will play when he is a man.'[271] John Wesley seems to

[269] Wesley Tracy, "Christian Education in the Wesleyan Mode," in *Wesleyan Theological Journal*, Vol. 17, No. 1, (Spring 1982), p. 39.

[270] Wesley Tracy, "Christian Education in the Wesleyan Mode," in *Wesleyan Theological Journal*, Vol. 17, No.1, (Spring 1982), pp. 39-40. cited by Elmer L. Towns, (ed)., *A History of Religious Educators*, p. 223.

[271] *The Works of John Wesley*, Vol. XIII, 3rd edition, (1998) "A Plain Account of Kingswood School," p. 294.

have had a strong aversion to play time as part of schooling. This rule has been rather strange for Methodists particularly Christian educators. However, present day schools and boarding homes have made some provision for playing along with gardening, cleaning and walking through the Woods for physical exercise. Because it is generally believed by various educational psychologists and physicians that play is a part of all round development of the learner/student. However, for Wesley play meant not cricket or football, but cards and dice. It was vanity and riches that had given cards, dice, and driniking so much credit in the world.[272]

This prohibition may have stemmed from John Wesley's memories of childhood when, as an undersized youth, John Wesley was often bullied and beaten for sport by his fellow students at Charterhouse. But more likely the rule reflects the practice of the Herrnhut Moravians where they let children walk through the woods to learn from the nature both morning and evening.

Children's sermons and hymns: John Wesley preached to children on many occasions, writing in his journal on 13 June 1790, for example, "In the morning I preached a charity sermon in Monkwearmouth Church, for the Sunday school; .... I preached at five near Pens, to several thousand people. Here it is our labour has not been in vain.[273]

In 1790, he published *Forty-Four Hymns for Children;* many hymns from which were later included in his Brother Charles's *Hymns for Children* and *Others of Ripe Years.* John introduced his *Forty-Four Hymns* with these words:

> There are two ways of writing or speaking to children; the one is to **let ourselves down to them**; the other, **to lift them up to us**. Dr. Isaac Watts has written in the former way and has succeeded admirably well speaking to children and leaving them as he found them. The following hymns are written on the other plain. They contain strong and manly sense, yet expressed in such plain and easy language a child may understand. But when they do, they will be children no longer, only in years and stature.[274]

This hymnal was one of Wesley's last publications, showing that even in his old age his concern for children did not decrease. One of the interesting facts to notice in John Wesley was that of inclusive nature. He was concerned about children, adults, women, miners, poor and everyone else too. John Wesley was equally concerned for the education of adult Methodists, and he did not leave it entirely to the preachers whom he helped in training to be preachers. During John Wesley's days at Oxford he, as well as Charles Wesley and George

---

[272] A. G. Ives, *Kingswood School in Wesley's Day and Since*, p. 241.

[273] Thomas Jackson, (ed). *The Works of John Wesley, Vol. IV, Journal* (Grand Rapids, Michigan: Baker Book House, 1998), p. 488.

[274] Elmer L. Towns, (ed). *A History of Religious Educators*, p. 224.

Whitefield, was part of the **Holy Club**[275], a small group organized for study, prayer, self-examination, and good works including the visitation of prisoners and the sick. Later, recognizing the value of small groups, he divided the Methodists into "bands," . . . putting the married and single men, and the married or single women, together. The following passage will help the reader to understand the role and the function of these small groups.

Methodist bands: The chief rules of the bands (that is, little companies) run thus: in order to confess our faults one to another, and pray one for another that we may be healed, we intend,

a. To meet once a week, at the least.
b. To come punctually at the hour appointed.
c. To begin with singing or prayer.
d. To speak, each of us in order, freely and plainly, the true state of oursoul, with the faults we have committed in thought, word or deed, and the temptations we have felt since our last meeting.
e. To desire some person among us (then called a leader) to speak his own state first, and then to ask the rest of them, in order, as many and searching questions as may be, concerning their state, sins, and temptations.[276]

Towards the end of his ministry John Wesley began to de-emphasize bands and emphasize the Sunday school. It is assumed that the activities of these bands were incorporated into Sunday schools in later years.

John Wesley did much to form popular opinion and advance the intellectual condition of the English people (he wrote 371 books [some say more than 400 books, cf. footnote 161, p. 42] on an enormous range of subjects), he was not an educational innovator; but rather used education to bring about change and transformation in the society.[277] John Wesley was a product of the eighteenth century and shared its blindness to the meaning of childhood. Nevertheless, his recognition of the crucial role that education must play in the Methodist revival and his educational achievements made John Wesley, a significant Christian educator of his century. In fact, motivated by John Wesley's whole programme **tens of thousands taught themselves to read,** writes J. W. Bready.[278] Indeed, interpreting education in terms of character building and acquiring the ability

[275] The nick name, which they earned while studying at Oxford from their contemporary student community.

[276] M. Piette, *John Wesley in Evolution of Protestantism* (London: Sheed and Ward, 1936), p. 457. Cf. Elmer L. Towns (ed)., *A History of Religious Educators*, pp. 224-225.

[277] Elmer L.Towns, "John Wesley" in *A History of Religious Educators*, edited by Elmer L. Towns (Grand Rapids: Baker Book House, 1975), p. 225.

[278] J. W. Bready, *This Freedom – Whence?, Faith and Freedom: The Roots of Democracy* (Indiana: Light and Life, 1952), n.p. Cf. John Wilkins Sigsworth, *World – Changers: Karl Marx and John Wesley* (Ontario: Easingwold Publications, 1982), p. 190.

to live usefully, Bready is prepared to rate John Wesley as the century's greatest educationist and one of greatest in history.[279]

While Robert Raikes is commonly regarded as the father of the Sunday School movement, the fact remains that John Wesley founded the World's first Sunday school (a catechizing programme) while in Georgia, what is now called Savannah's Christ Church (Episcopal). That was some 45 years before Raikes started his first Sunday school in Gloucester in 1780.[280] The more fascinating thing is that Raikes was drawn to the same educational goal as Wesley.

It will not be farfetched if one admits after reading his unflinching commitment to education that Wesley was a populariser of knowledge; he was determined to transform illiterates into literates.[281][Inspite of early Methodists being poor and could hardly afford education in those days].

However, John Wesley did synthesize as is mentioned earlier, a philosophy of education that was an amalgamation of the ideas of both religious and secular educators. From these educational convictions, he not only challenged the foundations of English education, but also called for reformation and reinvention of educational ideals and practices, particularly at the Kingswood School. John Wesley was a man of his time who advanced the cause of Christian education to the best of his ability. "It is only right," remarks G. R. Cragg, "to remember that few men in his period did more to promote the cause of education."[282]

The educational thoughts of John Wesley do offer some implications and indicate his vision for contemporary Christian education today:

i. A valid philosophy of Christian education cannot be formed in a vacuum, but needs to be formulated in the context of other educational philosophies, both religious and secular.
ii. A Christian philosophy of education needs to consider the perspective of Scripture and theology on child's education.
iii. The character and function of the teacher is paramount to the educational process, and is crucial to the success of any educational endeavour. Emphasis should be placed on the proper selection and training of faculty, both academically, and perhaps more importantly spiritually.
iv. Education is the means to a spiritual end, i.e., the call to reconciliation of the world to Christ is temporally accomplished through the education (or re-education) of the individual.

---

[279] John Wilkins Sigsworth, *World – Changers: Karl Marx and John Wesley* (Ontario: Easingwold Publications, 1982), p. 190.

[280] *Ibid.,* p. 189.

[281] John Wilkins Sigsworth, *World – Changers,* p. 190.

[282] G. R. Cragg, *The Church in the Age of Reason (1648-1789)* (New York: Penguin Books, 1970), p. 149.

v. Christian education must be critical of its own not only practices and contents, but offer a critique of the secular educational institutions and practices, particularly with regard to curriculum and discipline.[283]

John Wesley's vision for education amplifies his thoughts:[284]

- His unshakable faith that Christianity has something distinct to offer education;
- His emphasis on education as a search for the truth and on the need for a broad curriculum, i.e., inclusive education;
- The importance he attached to pupils really understanding what they were studying and encouraging a questioning approach, What Wesley thought was that interaction and dialogue method enrich learning;
- His concentration in encouraging young people to look beyond material pleasures to the things that really matter in life. An educational system is not worth a great deal if it teaches young people how to **make a living** but does not teach them how to **make a life**;
- His view of the school as an extended family and his passionate concern for the pastoral welfare of each individual pupil; he said, all **learning without love is but splendid ignorance**[285] and that all the people in a school should see themselves as *a family*,[286] **an ounce of love is worth a pound of knowledge.**[287] John Wesley was well aware that the context of the familial environment was paramount in the learning process;
- The importance he attached to acquiring a dedicated and caring teaching staff and seeing teaching as a vocation not a profession;
- His creation of bursaries to enable the school to be more socially inclusive to make provision for those who could not afford education;
- His desire was to enable the young to acquire a personal faith during their learning to guide them through the rest of their lives;
- His belief that religion should be of the mind as well as of the heart, in other words reason and feeling are two sides of same coin;
- His wish to educate the young to be responsible citizens, ready to challenge the current values of society and keen to serve the needs of others.

---

[283] James Riley Estep Jr. "John Wesley's Philosophy of Formal Childhood Education" in *Christian Education Journal*, Vol. INS, No. 2, (Fall 1997), p. 52.

[284] G. M. Best, the present Principal of Kingswood school, Kingswood, "Wesley and Education" Unpublished paper presented at Lincoln College, Oxford, 14 May (2003), pp. 16-17.

[285] Emphasis and highlights are mine to express the importance of Wesley's statements.

[286] G. M. Best, "John Wesley and A Christian Education," Unpublished paper sent by G. M. Best to the author, (2003), p. 4.

[287] *Ibid*, Cf. G. M. Best, the present Principal of Kingswood School, Kingswood, "Wesley and Education" Unpublished paper presented at Lincoln College, Oxford, 14 May (2003), p. 10. These papers are in possession of the author acquired with permission to quote in this book.

John Wesley knew that the only thing more expensive than education is **ignorance.**[288] In other words, he is saying that in civil society illiteracy has no place; every individual created in the image of God has a right to education. **Being ignorant of oneself, society and God is more costly than the cost of education.** John Wesley wrote that if the Methodists were not a reading people the work of grace would die out in a generation. Therefore, he encouraged his followers to practice daily Bible study, and weekly class meetings ensured the reading of the Scriptures.[289] This theory and approach was affirmed by Methodists in their educational statement and ministry in later years. The Wesleyan Methodists had to be taught to read and their Sunday Schools seemed admirably suited to meet this necessity.[290] Therefore, H. F. Mathew has pointed out that "Methodists had more Sunday schools than any other denomination other than the Church of England... in 1834."[291]

In the light of the above discussion then, John Wesley's voice need not be silenced by the passage of time, and though some of his practices may be antiquated, his pedagogical principles and methods do offer us a relevant direction for Christian education today. Therefore, Wesley's vision of education embraces heart and mind in the service of others.[292] The greatest contribution of Wesley to Christianity and in particular Christian education is through his numerous publications; his dream was to set up Christian library as part of educational project. Wesley believed in the importance of printed word.[293]

B. Wesley and Christian Education: A Biblical and Theological Perspective

Although John Wesley was not a systematic theologian, his theology can be described with reasonable clarity as a structured rationale from a biblical perspective, as evident from the study of his published sermons, tracts, treatises, and correspondence. In essence, John Wesley's theology affirms God's sovereign will to reverse our **sinful, devilish nature**, by the work of Holy Spirit, a process John Wesley named by their Augustinian terms: **prevenient, justifying** and **sanctifying grace.**[294]

---

[288] G. M. Best, the present Principal of Kingswood School, Kingswood, "Wesley and Education" Unpublished paper presented at Lincoln College, Oxford, 14 May (2003), p. 17.

[289] John T. Smith, *Methodism and Education, 1849-1902: J.H.Rigg, Romanism, and Wesleyan Schools* (Oxford: Oxford University Press, 1998), p. 1.

[290] Ibid.

[291] H. F. Mathew, *Methodism and the Education of the People, 1791-1851,* (London: The Epworth Press, 1949), p. 51.

[292] G. M. Best, "Methodist Education and the Board of Management," Unpublished paper (2003), p. 17.

[293] Ralph Waller, *John Wesley – A Personal Portrait* (London: SPCK, 2003), pp. 110-111.

[294] *The Concise Evangelical Dictionary of Theology,* 1991 edition, s.v. "Wesley John", by R. G. Tuttle Jr.

Christian perfection was the keynote of his theology, the highest expression of the love of God in the soul of man and the theme of holy living or sanctification runs as a main thread throughout John Wesley's sermons, determining both the shape of his theology and the tone of his preaching.[295]

William R. Cannon said: "so far as I have been able to determine, in the entire range of historical theology, there has never been a more orderly, well-arranged and consistent theologian than John Wesley."[296] At the same time, he acknowledged that others have been more profound than John Wesley. The range of his explorations was limited unlike Thomas Aquinas and John Calvin. However, John Wesley was always a people's theologian.[297] His sole purpose in thinking theologically at all was to help them. Their education leading to their salvation was the burden of his preaching. Consequently what salvation is was the theme of his theology. For John Wesley the question of how a sinner may be justified before God was the basic theological issue simply because it was the basic issue of human existence.[298] John Wesley had a strong belief that both social and spiritual liberation, is of central importance to every child of God.[299]

John Wesley believed that his own learning is not a ticket to preferment or privilege, but a tool of his ministry to the poor. His usual congregation was the working class; his most frequent pulpit was the nearest stump or a market cross. Observers of John Wesley noticed that he could preach in a learned style in the churches and among great people, but when he came among simple people he laid all his greatness aside. He says: I labour to avoid all words which are not easy to be understood, all which are not used in common life, and in particular those kinds of technical terms that so frequently occur in bodies of divinity- those modes of speaking which men of reading are intimately acquainted with, but which to common people are an unknown tongue. Though I slide into them unaware yet consciously make an effort not to use them.[300] John Wesley's views are plain and simple that every hearer and reader could follow his preaching and teaching.

1. Views on God, Man, Sin and Salvation

Wesleyan Christian Education could well be defined as Biblical Theism which is informed by Wesleyan – Arminian pre-suppositions which provide a foundation

[295] Richard P. Heitzenrater, *The Elusive Mr. Wesley*, 2nd edition (Nashville: Abingdon Press, 2003), p.145.

[296] William R. Cannon "Salvation in the theology of John Wesley", *Methodist History*, Vol. IX, No. 1, (October 1970), p. 3. He was a resident Bishop of the Raleigh area, the United Methodist Church USA and a noted theologian.

[297] William R. Cannon "Salvation in the theology of John Wesley", *Methodist History*, p. 4.

[298] William R. Cannon, *The Theology of John Wesley*, (New York: Abingdon Press, 1946), p. 49. Cf. *Methodist History*, Vol. IX, No. 1, (October 1970), p. 4.

[299] Thomas Jackson, (ed). *The Works of John Wesley*, Vol. V. Sermon, V, p. 53.

[300] Richard P. Heitzenrater, *The Elusive Mr. Wesley*, 2nd edition (Nashville: Abingdon Press, 2003), pp.141-142.

for structuring and communicating a view of God, man, and the universe.[301] In other words, Wesleyan Christian education is cognizant of a distinct theology with primary emphasis upon prevenient grace. God does not exclude any of His created order but the abiding grace is available to all irrespective of their status in the society. His prevenient grace covers all however, it depends on each individual's response to it. The following section will clarify his understanding of God's grace available for fallen humanity.

The Wesleyan doctrine of prevenient grace places man, even natural man (unregenerate man), as a recipient of God's grace. To be human is to be graced. Prevenient grace enables the unregenerate to recognize his need of salvation when he hears the gospel and moves toward God in repentance and faith that **God** might justify, regenerate, adopt, and begin sanctification in him with the gift of saving grace. It is the Wesleyan understanding of prevenient grace added to the concept that fallen man still has somewhat of the image of God. (in other words, total depravity is not absolutely total as Calvin taught); to which is added, the Wesleyan tenet that all men, fallen or redeemed, have free will; which interact to provide the bases for a **Christian education** which is distinctly Wesleyan. A Wesleyan Christian Education as is inferred from various writings has been developed upon the three-fold understanding of man.[302]

1) Humanity is graced (prevenient grace), 2) natural man can hear and understand the gospel, and 3) man is free to receive or reject, all or part of what he learns. One could then add a Wesleyan epistemology – the four-fold test of truth (Albert C. Outler[303] terms this as Wesleyan quadrilateral) – Scripture, reason, experience, and tradition. This three-fold understanding of man coupled with a Wesleyan epistemology provides a **minimal formula** for developing an approach to Christian Education that is distinctly Wesleyan. This **minimal statement not only has implications for Christian Education, but implications for evangelism as well**. Indeed, Wesleyans have been reticent to draw a line between Christian Education and Evangelism.[304]

This theoretical foundation has had a practical working out (though largely unconscious of its theoretical base) in the historical usage of the Sunday school

---

301 J. Duane Beals, "Doing Christian education in a Wesleyan Mode: A Response to Wesley Tracy", in *Wesleyan Theological Journal*, Vol. 17, No.1, (Spring 1982), p. 54.

302 *Ibid.*

303 Albert Cook Outler (1908-1989), was a 20th century American Methodist theologian and philosopher. Outler is generally considered to be one of the most important John Wesley scholars in the history of the Church as well as the first real *United Methodist* theologian. He was also a key figure in the 20th century ecumenical movement. A dean of Methodist Historians, philosopher; the pre-eminent Protestant ecumenists of the modern Methodists.

304 J. Duane Beals, "Doing Christian Education in a Wesleyan Mode: A Response to Wesley Tracy", in *Wesleyan Theological Journal*, Vol. 17, No.1, (Spring 1982), pp. 54-55.

as an evangelistic arm of the Church. For many Methodists there seems to be no problem with the relationship of evangelism and Christian education.[305]

Sin – Every person stands in need of salvation, and salvation is readily available to everyone that seeks it. Therefore, the universal sinfulness of humankind, original sin, and prevenient grace are inseparable and complementary concepts in Wesleyan theology. Neither has any meaning without the other since both together forms the basic understanding of John Wesley had of the human subject of salvation.[306]

It is said that:

> John Wesley was thoroughly Augustinian in his view of the scope and destructiveness of sin and man's inability through his own resources to cope with it. But Wesley, optimistic Englishman that he was, was not a disciple of either Augustine or Calvin in the ruthless way in which each of them carried out the implications of that concept, making salvation itself limited and restricted in its outreach and circumscribing the redemptive interests of God himself to a favoured few. Indeed, Wesley's position on sin and grace is the position of the Synod of Orange of A.D. 529. He, too, affirms the fall as over against Pelagianism and insists with Augustine that not only death fell on the human race as a result of Adam's disobedience but that a bent toward evil, sin itself, was transmitted by Adam to his posterity.
>
> He accepts the dictates of Orange, which were those of Augustine as well, that grace is the necessary antecedent to salvation, that it prepares the will and causes us to seek, to ask, and to knock, and that our nature is so weak and wounded by the fall that it can do nothing unaided by divine grace. Thus man's spiritual activity, always and invincibly, depends on God's grace to originate it, to assist it, and to sustain it to the very end.[307]

John Wesley, like the Synod of Orange, went all the way with Augustine on sin and grace just short of predestination. He could not accept this doctrine, harsh and forbidding to him as it was to the Ancient and Medieval Church as well.

How can one maintain the total depravity of man and yet man's ability either to accept or to reject divine grace? Augustine felt it was not possible to do

---

[305] J. Duane Beals, "Doing Christian Education in a Wesleyan Mode: A Response to Wesley Tracy", pp. 54-56.

[306] William R. Cannon "Salvation in the theology of John Wesley", *Methodist History*, Vol. IX, No. 1, (October 1970), p. 4. Cf. Wesley's "Original Sin" Works, Vol. IX, pp. 191-464.

[307] William R. Cannon "Salvation in the theology of John Wesley", *Methodist History*, Vol. IX, No.1, (October 1970), p. 4.

so, and therefore he left man's salvation or damnation entirely at the disposal of God. Calvin did the same.

John Wesley, however, both accepted human depravity and yet relieved it of its natural consequence of predestination by his concept of prevenient grace – surrounding man in his sinfulness is God in his love and relieving mercy.[308] This divine help is available to every man, no matter who he is and when and where he lives. God will **not permit him to be damned unless he damns himself**. This prevenient grace is like the sunshine which enables us to see, the air which we breathe, and the water which we drink. It is everywhere available to everybody, and it is entirely free. By the free Grace of God given to all men alike at the very moment of birth, they are able to turn again unto their Heavenly Father and to regain the privilege of which by nature they have been deprived.[309] Thus, John Wesley makes his Biblical teaching so simple that every person can follow and understand his views.

Salvation[310]- according to John Wesley salvation means holiness of heart and life that springs from true faith in Christ alone.[311] It is freely available to everybody, only a few are saved. The grace of God is universal not limited to any particular group. By divine design, it is all embracing, nothing withholding and free as it comes down in concrete instances to the most precious, and particular possession any person can obtain. What God intends for all, man by his recalcitrance limits to a few? Wesley while preaching a sermon – "On working out your own Salvation" explains thus:

> Salvation begins with what is usually termed as **preventing grace**;
>
> Including the first wish to please God, the first dawn of light concerning his will, and the first slight transient conviction of having sinned against him [this is the beginning of God's work of salvation, and this grace is present in all human beings]. All these imply some tendency towards life; some degree of salvation; the beginning of deliverance from a blind, unfeeling heart, quite insensible of God and the things of God. Salvation is carried on by **convincing grace**, usually in Scripture termed **repentance**; which brings a larger measure of self-knowledge, and a farther deliverance from the heart of stone.

---

308 Wesley has taken pains to explain his stand on the "Original Sin" at length; Cf. *The Works of John Wesley*, Vol. X, "Doctrine of Original Sin" pp. 191-464. Here, it suffices to serve the purpose of this research to understand his basic theological understanding of sin.

309 William R. Cannon, *The Theology of John Wesley* (New York: Abingdon Press, 1946), p. 200. Cf. *Methodist History*, Vol. IX, No.1, (October 1970), p. 5.

310 *The Works of John Wesley*, Vol. V, Sermon, I, "Salvation by faith", pp. 7ff.

311 Richard P. Heitzenrater, *The Elusive Mr. Wesley*, 2nd edition (Nashville: Abingdon Press, 2003), p. 146.

> Afterwards we experience the proper Christian salvation; whereby, "through grace," we are "saved by faith;" consisting of those two grand branches, justification and sanctification. By **justification** we are saved from the guilt of sin, and restored to the favour of God; by **sanctification** we are saved from the power and root of sin, and restored to the image of God. All experience as well as Scripture show this salvation to be both instantaneous and gradual. It begins the moment we are justified, in the holy, humble, gentle, patient love of God and man.
>
> It gradually increases from that moment, as "a grain of mustard-seed," which, at first, is the least of all seeds, "but afterwards puts forth large branches, and becomes a great tree;" till, in another instant, the heart is cleansed from all sin, and filled with pure love to God and man. But even that love increases more and more, till we "grow up in all things into Him that is our Head;" till we all attain the measure of the stature of the fullness of Christ.[312]

The expression of salvation, in Wesleyan theology, is justification and regeneration. The two words are not synonymous, yet each is essential to the other. Justification[313] is the ***objective act*** of God in which a sinner is absolved of his sin and is pronounced to be righteous and upright before his divine judge – God. Regeneration[314] is the **subjective experience** in which the person himself knows that he is justified, feels cleansed of his sin, and by divine grace is really made righteous by the transformation of his life. John Wesley believes that justification and regeneration are concomitants. They take place simultaneously. The twin acts of justification and regeneration, both the divine bestowal of grace and the human reception of what is bestowed are present and are equally effective. John Wesley's stand is that an act of salvation cannot come about without the individual's willingness to take what God gives. It does not mean that faith is the human response to divine initiative in salvation. Faith belongs to the divine side of the process as much as grace. Bishop Cannon explains Wesley's idea of grace as:

> Grace may be characterized as the big, broad ocean of God's mercy, while faith is the refreshing wave from that ocean that washes up

---

[312] Collin W. Williams, *John Wesley's Theology Today* (New York/Nashville: Abingdon Press, 1970), p. 40

[313] *The Works of John Wesley*, Vol. V, Sermon, V, "Justification by Faith" pp. 53ff. Cf. William R. Cannon "Salvation in theology of John Wesley," *Methodist History*, Vol. IX, No. 1, (October 1970), p. 6.

[314] *Ibid.*, Vol. VI, Sermon XLV, "The New Birth," pp. 65ff.

on one, particular desolate human shore to quicken it and make it productive and capable of Christian growth.[315]

On the other hand, John Wesley also writes, neither your faith nor your salvation is human efforts but the gift of God. "By grace ye are saved through faith," grace is the source; faith is the condition of salvation.[316] Wesley repudiates such doctrines as election and predestination taught by Luther and Calvin who both made use of and interpreted the views of Augustine. To say that Jesus did not intend to save all sinners but the elect only is to represent Christ as a gross deceiver of the people.[317] Therefore, John Wesley taught that salvation is made available freely for all, but the individual is the sole determinative factor in his own salvation. God does not impose anything on human beings. This fact has to be made clear to the common people through education so that they may make the right choice in life.

John Wesley's sole concern was human liberation in Christ; the liberation of individuals could be translated into societal transformation. Society can be transformed only through the transformation of all its members individually and personally by the grace of God.[318] Liberation of human beings is the act of God.[319] God works in each individual. It is the effect of his great and wonderful act of liberation, which he wrought for all humankind.[320] The central focus of John Wesley's theology is on the liberative work of Christ and the human appropriation of that liberation. However, Wesley was neither education philosopher nor a theologian in strict sense of those terms but a man with deep sense of conviction that God loves all and had sincere compassion for humanity. It is befitting to note the comments and observations of Albert Outler a Methodist theologian. Outler portrays Wesley as a "folk theologian"[321] because unlike Martin Luther and Halle Pietists, he had no academic base and unlike Calvin and Knox he had no political base. Indeed outside the Methodist tradition, Wesley largely went unnoticed by theologians since the eighteenth –century leader was not a theologian's theologian partly because he belonged to no single school of thought and founded none.[322]

---

315 William R. Cannon, "Salvation in the Theology of John Wesley," *Methodist History*, Vol. IX, No. 1, (October 1970), p. 6.

316 Ephesians 2:8, The Bible, King James Version Cf. Works, Vol. V, Sermon I, "Salvation by faith", pp. 7-8.

317 *The Works of John Wesley*, Vol. VII, Sermon, 128, section 24, p. 382.

318 William R. Cannon, "Salvation in the Theology of John Wesley," *Methodist History*, Vol. IX, No. 1, (October 1970), p. 10.

319 *Ibid.*

320 *Ibid.*, p. 9.

321 Kenneth J. Collins, "Rethinking the systematic nature of John Wesley," in *Bulletin of the John Rylands University Library of Manchester*, Vol. 85, Number 2 and 3, (Summer and Autumn, 2003), p. 309.

322 Albert C. Outler, "The Place of Wesley in the Christian Tradition," in *The Wesleyan Theological Heritage*, edited by Thomas C. Oden and Leicester R. Longden (Grand Rapids: Zondervan

This is a proof that Wesley was an eclectic and synthesizer of various views and ideas in his ministerial endeavour.

2. Understanding humanity

John Wesley's doctrine of man receives full meaning when it is seen in its relation to salvation as was discussed above. He believes that the image of God in man which is marred by sin is restored by the liberative process in Jesus Christ. John Wesley distinguishes between the guilt of sin, which is forgiven in justification (regeneration), and the depravity or the power of sin which is removed in sanctification. Unfortunately, Wesley only outlines this distinction briefly and never developed it in further detail. According to John Wesley a purely **natural man**[323] does not exist, because a human being is never wholly devoid of grace.[324] Each person is created in the image of God. "God created man in His own image, in the image of God created He him" (Gen.1: 26-27), not barely in his **natural image**, a picture of God's own immortality, a spiritual being, endued with understanding, freedom of will, and various affections; man was not created merely in his **political image**; the governor of this lower world, having dominion over the fishes of the sea, and over all the earth but chiefly in his **moral image**; which according to the Apostle Paul, is "righteousness and true holiness", (Ephesians 4:24). Accordingly man at his creation was full of love; which was the sole principle of all his tempers, thoughts, words and actions. God is full of justice, mercy and truth, so was man as he came from the hands of his creator. God is spotless purity so was man pure from every sinful blot,[325] otherwise God could not have pronounced him, as well as all the other works of his hands, "very good" (Gen.1:32). The Creator is holy so is His creation, merciful as the author of all is merciful, perfect as His father in heaven is perfect. God made man and woman to be an image of His own eternity. Human beings knew not evil in any kind or degree but were sinless and undefiled. Therefore, God required full and perfect obedience in every point. No allowance was made for any falling short. On the other hand he was endued with understanding, judging and a will exerting itself in various affections and passions. And lastly, he was endued with liberty, or freedom of choice without which all the rest would have been in vain and man would have been no more capable of serving his creator than a piece of earth or a marble or he would have been as incapable of vice or virtue, as any part of inanimate creation.[326] But the abuse of liberty led to the fall of man and the introduction of evil into the world.[327] When Man the lord of the visible creation rebelled against God, every part of the creation began to

---

Publishing House, 1991), p. 77.

323 Robert W. Burtner & Chiles Robert E., *A Compend of Wesley's Theology* (Nashville: Abingdon Press, 1954), p. 109.

324 *Ibid*, p. 139.

325 Robert W. Burtner & Chiles Robert E., *A Compend of Wesley's Theology*, p. 111.

326 *Ibid.*

327 *Ibid.*, p. 112.

suffer on account of his sin.[328] The effect was that man's perversion expressed itself in spiritual blindness, smugness, atheism, idolatry, pride, self-will, wicked desire and acts of disobedience. John Wesley readily admitted that he knew not how this inclination is transmitted from father to son but despite the popular picture of the dignity and virtue of natural man, he judged that evidence to the contrary was undeniable in both children and adults.[329] He incorporated this understanding in his theory of education as is discussed earlier in this chapter. On the other hand, Wesley affirmed that man, through receiving Christ could know his sins forgiven and enter into the kingdom of God. This new birth, according to John Wesley, would solve society's problems. In a bold pamphlet John Wesley declared "this we believe to be the never failing remedy for all the evils of a disordered world, for all the miseries...of man."[330]

Though man fell from the favour of God, He did not abandon humanity, instead He prepared a way of liberation/salvation by sending His only begotten son Jesus Christ. This liberation in Christ has to be proclaimed via teaching and preaching that humanity could be restored back to their intended status in Christ. Depraved humanity has to find deliverance in Christ through faith which could transform the given society. This leads then, to a further discussion about society and community of people.

3. Community and Society

England in the eighteenth century is often called the Age of Enlightenment. Yet to a great extent that century in which Wesley appeared was dissolute, irreligious and corrupt. Carlyle rated it to be "a bankrupt century."[331] And Lord Action (*Cambridge Modern History*) called it a period of dim ideals and expiring hopes.[332] John Wesley himself in 1745 wrote: **Our nation stands on the very brink of destruction**. And he said, because the cry of our wickedness is gone up to heaven and we have so exceedingly, abundantly, beyond measure, corrupted our ways before the Lord.[333] The evidences of decadence are overwhelming as one looks at the following issues and could be ashamed of the condition that existed then.

Class distinctions were fairly obvious, and *moral standards*, even among the elite, had reached an all time low. Marriage vows were sneered at by many in the same circles. Even court life was corrupt with one queen encouraging her husband to be unfaithful.

---

[328] Robert W. Burtner & Chiles Robert E., *A Compend of Wesley's Theology*, pp. 115-116.

[329] John Wilkins Sigsworth, *World – Changers : Karl Marx and John Wesley* (Ontario: Easingwold Publications, 1982), p. 84.

[330] *Ibid.*, p. 85.

[331] *World – Changers: Karl Marx and John Wesley*, p. 39.

[332] *Ibid.*

[333] *Ibid.*

Smuggling in seaport areas was widespread. Off the rocky coast of Cornwall another game was played, decoy lights were planted to lure nearby ships into shore in the hope they might be wrecked and subsequently plundered.

Gambling was almost a national disease. One person by the name Charles James Fox owed 5,00,000 pounds in gambling debts by age 24.[334] The spirit of gambling was rife among all classes, and in polite society both men and women were much addicted to it. "The English at this time," says Fielding, "were so addicted to gambling that several of the great men used to make it the sole business of their lives; and not only the wives these men but also their dames used to spend whole days and nights at their cards."[335]

Alcoholism was devastating the society. London gin-shops invited passersby to get drunk for a penny or dead drunk for two pence, with free straw to lie on. London at the middle of the century had an estimated 17,000 private shops so that after sundown it was unsafe to be abroad alone. The consumption of distilled spirits between 1684 and 1750 more than doubled. Sometimes Parliament had to adjourn early because members were too drunk to legislate.[336] Heavy drinking was nearly a universal vice. It is not the lower population alone that was addicted to drunkenness; numbers of persons of high rank and even of distinction were over fond of liquor. No one can study the public or personal history of the eighteenth century without being impressed by the truly immense space which drinking occupied in the mental horizon of the young, and the consequences of drinking in that of the old.[337]

Corruption, Speaking further of things about the government, it should be noted that bribery kept Walpole's government in power and that "rotten boroughs" – constituencies with few or no voters because of migrations – were selling votes readily at prices up to 5,000 pounds. Such constituencies sometimes sent more than one member, while some populous areas – particularly new towns – were scarcely represented in the House of Commons at all.[338]

Highway robbery was so common that many travellers were afraid to drive after dark. Robberies were of common occurrence. In London, the streets were never safe at night, and in the country highway men often operated in the full day light. Even the threat of capital punishment or hanging did not deter the thief.[339]

Slaves by the thousands were being brought into England and sold by auction to work on estates there with rich landlords. The usual price of a slave was a pound, the equivalent of eight oxen, and the sale of a slave took place, like

---

[334] *World – Changers: Karl Marx and John Wesley*, p. 39.

[335] W. E. Lunt, *History of England,* 3rd edition (London: Harper and Brothers, 1946), p. 534.

[336] *World – Changers : Karl Marx and John Wesley*, p. 39.

[337] W. E. Lunt, *History of England,* 3rd edition (London: Harper and Brothers, 1946), pp. 535-536.

[338] *World – Changers : Karl Marx and John Wesley*, p. 39.

[339] W. E. Lunt, *History of England,* 3rd edition (London: Harper and Brothers, 1946), p. 537.

that of cattle or other goods, before proper witnesses, so that the purchases could vouch the seller to warranty if later anyone claimed that the slave had been stolen. As a slave, person had no property of his own in the eyes of the law. Slaves often ran away. The law tried to put a stop to this by harsh penalties if the runaway slaves were caught. According to the laws of King Athelstan, runaway slave is to be stoned to death.[340] In times of great dearth men were reduced to the extremity of selling their children or other kin into slavery.[341]

Cruelty - Popular sports were often sordid. Bear, bull and badger-baiting, cock-fighting, bare-fisted humans (even women) fighting – these are typical of entertainment in that day. The theatre had sunk to a point where Sir John Hawkins could refer to it and its surroundings as hot-beds of vice.[342]

Diseases - Lack of medical care and unsanitary methods of treatment resulted in a high death rate. Many medical practitioners had limited training.[343]

Ignorance – for masses education[344] was almost non-existent. Religious education fared about the same. The state of society, as many contemporary observers pointed out, existing situation was largely due to ignorance. So, strongly did common sense rule the day that the need of an education was not recognized. The children of the workmen had small chance to acquire an adequate education, had they wanted to educate themselves. The state maintained no schools, and the schools supported in part by endowments were inadequate. But even those who could afford to pay for the education of their children often neglected it.

Religion was taken seriously by only a few. The French political philosopher Montesquieu observed that among the English society he visited "If one speaks of it (religion), everyone begins to laugh." Christianity to many had become a fiction. The celebrated legal lecturer at Oxford called Blackstone, after listening to many of the prominent clergy in London confessed that he had heard not a single sermon with more Christianity than the writings of Cicero. Wesley's own blunt mid-century estimate was that nine-tenths of the English people had no more religion than horses.[345]

Absentee Bishops were free to do what they chose in their own dioceses and, since they were obliged to spend two-thirds of their time anyway in political duty in London, sometimes scarcely visited their dioceses.[346]

Civil-disorder - The 18th century was also a time of almost continuous disorder. Wearmouth (*Methodism and the Common People of the Eighteenth Century*) mentions riot after riot beginning with one in 1740 when a mob in

---

340 Dorothy Whitelock, *The Beginnings of English Society* (Harmondsworth, Middlesex: Penguin Books Ltd, 1952), p. 108.

341 *Ibid.*, p. 109.

342 *World – Changers: Karl Marx and John Wesley*, pp. 39-40.

343 *Ibid.*

344 W. E. Lunt, *History of England*, 3rd edition (London: Harper and Brothers, 1946), p. 538.

345 *World – Changers: Karl Marx and John Wesley*, p. 40.

346 *Ibid.*

south Yorkshire tried to stop a load of meal and flour en-route to Lancashire and precipitated a four-day riot. It seems that many of the later local disturbances, as one in London in the spring of 1768, were also associated with shortages of food or the high price of food, but discontent with enclosures and wage conditions were sometimes causal factors also. Stories of the distress and suffering at times endured in rural areas are appalling. The riots threatened the destruction of London.[347]

Lawlessness – The hard drinking and the immorality prevailing among the lower orders produced a large amount of lawlessness. Swearing, vulgarity, drinking and gambling moreover, were sufficiently common to give the tone to society.[348]

After analyzing the general lawlessness and degradation in the society and communities, John Wesley declared as is quoted earlier in the same section - Our nation stands on the very brink of destruction. Therefore, his vision and dream was to liberate (reform) society and the nation with all its ills using education as his major tool, God's free gift of salvation as his source of strength and inspiration.

John Wesley's work was mainly among the poor because these people were in dire need and more receptive to his teaching. In addition, such ministry was long overdue. It is believed that John Wesley and his helpers were the first preachers since the days of the Franciscan friars in the middle Ages to reach out to the working classes.[349] It is not exaggeration to say that John Wesley had a wider constructive influence in the sphere of practical religion than any other person who has appeared since the sixteenth century and by his humane endeavours a sense of decency in morals and religion was introduced in the lowest classes of humankind.[350] John Wesley was indeed a **Social, Moral, and Spiritual** revolutionary similar to what Paulo Freire did with education in Latin America after two hundred plus years. The politician Lloyd George affirmed that his native Wales owed more to the Wesleyan movement than to any other movement in the whole of history- **It civilized the people**, he said succinctly. The clergyman-chemist Joseph Priestly commended the Wesleyan movement for their contribution to the **civilization,** the **industry,** the **sobriety** of the labouring group. It is generally acknowledged that in the wake of the revival came behavioural changes in English society.[351] J. W. Bready estimates that John Wesley's influence on the consciences of Englishmen [women] was more widespread than that of any other person of his day.[352]

4. Church and Mission

John Wesley envisioned the Methodist movement to be a movement of revitalization. The movement was to revitalize not only the Church of England

---

[347] *World – Changers : Karl Marx and John Wesley*, p. 41.

[348] W. E. Lunt, *History of England,* 3rd edition (London: Harper and Brothers, 1946), pp. 537-536.

[349] *World – Changers: Karl Marx and John Wesley*, p. 251.

[350] *Ibid.*, 363.

[351] *World – Changers: Karl Marx and John Wesley,* pp. 364-365.

[352] *Ibid.*, p. 366.

outside, but also the hearts of men and women within. The grace of God to be found in the means of grace and the life lived in the love of Christ are seen as the essential elements of John Wesley's theology. Albert C. Outler has stated, "The heart of John Wesley's gospel was always its lively sense of God's grace at work at every level of creation and history in persons and communities"[353]

John Wesley makes an earnest effort to define **Church** based on the scripture, in a way the common people could understand.

> The Church at Ephesus, as the Apostle Paul himself explains it, means, the **saints**, the holy persons, that God the Father, and His Son Jesus Christ being the head; whether they did this in one or in several places. But it is the Church in general, the universal Church, which the Apostle here considers as one body: Comprehending not only the Christians... of one congregation, of one city, of one province, or nation; but all the persons upon the face of the earth.[354]

John Wesley further considers several particulars in the above definition and explains this to common people.

> There is one Spirit who animates all these, all the living members of the Church of God. Some understand hereby the Holy Spirit himself, the Fountain of all spiritual life; and it is certain, if any man has [sic] not the Spirit of Christ, he is none of his.... There is one Lord, who has now dominion over them; who has set up His kingdom in their hearts, and reigns over all those that are partakers of this hope.... There is one faith which is the free gift of God, and is the ground of their hope....There is one baptism which is the outward sign, our Lord has been pleased to appoint, of all that inward and spiritual grace which He is continually bestowing upon His Church....There is one God and Father of all that have the Spirit of adoption, which cries in their hearts, **Abba, Father** which **witnesses** continually **with their spirits**, that they are the children of God: Who is above all, – the Most High, the Creator, the Sustainer, the Governor of the whole universe:
>
> And through all, – pervading all space; filling heaven and earth ... And in you all, – in a peculiar manner living in you, that are one body, by one Spirit: **Making your soul His loved abode, the temples of indwelling God**. The universal Church is, all the persons in the universe whom God hath so called out of the world as to entitle them to the preceding character; as to be **one body**, united by **one Spirit**;

---

[353] Albert C. Outler (ed), *The Works of John Wesley: Volume I, Sermons I, 1-33* (Nashville: Abingdon Press. 1984), p. 98.

[354] Robert W. Burtner & Robert E Chiles, *A Compendium of Wesley's Theology* (Nashville: Abingdon Press, 1954), p. 253.

having one faith, one hope, one baptism; one God and Father of all, who is above all, and through all, and in them all.[355]

John Wesley says here is a native specimen of a New-Testament church, which is a company of men, called by the Gospel, grafted into Christ by baptism, animated by love, united by all kinds of fellowship.[356]

John Wesley's primary **mission** was always to present the gospel as well as he could with the best understanding. He firmly believed that the grace of our Lord Jesus Christ was sufficient to cure the oppression of sin found in the human heart.

John Wesley's homeland conference of 1769 meeting at Leeds sent out the first two missionaries, Richard Boardman and Joseph Pilmoor. Two years later in 1771 Francis Asbury, a man destined to provide impressive leadership for half a century, followed. The growth of Methodist missions, during the Asbury years and beyond is almost unbelievable, as statistics in the following chapter clearly demonstrate.[357]

The statements and evaluation of numerous responsible people in both the religious and secular world undoubtedly recognize John Wesley's missionary zealous, commitment; and secular lifestyles, have attested to the enormous impact that Wesley and his mission made on the religious world of his day and since. Kenneth Slack, a Presbyterian divine commented about John Wesley: incomparably the most influential English figure in the religious story of the world. W. H. Fitchett, an Australian Methodist biographer says: Wesley restored Christianity to its place as a living force in the personal creed of men .... T. R. Glover, a Baptist scholar at Cambridge, called Wesley, one of the four intellectuals through whom God put a new heart into Christendom on both sides of the Atlantic. - The others in Glover's mind were Paul, Augustine, and Luther. Johann Dollinger, a distinguished German Roman Catholic historian of the last century, considered Wesley, the most significant Protestant figure since the Reformation. W. E. Lecky, regarded as one of the most unbiased of historians, judged the Wesleyan revival to the most important event in the history of modern Christianity. Moreover, Sir Leslie Stephen, a nineteenth century critic, called the Wesleyan movement the most important phenomenon of the eighteenth century.[358] Although, John Wesley did not set out to create a new denomination, his hard labour resulted in the formation of one, a distinctly new self-conscious religious community called Methodists. Overall John Wesley's influence extended far beyond the Methodist communion.

At the time of John Wesley's death, over 500 Anglican clergy could be classed as evangelicals within the Anglican establishment. Thus, in Fitchett's words,

[355] Robert W. Burtner & Robert E Chiles, *A Compendium of Wesley's Theology*, pp. 254-255.

[356] *Ibid.*, p. 255.

[357] *World – Changers: Karl Marx and John Wesley*, p. 273.

[358] *Ibid.*, p. 344.

Wesley **created a new conscience** in his mother Church.[359] In comparison with the total clergy at that time, the evangelicals were only five or six per cent of the total. Yet Canon Overton *The Evangelical Revival in the Eighteenth Century* has conceded that around 1800 A.D., these evangelicals were "morally and spiritually the dominant religious power both inside and outside the church ..."[360]

John Wesley's movement at his death in 1791 embraced some 71,000 members in the Great Britain **societies**, with 1,000 local preachers and nearly 300 itinerant preachers. It was, in fact, the second largest religious group in both England and Wales and its strength so frightened the Anglican establishment that an Act of Parliament in 1792 ordered more churches to be built to counter the spread of Wesley's mission.[361]

On the other hand, American contingent embraced another 6,000 members served by nearly 200 preachers in 14 Annual Conferences. In addition, the Methodists in British North America (Canada) and those in the West Indies and the Channel Islands put together were about 40,000 members in all. Adherents of Methodist faith & practices especially in Britain have been more in numbers than those claimed to be Methodist members. Yet to John Wesley, the Methodist Societies, at least those in Britain were still in the Anglican Church.[362] As George Grant Cell correctly states it in *The Rediscovery of John Wesley*, "John Wesley became the founder of a Church against his will." To illustrate this, one finds as late as 1789 that John Wesley was expressing his desire that the societies remain in Mother Church.[363]

John Wesley's brother, Charles, used to say, "God buries His workmen but carries on His work."[364] Surely enough, the revival persisted and Methodists continued to increase even after John's death. In 1810, 19 years later – the total number worldwide apart from United Kingdom was approximately 3,50,000. In the decades that followed, the world membership continued to mushroom, despite some homeland stagnation in the 1830s under John Wesley's autocratic successor, Jabez Bunting.[365] By 1860, the world figure exceeded 10,00,000 and it was nearly 15,00,000, if all Methodist bodies are included. (What an exception to Luther's observation that "a revival of religion seldom continues above thirty years"!) By 1935, the fellowship numbered 4,00,00,000 (four crores) around the world.[366]

In recent decades, the overall rate of gain has tapered off but recent estimates of members and adherents in over 80 countries suggests a total of nearly

[359] *World – Changers: Karl Marx and John Wesley*, p. 344.

[360] *Ibid.*, p. 345.

[361] *World – Changers: Karl Marx and John Wesley*, p. 272.

[362] *Ibid.*

[363] *Ibid.*

[364] *World – Changers: Karl Marx and John Wesley*, p. 273.

[365] *Ibid.*

[366] *Ibid.*

5,00,00,000, about half of these being actual members. This makes Methodism the largest of all churches that enjoy no favoured connection with a political state. Roy Smith, a knowledgeable Methodist writer in America conjectured a few decades ago, "it is probable that the Methodist Church is at work in more fields and under more flags than any protestant church in the world."[367] John Wesley once wrote to a friend shortly after he began field preaching: **I look upon the world as my parish.**[368] Those words have surely inspired Methodists since, as they have gone to the ends of the earth with the Christian gospel.

By 1865, ten Methodist bodies flourished in the U.S. with a total membership of 20,00,000. Interestingly by then, one out of five U.S. church members in the U.S. was a Methodist.[369]

John Wesley has had an impact on missions outside official Methodism. For instance, J. Hudson Taylor whose father was a Yorkshire Methodist lay evangelist founded the China Inland Mission, one of the earliest of the so-called interdenominational "faith" missions, in 1865.[370]

The largest single Christian denomination in the Republic of South Africa in the mid 1970s was the Methodist Church. It had something in excess of twenty lakh[371] members.[372]

Being an established organization, Methodists naturally participated in the organization of the World Council of Churches in 1948 in Amsterdam and have been active in it ever since. Dr. John R. Mott, a Methodist layperson known worldwide through his associations with the Young Men's Christian Association (YMCA) and the Student Volunteer Movement (SVM). Later it was rechristened as the Student Christian Movement (SCM). Mott was named as the first honorary president of the World Council of Churches, an ecumenical body. Some evangelicals regret that in recent decade's theological liberals and political activists who sometimes have seemed to display more concern for social justice and Marxist ideology than for spiritual values and national survival have heavily captured the key leadership of the ecumenical bodies that began with much to commend them.[373] Many regret that the social gospel bandwagon, which seemed one-sided in American Churches, is almost overtaken by liberal ecclesiastics today.[374]

John Wesley's watchword – **World is my Parish**, proved beyond any one's doubt the extent of his vision and made his mission's presence felt in almost every

[367] *World – Changers: Karl Marx and John Wesley*, p. 273.

[368] These are Wesley's own words, *the world is my parish* is a paraphrased by the subsequent Writers. *World – Changers: Karl Marx and John Wesley*, p. 273.

[369] *Ibid*, p. 274.

[370] *Ibid.*, p. 277.

[371] *An Indian term for hundred thousand.*

[372] *World – Changers : Karl Marx and John Wesley*, p. 278.

[373] *Ibid.*, p. 282.

[374] *Ibid.*, p. 278.

part of this universe. Wesley's mission transcended the denominational divisions of the Church including the Catholics and Protestants as well as East and West. Such was the impact of his vision and mission during his lifetime and since.[375]

5. Family and Education

While the whole world was Wesley's parish, his focus was always on the salvation of the individual's soul. For John Wesley everyone that lives under one roof is a family and it is knit by love, understanding, sharing, caring and teaching one another. Christian family and religion are two sides of the same coin and cannot be separated easily. Family is a key unit of the society for any transformation to usher in.

John Wesley's emphasis on the role of each key person in the family shows his concern for each member of the household. He educates a man of the house through his sermon (*sermon no.94, "on family Religion"*) as is discussed below.

The person in your house that claims your first and nearest attention, is, undoubtedly, your wife; seeing you are to love her, even as Christ hath loved the Church, when he laid down his life for it, that he might "purify it unto himself, not having spot, or wrinkle, or any such thing." The same way is the duty of every husband to pursue, in all his relationship with his wife; to use every possible means ...[376] to make her feel that she is being loved and cared for, as Christ loved his church.

Next to your wife are your children; immortal spirits whom God hath, for a time, entrusted to your care, that you may train them up in all holiness, and fit them for the enjoyment of God in eternity." Every child, therefore, you are to watch over with the utmost care, that, when you are called to give an account of each to the Father of heaven, you may give your accounts with joy and not with grief.[377]

About the servants: you are to look upon them as a kind of secondary children.

These, likewise, God has committed to your charge, as one that must give account. For every one under your roof that has a soul to be saved is under your care; not only indented servants, who are legally engaged to remain with you for a term of years; not only hired servants, whether they voluntarily contract for a longer or shorter time; but also those who serve you by week days: For these too are, in a measure, delivered into your hands. And it is not the will of your Master who is in heaven, that any of these should go out of your hands before they have received from you something more valuable than gold or silver. Yea and you are in a degree accountable even for **the stranger that is within your gates**.[378]

---

[375] Ryan Danker, *Introduction, The Sermons of John Wesley*, 1872 edition, This article was down loaded from the internet and it is in the possession of the author, p. 4.

[376] *The Works of John Wesley, Vol. VII, Sermon 94*, p. 79.

[377] *Ibid.*

[378] *The Works of John Wesley, Vol. VII, Sermon 94*, pp. 78-79.

John Wesley also described proper techniques to be used with the various members of the household.

Firstly, your children, while they are young, you may restrain them from evil, not only by advice, persuasion, and reproof, but also by **correction**; only remembering, that this means is to be used last, ... not till all other have been tried, and found to be ineffectual. Even then, you should take the utmost care to avoid the very appearance of passion. Whatever is done should be done with mildness; nay, indeed, with kindness too. Otherwise, your own spirit will suffer loss, and the child will reap little advantage.

> But some will tell you, "All this is lost labour: A child need not be corrected at all. Instruction, persuasion, and advice, will be sufficient for any child without correction; especially if gentle reproof be added, as occasion may require." I answer; there may be particular instances, wherein this method may be successful. But you must not, in anywise, lay this down as a universal rule; unless you suppose yourself wiser than Solomon, or, to speak more properly wiser than God. For it is God Himself, who best knows His own creatures, that has told us expressly, "He that spares the rod, hates his son: But he that loves him chastens him betimes." (Proverbs 13:24.) And upon this is grounded that plain commandment, directed to all that fear God, "Chasten thy son while there is hope, and let not thy soul spare for his crying." (Prov. 19:18.)[379]

Secondly, to **instruct** them, to take care that every person who is under your roof have all such knowledge as is necessary to salvation, to see that your wife, servants, and children be taught all those things which belong to their eternal peace? In order to do this you should provide that, not only your wife, but your servants also, might enjoy all the public means of instruction. On the Lord's Day in particular, you should so forecast what is necessary to be done at home, that they may have an opportunity of attending all the ordinances of God. Yes, and you should take care that they have some time every day for reading, meditation, and prayer; and you should inquire whether they do actually employ that time in the exercises for which it is allowed. Neither should any day pass without family prayer, seriously and solemnly performed.[380]

> You should particularly endeavour to instruct your children, early, plainly, frequently, and patiently. Instruct them **early**, from the first hour that you perceive reason begins to dawn. Truth may then begin to shine upon the mind far earlier than we are apt to suppose. Moreover, whoever watches the first openings of the understanding, may, by little

[379] *The Works of John Wesley, Vol. VII, Sermon 94,* p. 81.

[380] *Ibid.*

> and little, supply fit matter for it to work upon, and may turn the eye of the son (sic), toward good things, as well as toward bad or trifling ones. Whenever a child begins to speak, you may be assured reason begins to work. I know no cause why a parent should not just then begin to speak of the best things, the things of God. And from that time no opportunity should be lost, of instilling all truths as they are capable of receiving.[381]

Speaking to them early will not avail, unless you likewise speak to them **plainly**. Use such words as little children may understand, just such as they use themselves.

If you wish to see the fruit of your labour, you must teach them not only early and plainly, but **frequently** too. It would be of little or no service to do it only once or twice a week. How often do you feed their bodies? Not less than three times a day. And is the soul of less value than the body? Will you not then feed this as often? If you find this a tiresome task, there is certainly something wrong in your own mind.[382]

However, it will not avail to teach them both early, plainly, and frequently, unless you **persevere** therein. Never leave off; never intermit your labour of love, till you see the fruit of it.[383]

Let it be remembered, said Wesley:

> that I do not speak to the wild, giddy, thoughtless world, but to those that fear God. I ask, then, for what end do you send your children to school? "Why, Children may be taught to live in the world." In which world do you mean this or the next? Perhaps you thought of this world only; and had forgot that there is a world to come; yea, and one that will last forever! Please take this into your account, and send them to such masters as will keep it always before their eyes. Otherwise, to send them to school (permit me to speak plainly) is little better than sending them to the devil. At all events, then, send your boys, if you have any concern for their souls, not to any of the large public schools, (for they are nurseries of all manner of wickedness,) but private school, kept by some pious men, who endeavours to instruct a small number of children in religion and learning together.[384]

You may ask what I shall do with my girls." By no means, send them to large boarding schools. In these seminaries too the children teach one another pride,

[381] *The Works of John Wesley, Vol. VII, Sermon 94,* p. 81.

[382] *Ibid.*, p. 82.

[383] *Ibid.*

[384] *The Works of John Wesley, Vol. VII, Sermon 94,* p. 83.

vanity, affectation, intrigue, artifice, and, in short, everything which a Christian woman ought not to learn.[385]

After speaking comprehensively about family religion, John Wesley admonishes parents with regard to educating children. John Wesley while quoting William Law says, the ground of this is admirably well laid by Mr. Law, in his *Serious Call to a Devout Life*. This is what he said:

> Had we continued perfect as God created the first man, perhaps the perfection of our nature had been a sufficient self-instructor for every one. But as sickness and diseases have created the necessity of medicines and physicians, so the disorders of our rational nature have introduced the necessity of education and tutors.[386]

Therefore, as the only end of a physician is, to restore nature to its own state, so the only end of education is, to restore our rational nature to its proper state. John Wesley said, the education under Pythagoras or Socrates had no other end, but to teach children to think and act as Pythagoras and Socrates did.

> Is it not then, reasonable to suppose that a Christian education should have no other end but to teach them how to think, and judge, and act according to the strictest rules of Christianity?
>
> At least one would suppose, that in all Christian schools, the teaching them to begin their lives in the spirit of Christianity, ... in such abstinence, humility, sobriety, and devotion as Christianity requires, should not only be more, but a hundred times more. [387]

The major role of Christian education is to restore humanity to its original nature and liberty in Christ. John Wesley calls those actions that keep human beings away from God as diseases. They are briefly mentioned earlier in the same chapter.

What are those spiritual diseases, which every one that is born of a woman brings with him/her into the world? Following discussion is a summery taken from John Wesley's Sermon no. 95: "On the Education of Children."[388]

Is not the first of these, Atheism? That man has naturally any more idea of God than that any of the beasts of the field; he has no knowledge of God at all; no fear of God at all; neither is God in all his thoughts. Whatever change may afterwards be wrought, (whether by the grace of God or by his own reflection, or by education) he is, by nature, a mere Atheist.

---

[385] *The Works of John Wesley, Vol. VII, Sermon 94*, pp. 83-84.

[386] *Ibid.*, p. 87.

[387] *Ibid.*, p. 88.

[388] *The Works of John Wesley, Vol. VII, Sermon 94*, pp. 89-90.

Indeed, it may be said that every man is by nature, as it were, his is own god. He worships himself. He is, in his own conception, absolute lord of himself. **His own will** is his only law; he does this or that because it is his good pleasure.

Another evil disease, which every human soul brings into the world with him, is ***pride*** a continual proneness to think of him more highly than he ought to think. Every person can discern more or less of this disease in everyone... excluding himself. Moreover, indeed, if he could discern it in oneself, it would subsist no longer; for he would then, in consequence, think of himself just as he ought to think.[389]

The next disease natural to every human soul, born with every man, is **love of the world**. Every man is, by nature, a lover of the creature, instead of the Creator a "lover of pleasure," in every kind, "more than a lover of God." He is a slave to foolish and hurtful desires, in one kind or another; either to the "desires of the flesh, the desires of the eyes or the pride of life." "The desires of the flesh" is a propensity to seek happiness in what gratifies one or more of the outward senses. "The desires of the eyes" is a propensity to seek happiness in what gratifies internal sense, the imagination, either by things grand, new, or beautiful. "The pride of life" seems to mean a propensity to seek happiness in what gratifies the sense of honour. To this head is usually referred "the love of money;" one of the basest passions that can have place in the human heart. However, it may be doubted whether this be not an acquired rather than a natural, distemper.[390]

Whether, the love of the world is a natural disease or not, it is certain that the **anger** is. Now, was there ever anyone born of a woman who did not labour under this? Indeed, like other diseases of the mind, it is far more violent in some than in others. It is a real, though short, madness wherever it is.[391]

A **deviation from truth** is equally natural to all the children of men. One said in his haste, "All men are liars;" but we may say, upon cool reflection, all natural men will, upon a close temptation, vary from, or disguise, the truth. If they do not offend against veracity, if they do not say what is false, yet they frequently offend against **simplicity**. "Behold an Israelite indeed, in whom is no guile!"[392]

Wesley continues his discussion further saying, everyone is likewise prone, by nature, to speak or act **contrary to justice**. This is another of the diseases, which we bring with us into the world. All human creatures are naturally partial to themselves, and, when opportunity offers, have more regard to their own interest or pleasure than strict justice allows. Neither is any man, by nature, **merciful** as our heavenly Father is merciful; but all, more or less, transgress that glorious rule

---

[389] *The Works of John Wesley, Vol. VII, Sermon 94*, p. 89.

[390] *Ibid.*, pp. 89-90.

[391] *Ibid.*, p. 90.

[392] *Ibid.*

of mercy as well as justice, "Whatsoever ye would that men should do unto you, the same do unto them."[393]

Now, if these are the **general diseases of human nature**, is it not the **grand end of education to cure them**? And is it not the part of all those to whom God has entrusted the education of children, to take all possible care, first, not to increase, not to feed, any of these diseases; (as the generality of parents constantly do) and next, to use every possible means of healing them? [394]

Most parents increase the natural tendency to **injustice** in their children, by conniving at their wronging each other; if not laughing at, or even applauding, their witty contrivances to cheat one another. Beware of everything of this kind; and from their very infancy sow the seeds of justice in their hearts, and train them up in the most exact practice of it. If possible, teach them the love of justice, and that in the least things as well as the greatest. Impress upon their mind the old proverb: "He that will steal a penny will steal a pound." Habituate them to render unto all their due, even to the uttermost farthing.[395]

Many parents connive likewise at the **ill nature** of their children, and thereby strengthen it. Nevertheless, truly affectionate parents will not indulge them in any kind or degree of un-mercifulness. They will not suffer them to vex their brothers or sisters, either by word or by deed. They will not allow them to hurt, or give pain to, anything that has life. They will not permit them to rob birds' nests; much less to kill anything without necessity, -- not even snakes, which are as innocent as worms, or toads, which, notwithstanding their ugliness, and the ill name they lie under, have been proved repeatedly to be as harmless as flies. Let them extend in its measure the rule of doing, as they would be done by, to every animal whatsoever. You that are truly kind parents, press upon all your children, "to walk in love, as Christ also loved us, and gave himself for us." To mind that one point, "God is love; and he that dwells in love, dwells in God, and God in him." [396]

John Wesley's advice to parents is not just in the area of spirituality, morality, social behaviour alone but includes ecological concerns and just behaviour with even the natural and animal world. This is truly an inclusive and wholesome education. There are several other related issues, which John Wesley talks about such as children's obedience to the parents and pastors, use of time, charity, conscience, ethical behaviours etc. Since the focus of this book is limited to Wesley's educational thoughts, those issues mentioned above are not discussed in this research work.

John Wesley indeed was a pioneer in popularizing education in his century. Researcher's assumption is that most of his educational thoughts, if used properly

---

[393] *The Works of John Wesley, Vol. VII, Sermon 94*, p. 90.

[394] *Ibid.*

[395] *The Works of John Wesley, Vol. VII, Sermon 94*, p. 97.

[396] *Ibid.* p. 97-98.

could revitalize the present Christian education programmes of Methodists in Karnataka today. The next section will then discuss his educational theory and approach briefly.

C. Distinct Characteristics of Wesley's Educational theory and Approach

John Wesley believed that religion and education are inseparable and should always proceed hand in hand.[397] He evolved educational theory and philosophy based on his theological conviction and personal experiences.

1. Learning Theory[398]

Wesley scholars, especially Tracy suggests John Wesley's learning theories under three headings:

a. Personologism

This declares the human personality to be generative and active. It acts upon environment shaping it and at times follows its own ends inspite of environment. Human beings are uniquely persons with inner potential and functioning organisms, subject to forces from the environment that cause them to behave the way they do.[399] Therefore, Wesley sets forth a basis for dialogue with human potential and environmental influences, but it begins with human nature and sin as a first consideration.

b. Situationalism

Declares the personality or intellect to be a passive lump upon which environment works with a free hand shaping and forming the person in its environment's own image.[400]

c. Interactionism

It says that the person is indeed generative and active but not impervious to environment.[401] Interaction or dialogical approach is an important method in teaching and learning process. Most of the educators in the history of educational philosophy have advocated interaction or dialogical method either directly or indirectly as is discernable in their writings.

2. Practice of Christian Education

John Wesley's theory and approach evolved out of his main objectives of Christian education that he had proposed for Kingswood School near Bristol. These

[397] Alfred H. Body, *John Wesley and Education* (London: The Epworth Press, 1936), p. 67.

[398] Wesley Tracy, "Christian education in Wesleyan Mode," pp. 45-46.

[399] *Ibid.*, p. 47.

[400] *Ibid.*, p. 45.

[401] Wesley Tracy, "Christian education in Wesleyan Mode," p. 46.

objectives were framed after studying the educators of his time, the educational institutions and their conditions. John Wesley's unique objectives of Christian Education inferred from his writings are:

a. Objectives of Christian Education

First of all, says John Wesley, it is our particular desire that all who are educated here may be brought up in the fear of God and of course learners must be kept at the utmost distance from vice in general, idleness and effeminacy in particular.[402]

Secondly, the main point was, to fulfill the purpose of Christian education, by forming their minds, through the help of God, to wisdom and holiness, by instilling the principles of true religion, speculative and practical, and training them up in the ancient way, that they might be rational, scriptural Christians.[403]

Thirdly, the aim is not so much to teach Greek and Latin as much as to train up soldiers for Jesus Christ, men [women] who could fight and sacrifice like the early Church.[404]

Fourthly, John Wesley proposed to educate a few children according to the accuracy of the Christian model,[405] instead of being ambitious to have a large numbers. John Wesley says, "I was afraid of having too many at once, knowing how difficult it was to govern a large number; children being so apt, when many of them are together, to hinder and corrupt one another."[406]

Fifthly, he says, the design is, with God's help to train up children in every branch of useful leaning.[407]

b. John Wesley's Theory and Method

John Wesley instructed his followers concerning the methods which a teacher should use and the characteristics of a good teacher. The principle of **known to unknown** was a key for an orderly progression in teaching. The **pedagogical** methods which he advocated could be summarized in five points,[408] which established as a priority enabling the learner to understand what is being taught.

i. Secure the students' attention before teaching. John Wesley recognized that "to draw and fix the attention of the children is one of the greatest difficulties in speaking to them."

---

[402] *The Works of John Wesley, Vol. XIII*, "A Short Account of the School in Kingswood, Near Bristol" (1768), p. 284.

[403] *Ibid.,* p. 293.

[404] John Telford, (ed), *The Letters of the Rev. John Wesley A.M. Standard edition*, Vol. II, May 17, 1742-Jan 4, 1749 (London: The Epworth Press, 1931), p. 128.

[405] *The Works of John Wesley, Vol. XIII,* "Remarks on the State of Kingswood School," (1783), p. 301.

[406] *The Works of John Wesley, Vol. XIII*, "A Plain Account of Kingswood School," (1781), p. 293.

[407] *The Works of John Wesley, Vol. XIII*, "A Short Account of the School in Kingswood, Near Bristol" (1768), p. 283.

[408] James Riley Estep Jr. "John Wesley's Philosophy of Formal Childhood Education" in *Christian Education Journal*, Vol. INS, No. 2, (Fall 1997), p. 50.

ii. Use words that the children understand. He advised parents and teachers not to make schools the 'slaughter house of the mind'[409] instead insisted on understanding. Take time to make them understand and explain things in their words which they use themselves. Carefully observe the few ideas the children already have and graft into them what is being taught. To speak of God and use the words of the assembly's Catechism, that "the chief end of human being is to glorify God and enjoy Him forever," is to employ terms beyond any capacity of little children.

iii. Use illustrations from everyday life. In speaking of God, interest children first in the sun, in its warmth, its work in causing flowers and grass to grow. Then point to God as the power behind the sun, causing it to shine, giving it its warmth. From that, it is easy to speak of His power and love, even to the smallest persons such as children.

iv. Establish a relationship of love. The teacher can then say to the student: God loves you. He loves to do you good. He loves to make you happy. Would you then not love Him? You love me, because I love you and do you good. But it is God that makes me love you. Therefore, you should love Him. He will teach you how to love Him.[410]

v. Be Patient, and repeat yourself many times. ". . . If teaching is to bear any fruit," wrote John Wesley, one must "teach patiently." You must tell them the same thing ten times over and over again or you do nothing.[411] He insisted that the teachers to adapt content to the learners level of thinking. In fact, he demonstrated it in his preaching to 550 children and thereby taught a lesson to his preachers.[412] This indicates that he was conscious of developmental stages of the learners. These stages were classified much later than Wesley's time.

Here is a classic illustration that John Wesley records in his *Works* about his mother's patience with her children some of them who were slow of learning, as an encouragement to the teachers.

> Some children are inconceivably dull, others so giddy and perverse that if the teacher follows his own inclination he will give up in despair. I remember to have heard my father asking my mother, "How could you have the patience to tell that blockhead the same thing twenty times over?" She [Susanna Wesley] answered, "Why if I had told him but nineteen times I should have lost all my labours." What patience indeed, what love, what knowledge.[413]

---

[409] Wesley Tracy, "Christian Education in the Wesleyan Mode", in *Wesleyan Theological Journal*, Vol. 17, No. 1, (Spring 1982), p. 45.

[410] John Wesley, *The Works of John Wesley*, Vol. II, pp. 304-305.

[411] *Ibid.*, Vol. VII, p. 91.

[412] Wesley Tracy, "Christian Education in the Wesleyan Mode", in *Wesleyan Theological Journal*, Vol. 17, No. 1, (Spring 1982), pp. 44-45.

[413] John Wesley, *The Works of John Wesley*, Vol. I, p. 68.

This is a grim reminder to those teaching faculty who is under tremendous pressure to complete the syllabus for that academic year. It is not the completion of the course that matters but making the learners understand is the key in teaching vocation.

Moreover, John Wesley did not limit teaching to the four walled classrooms or traditional schools but engaged his preachers, societies, parents, and every one that mattered in this business. For him it was teamwork.

c. Pedagogy of Liberation

Do not force religion on children but inculcate it in them.[414] It will only lead to domestication and not learning with freedom. Any pedagogy that one applies in teaching must be liberative and not lead to domestication, was Wesley's advice to his teachers and house masters.

Be tender and compassionate in correcting their wrongs.[415] Neither severity nor leniency is appreciated in learning teaching process. One must balance discipline with love and understanding.

Do not follow extremes either in discipline or in teaching religion. A teacher should proportionately administer be it religion or discipline as is necessary.

Do everything within your power to shape them as God intended them to be.[416] A duty of a teacher is to draw out as best as possible from the learners. One must not settle with second best attitude.

d. The Preachers as Teachers

John Wesley emphasised that education was a preacher's priority. They were encouraged to teach the children and adults in the homes of his people. A preacher seeking membership into the conference was asked – Will you diligently and earnestly instruct the children and visit from house to house?[417] John Wesley counselled his preachers to deal gently with the children and encourage them to learn the document- *Instructions for children,* which he translated from French.[418] 'Take each person alone aside and deal closely with him about his sin, misery, and duty'.[419]

---

[414] John Wesley, "A Thought on the Manner of Educating Children" *The Works of John Wesley*, 3rd edition, complete and unabridged, Vol. XIII (Grand Rapids, Michigan: Baker Books, 1998), p. 476.

[415] John Wesley, "A Thought on the Manner of Educating Children," pp. 476-77.

[416] *Ibid.*, p. 477.

[417] John Wesley Prince, *Wesley on Religious Education* (New York: Methodist Book Concern, 1926), p. 134.

[418] The Instructions for Children, translated from *Les Principes solides de la religion et de la vie Chretienne appliqués a l'educateur des enfants* by Abbe Fleury and M. Pierre Poirot. Cf. Wesley Tracy, "Christian Education in the Wesleyan Mode", in *Wesleyan Theological Journal*, Vol. 17, No. 1, (Spring 1982), pp. 32, 34.

[419] John Wesley, *The Works of John Wesley*, Vol. VIII, p. 305. Cf. Wesley Tracy, "Christian Education in the Wesleyan Mode", in *Wesleyan Theological Journal*, Vol. 17, No. 1, (Spring 1982), p. 32.

John Wesley goes systematically and tells the preachers how to conduct such religious education sessions. In 1766, he outlined the preacher's responsibility for the religious education of children.

i. Where there are ten children in a society, meet them at least an hour every week.
ii. Talk with them every time you see any of them at home.
iii. Pray in earnest for them.
iv. Diligently instruct and vehemently exhort all parents at their houses.
v. Preach expressly on education.[420]

After listening to John Wesley's instructions - one preacher objected, "But I have no gift for this," John Wesley replied, "Gift or no gift, you are to do it; else you are not called to be a Methodist Preacher."[421]

Again the Methodist Conference of 1768 legislating programmes for religious education in the larger parishes, instructed the preachers to meet with the children an hour a week "whether you like or not."[422] "For what avails preaching alone, though we could preach like angels?" John Wesley asks. "We must, yea, every travelling Preacher must, instruct them [children] from house to house.[423]

e. The Parents as Teachers

Of course, Wesley knew that the preachers alone could not do the task of educating the young and the adults. Parents were strongly urged to carry on family education. Repeatedly Wesley told his people that the Methodist **revival would dissipate in one generation without a vigorous programme of Christian Education in the home.**[424] John Wesley had almost a fanatic belief in education.

John Wesley spoke to his congregations that their children were 'immortal spirits whom God hath, for a time, entrusted to your care." Moreover, this He has done 'that you may train them up in all holiness.[425]

---

[420] Wesley Tracy, "Christian Education in the Wesleyan Mode," in *Wesleyan Theological Journal*, Vol. 17, No. 1, (Spring 1982), p. 32.

[421] John Wesley, *The Works of John Wesley*, Vol. VIII, p. 316. Cf. Wesley Tracy, "Christian Education in the Wesleyan Mode," in *Wesleyan Theological Journal*, Vol. 17, No.1, (Spring 1982), p. 33.

[422] John Wesley Prince, *Wesley on Religious Education* (New York: Methodist Book Concern, 1926), p. 135. Cf. Wesley Tracy, "Christian Education in the Wesleyan Mode", in *Wesleyan Theological Journal*, Vol. 17, No.1, (Spring 1982), p. 33.

[423] John Wesley, *The Works of John Wesley*, Vol. VIII, p. 302. Cf. Wesley Tracy, "Christian Education in the Wesleyan Mode", in *Wesleyan Theological Journal*, Vol. 17, No.1, (Spring 1982), p. 33.

[424] Wesley Tracy, "Christian Education in the Wesleyan Mode", in *Wesleyan Theological Journal*, Vol. 17, No.1, (Spring 1982), p. 33.

[425] John Wesley, "On Family Religion," Sermon 94, section II in his *Works*, Vol. VII, p. 79. Cf. Wesley Tracy, "Christian Education in the Wesleyan Mode," in *Wesleyan Theological Journal*, Vol. 17, No.1, (Spring 1982), p. 33.

> Preaching from the text, "as for me and my house we will serve the Lord" (Joshua 24:15) John Wesley told parents they must restrain their children through advice, persuasion, and reproof, but also by correction; only remembering, that this means is to be used last,... not till all other have been tried and found to be ineffectual. And even then you should take the utmost care to avoid the very appearance of passion. Whatever is done should be done with mildness, nay indeed with kindness too. Otherwise your own spirit will suffer loss, and the child will reap little advantage."[426]

However, he declared that those who tried to thrash their children into heaven and out of hell should not think it strange **if religion stinks in the nostrils of those that were so educated**. Those children will hate such religious education and will naturally look upon it as an austere, melancholy thing.[427]

To **advice, persuasion** and **correction** the Christian parent was to add **instruction**. This **instruction** was to be done **early, plainly, frequently,** and **patiently.**[428] From the first sign that you perceive reason begins to dawn, instruct them to turn their eyes toward good things as well as trifling ones. John Wesley said, 'I know no cause why a parent should not just then begin to speak of the best things, the things of God. And from that time no opportunity should be lost, of instilling all truths as they are capable of receiving.'[429] John Wesley reasons that this project should start as soon as the child begins to speak and understand.[430]

Apart from this, parents were encouraged to inculcate in each child daily Bible reading, meditation, and prayer along with morning and evening family worship, which included prayer, Bible reading, and singing. John Wesley, realizing that not all parents may know how to go about it daily, prepared an order of service, which included – a short prayer, brief Bible explanation by the parent, doxology, and benediction. Besides this, Thursday evening was set aside for

---

[426] John Wesley, "On Family Religion," Sermon 94, section III, point 3, in his *Works*, Vol. VII, p. 80.

[427] John Wesley, "A Thought on the Manner of Educating Children," *Works*, XIII, p. 476.

[428] Wesley Tracy, "Christian Education in the Wesleyan Mode", in *Wesleyan Theological Journal*, Vol. 17, No. 1 (Spring 1982), p. 33. Cf. John Wesley, "on Family Religion," Sermon 94, section III, point 6. *Works*, Vol. VIII, p. 81.

[429] John Wesley, "on Family Religion," Sermon 94, section III, point 6, in his Works, Vol. VII, p. 80.

[430] Because the bias of nature is set the wrong way; education is designed to set it right." Education aided "by the grace of God is to turn the bias from self-will, pride, anger, revenge, and love of the world," John Wesley goes on to say, "to resignation, lowliness, meekness, and the love of God. John Wesley, "A thought on the Manner of educating Children," *Works*, XIII, p. 476. Wesley Tracy, "Christian Education in the Wesleyan Mode", in *Wesleyan Theological Journal*, Vol. 17, No. 1, (Spring 1982), p. 33.

religious education and Saturday night was a special review time when each child was encouraged to recite what they had learnt during the week.[431]

John Wesley made available to both parents and preachers resources for the *Christian nurture* of children. He published *Prayers for families* and *Prayers for Children*, in addition "A Collection of Forms of Prayer" which included morning and evening prayers for private devotion and added questions for self-examination as well. He also suggested some moving biographies to be included in private devotions such as the *Life of Philip Henry*, the father of Matthew Henry who is well known for his Bible commentary.[432]

Apart from small booklets of instruction, John Wesley himself prepared an important document for the education and spiritual nurture of children in the parish and in the home: *Lessons for Children*. It is a series of 200 Bible studies for children. All based on the Old Testament. In addition, he edited a French document and called it "Instructions for Children." Fifty-eight lessons are summarized under six sections and include the following subjects:[433]

i. God, Creation, Man, Sin, Redemption, Heaven and Hell
ii. God and the Soul of Man
iii. How to regulate our Desires
iv. How to regulate our Understanding
v. How to regulate our Joy
vi. How to regulate our Practice.

Beyond the preceding exhortations and ample materials for the Christian religious education and nurture of Methodists, John Wesley successfully made use of the **Societies, Classes, and Bands** to perpetuate his teachings and concern for Church's liberation. Added to this successful method, he established special schools to carry on his liberative and transformative teaching and preaching. One of the major differences and probable cause for John Wesley's success that one could notice is, he did not give instructions for the instruction sake, be it the parents, preachers, or congregants. He prepared materials befitting the needs of the peoples group and made them available easily so that no one could give any poor excuses for failing in their expected duties.

3. Christian Education for Humanization, Liberation and Justice

a. Education for Humanization

Wesley believed that personalistic love for the pupil will have a humanizing effect.[434] His heart went out for dehumanized, marginalized, poverty stricken

---

[431] Wesley Tracy, "Christian Education in the Wesleyan Mode", in *Wesleyan Theological Journal*, Vol. 17, No. 1, (Spring 1982), pp. 33-34.

[432] Wesley Tracy, "Christian Education in the Wesleyan Mode", pp. 33-34.

[433] *Ibid.*

[434] Wesley Tracy, "Christian Education in the Wesleyan Mode", p. 44.

colliers and their family members. Education was the only hope that Wesley thought that would humanize the dehumanized, recognize the marginalized and lift up the poor. Thus, he stood his ground to change the socio-economic status of both colliers and slaves. Education for the poor was key note of Wesley. He believed that education itself transforms and liberates people from their present plight. Wesley effectively made use of pulpit and print media to educate people of his days about the ills of drinking, bribing, smuggling, plundering, and slave trade.[435] Joseph Priestly (discoverer of oxygen) immediately after Wesley's death said that John Wesley and his company in liberating the poor and depraved had exceeded all.[436] Wesley's words and work went hand in hand, he practiced what he preached. He and his society actively worked for the upliftment of the poor and the needy. He not only educated them but provided immediate needs with such as used clothes, medicine to the sick, opened a dispensary to treat the poor etc. It is estimated that he distributed some 30,000 sterling pounds during his life time which he collected from the rich for the sake of deserving poor.[437]

b. Education is Liberation and for Justice

John Wesley fought against injustices and exploitation by industrialists and the powerful. He proposed to outlaw distilling, wrote to the then prime minister Pitt to classify industry as felony[438]. He wrote to the 'Anti-Slavery Society' promising his support to abolish slave trade. In 1791, four days before his death wrote a letter to Wilberforce who led the Parliamentary drive to abolish the trade: "go on in the name of God, and in the power of his might, till even American slavery, the vilest that ever saw the sun shall vanish away."[439] He considered slavery the greatest evil and raised his voice from the pulpit and through booklets to conscientize people to stand against such evil practices.[440] Such was Wesley's stand for justice and liberation of those victims of his time. He did not believe in mere socio-economic and political liberation but spiritual transformation and human liberation was his ultimate intent. Because he believed that every human being is created in the image of God and had equal right to live with respect and dignity in the world. John Wesley was indeed a reformer, politician, preacher and educator.

In fact, the humanitarian tone of the Methodist revival is the foundation of a humane face of Methodist education today.[441]

Summary: Wesley the synthesist, the eclectic, studied the schools, scholars and educational literature available to him and critically selected what he considered

[435] *World – Changers: Karl Marx and John Wesley*, pp. 139-140.

[436] *Ibid.*, p. 191.

[437] *World – Changers: Karl Marx and John Wesley*, pp. 192-193.

[438] *Ibid.*, 139.

[439] *World – Changers: Karl Marx and John Wesley*, p. 140.

[440] *Ibid.*

[441] Wesley Tracy, "Christian Education in the Wesleyan Mode," in *Wesleyan Theological Journal*, Vol. 17, No.1, (Spring 1982), p. 45.

to be strengths of each.[442] Moravians had two sessions of walking in the woods to "learn from nature"- taking a cue from them, Wesley decided that his students could use that time to get acquainted with nature even better through work – so pulling weeds, cutting fire wood, and hoeing in the garden were prescribed.

Effective learning occurs in an atmosphere of pleasant emotion. The Best education is pleasurable but for Wesley education is to be *painful to be profitable,*[443] Wesley believed Knowledge as the root of Virtue and Piety which is unfolded through education. This in turn is hoped to create a just society and to bring about liberation and humanization

Personalized *love for the pupil* was the bed-rock of the Port Royal discipline and teaching. Port Royal educators' severity and love were admirably combined which Wesley copied without hesitation and practiced at Kingswood school.[444]

Wesley had some strong views about education such as this "Will breaking" Doctrine. Though he modified later in saying that there should be no extremes either in discipline nor in religion. Another stand which many educational theorist would disagree is about having no room for playing in his scheme of educational curriculum. He was bullied while schooling by other students and witnessed fighting in the name of play. This may have played strongly to evolve 'no play theory' in his schools. Instead he advocated work and walk to learn from the nature.

Based on such available information and experience, he evolved his own educational theory, and pedagogical approach.

D. Limits in John Wesley's Method and Pedagogical Approach to Christian Education

There are certain views and concepts in Wesley's pedagogy that needs deconstruction as well as reconstruction because of certain limitation inherent in them. Following statements and views reveal their limitation in comparison to modern Christian educators.

1. Is it fair to deal with a child's sinful nature and adult's acts of sin on the same pedagogical parameters? Wesley's view that children so young are capable of mature religious consciousness is based on his theological convictions and his doctrine of grace.[445] However, it seems unfair to deal with children's sins of omission and adult's sins of commission on same level.

---

[442] Wesley Tracy, "Christian Education in the Wesleyan Mode, p. 45.

[443] *Ibid.*

[444] John W. Prince, *Wesley on Religious Education* (New York: The Methodist Concern, 1926), p. 121. Cf. Wesley Tracy, "Christian Education in the Wesleyan Mode," in *Wesleyan Theological Journal*, Vol. 17, No. 1, (Spring 1982), p. 44.

[445] James Riley Estep Jr. "John Wesley's Philosophy of Formal Childhood Education" in *Christian Education Journal*, Vol. INS, No. 2, (Fall 1997), p. 48.

2. Is a militant approach to education a necessity to curb a child's misbehaviours/or strong will? Child's will must be curbed to save the soul.[446]

3. Will a rigid and orthodox disciplinarian approach to education work in today's context? Wesley seems to contradict his own views in many instances. For example, he says anything too much either freedom or punishment can adversely affect the young lives.[447] However, his approach to education in practice appears rigid disciplinarian.

4. While saying no to play, was Wesley oblivious of children's natural instincts? Psychologists would argue then, that, how can a growing child be deprived of natural instinct to play with peers? In this context one could quote again, Horace Bushnell who, advocated play "as the symbol and interpreter of Christian Education liberty."[448] To authenticate his argument he quotes a harsh German proverb – "He that plays when he is a boy will play when he is a man."[449] Southey calls this a "sour German proverb" and that Wesley had forgotten the sensible English one, "All work and no play makes Jack a dull boy."[450] When seen in perspective that play in Eighteenth Century School did not consist of football, cricket or hockey but bestial sports like cockfighting, bearbaiting, and prize fighting. In addition to German influence, Wesley's memories at Charterhouse may have formed his attitude towards recreation.[451] However, Wesley is not the only person to have made such a statement, even August Hermann Francke,[452] a leading German educator of eighteenth century said, "Play must be forbidden in all its forms."[453]

5. Wesley proposes too many things too early for young children to learn which is beyond their natural - cognitive and physical development.

6. Wesley regarded secular education as equivalent to 'sending children to the devil' and large public schools as nurseries of all matter of wickedness.[454] What did Wesley mean by his over-generalization? Apart from his schools and few other private schools, rest were nurseries of wickedness. It sounds rather subjective and fundamentalist's statement.

---

[446] Elmer L. Towns, (ed). *A History of Religious Educators,* p. 221. Cf. James Riley Estep Jr. "John Wesley's Philosophy of Formal Childhood Education" in *Christian Education Journal,* Vol. INS, No. 2, (Fall 1997), p. 49.

[447] Alfred H. Body, *John Wesley and Education,* p. 68.

[448] James Riley Estep Jr. "John Wesley's Philosophy of Formal Childhood Education" in *Christian Education Journal,* Vol. INS, No. 2, (Fall 1997), p. 49. Cf. J. E. Reed, and R. Prevost, *A History of Christian Education* (Nashville: Broadman and Holman, 1993), p. 319.

[449] Alfred H. Body, *John Wesley and Education,* p. 60.

[450] John Owen Gross, John Wesley: Christian Educator (Nashville: Board of Education, The Methodist Church, 1954), p. 14.

[451] John Owen Gross, John Wesley: Christian Educator, pp. 13-14.

[452] Elmer L. Towns, (ed). *A History of Religious Educators,* p. 190ff.

[453] John W. Prince, *Wesley on Religious Education* (New York: Methodist Book Concern, 1926), p. 145.

[454] John Wesley, Sermon 94, "On Family Religion" *The Works of John Wesley,* Vol. 7, p. 83.

7. "A Religious education can only be successful under the guidance of a teacher in whom is the spirit of true religion."[455] How to know whether one has the spirit of true religion or not? What were the parameters that Wesley used to judge one's spirit of true religion?

8. Some of Wesley's contemporaries objected strongly to the bringing up of children too strictly; giving them more of religion than they liked; telling them of it too often; or pressing it upon them whether they will or not. His critics thought that the common methods that are used in those, that are called religious schools… did abundantly more harm than good; especially if any severity were used; and concluded with saying that those children who had been trained up in this manner, as soon as the restraint was taken off, were commonly worse than others.[456] Researcher agrees with the critics' view, for his personal experience as a boarder and many of his co-boarders were repulsive to the spiritual activities in the boarding homes, though dare not to rebel openly against the authorities concerned.

9. By modern standards, Wesley tried to impose maturity too fast on his Kingswood children. It seems to contradict his own advice to teachers that if teaching is to bear fruit – you must tell them ten times over or you do nothing.[457] That is to say, repeat yourself, do not impose too much at a time, but wait for them to understand before you proceed further in teaching. "Beware of that common, and accursed, way of making children parrots."[458]

10. W. H. Fitchet wrote that, Wesley tried on a large scale; "to transfigure boys of seven or eight and ten into middle-aged saints"[459] His quick fix solution to so called sinful behaviours seems farfetched in today's context.

11. The plethora of subjects that included French, Latin, Greek, Hebrew, history, geography, chronology, rhetoric, logic, ethics, geometry, algebra, physics, music, biographies, and other religious material, would seem to an outsider that Wesley was providing a constipating intellectual diet.[460]

12. Wesley was the product of the eighteenth century and seemed to have shared its blindness to the meaning of childhood.[461] Wesley perceived every child as "bred in sin, apt to evil and altogether as a 'brand to be plucked out of the

---

455 Alfred H. Body, *John Wesley and Education*, p. 67.

456 *Ibid.*

457 Elmer L.Towns, *A History of Religious Educators*, p. 222. Cf. *The Works of John Wesley*, Vol. 7, p. 82.

458 James Riley Estep Jr. "John Wesley's Philosophy of Formal Childhood Education" in *Christian Education Journal*, Vol. INS, No. 2, (Fall 1997), p. 48.

459 John Wilkins Sigsworth, *World-Changers: Karl Marx and John Wesley*, p. 189. Quoted from W. H. Fitchett, *Wesley and His Century* (Cincinnati: Jennings and Graham), 1966.

460 John Wilkins Sigsworth, *World-Changers: Karl Marx and John Wesley*, p. 189. See also, details of course of academical learning at Kingswood School, *John Wesley and Education*, by Alfred H. Body (London: The Epworth Press, 1936), p. 162.

461 Elmer L.Towns, *A History of Religious Educators*, p. 225.

burning."[462] This perception may have hindered John Wesley to understand the nature of child objectively.

13. Wesley encouraged the Kingswood masters to make sure that the pupils were all fully saved. A rather unstable English master by name James Hindmarsh instilled such a fear of damnation in the children that they became hysterical. He delighted in their utmost distress because he believed their screams indicated that the devil was being driven out of their lives. In September 1770, he took them to see a dead body to reinforce the impact of his words about their mortality and it resulted in thirteen days of religious fervour in which the Lord seemed to have rested on them and pierced their hearts with conviction. Wesley seemed to have approved it. On one occasion, Wesley himself placed a child's finger into the flame of a candle to convey a sense of the pain in hell.[463] This is an extreme and fanatical approach to teaching. Today, such acts are considered outrageous and primitive; no doubt, modern educators would not appreciate or recommend such an approach to education.

However, there is a huge time gap between Wesley and the author. Today's methods and approaches have been modified keeping child's level of comprehension and cognition. These contentious points will be analysed in view of empirical findings. This discussion then, leads into the details of empirical study and interpretation of the same in the next chapter. Thereafter, the above issues are discussed under the section re-reading of John Wesley's Christian education methods and pedagogical approaches in subsequent sections.

[462] James Riley Estep Jr. "John Wesley's Philosophy of Formal Childhood Education" in *Christian Education Journal*, Vol. INS, No. 2 (Fall 1997), p. 47.

[463] Gary Best, "Wesley and Education," A paper presented at Lincoln College, Oxford on 14 May 2003, p. 9.

Chapter 3

Analysis of the Empirical Data Tracing the Link in the Use of Wesley's Educational Method in the Christian Education Ministry of the Methodist Churches in Karnataka

Introduction 111

Hypothesis 111

A. Biblical and Theological Foundations of Educational Ministry 112

B. Board of Education Ministry of the Methodist Church in Karnataka 113

  1. Sunday Schools 114
  2. Methodist Youth Fellowships 114
  3. Women's Christian Fellowship 115
  4. Christian Boarding Schools 115

C. Analysis and Assessment of Christian Education programmes based on Empirical study 116

General profile of the Respondents 116

Questionnaire I: Information about the Church/Ministry 119

Questionnaire II: Ministerial Activities of the Church 128

Questionnaire III: John Wesley and his thoughts on Christian Education 138

Questionnaire IV: Christian Education as understood by Respondents 143

Chapter 3

Analysis of the Empirical Data Tracing the Link in the Use of Wesley's Educational Method in the Christian Education Ministry of the Methodist Churches in Karnataka

Introduction

The previous chapter highlighted the factors concerning John Wesley the educator, who synthesized a theory of education from an amalgamation of the ideas of both religious and secular educators. He sought to improve the quality of the education system of his time by adapting methods and approaches peculiar to his convictions. Wesley's theological and experiential convictions forced him to challenge the foundations of English education. He voiced his concerns at the then poor state of affairs and called for transformation and re-invention of educational ideals and practices at schools of his time. He was a man of his time and so advanced the cause of Christian education to the best of his ability.[464] In the light of this, the present chapter analyses the empirical data to ascertain the use and implementations of Wesley's thoughts on Christian Education and its implications for contemporary Christian Education particularly for Methodists in Karnataka.

Hypothesis

Wesley as such had disapproved certain practices of the Church of England, and the present day Methodists seem to have not given the same emphasis to the vision and the teaching objectives of Wesley which were the basis of Methodist movement's emergence and existence. It may be assumed that the changes were

---

[464] James Riley Estep Jr., "John Wesley's Philosophy of Formal Childhood Education" in *Christian Education Journal,* Vol. INS, No. 2 (Fall 1997) p. 52.

caused by socio-cultural, spiritual, structural and leadership crises in the last forty years or so. Some changes were probably necessary as the Church came of age.

Reacting to the then decadence in society, Wesley had embarked on a programme with a strong emphasis on Biblical teaching, Preaching and Christian education. Would that the Scripture-centred education programmes be relevant or is it the need of the hour, then as it would be now needs to be discovered. Now, as it appears the Methodist Church in Karnataka has gone through a sea change over the years and so are Wesley's thoughts on Christian education, spirituality, and teaching as is implied in the data analysis of empirical research. It is presumed that a fresh look at his educational thoughts, theory and approach may enable one to take a stand and revitalize the present conditions as it did in his times, to bring about an effective form of Christian education programme.

A. Biblical and Theological Foundations of Educational Ministry

The Methodist Theological and Educational Policy in general concerning Christian Education, asserts that 'education is the gift of hope.'[465] The Founder of Methodism believed that the best gift one could give to the society and the world at large is education. Education means change and transformation leading to liberation of those groping in darkness of ignorance, and illiteracy. Education is indeed the gift of hope to the hopeless. It is interesting to note that the followers of Wesley did continue with his legacy of the deep-seated conviction that education itself was the most probable method of teaching religion to children and making them Christians.[466] Wesley believed that Christian education paved the way for true liberation.

Methodists, as Christians and followers of John Wesley are passionate in belief that education is a right of every one. For them, education is about values and the Methodists believe that it is part of Christian mission.[467] For Wesley, teaching and preaching were the two sides of the same coin. This legacy was carried on by his successive followers in earnest. The Great commission in Matthew 28:18-20 - Then Jesus came to them and said, "All authority in heaven and earth has been given to me. Therefore, go and make disciples of all nations, baptizing them in the name of the Father and of the Son and of the Holy Spirit, and teaching them to obey everything I have commanded you. And surely I am with you always, to the very end of the age."[468] and the Nazareth manifesto in

---

[465] Sharon Hels, "Educating for the World Citizenship" *The Seventeenth World Methodist Conference, held at Rio-de Janeiro, Brazil, 7-15 August, 1996*, edited by Joe Hale (Ashville, NC: World Methodist Conference, 1997), p. 205.

[466] John W. Prince, *Wesley on Religious Education: A Study of John Wesley's Theories and Methods of the Education of Children in Religion* (New York: The Methodist Book Concern, 1926), p. 148.

[467] John C. A. Barret, "Education Committee Report" *The Seventeenth World Methodist Conference, held at Rio-de Janeiro, Brazil, 7-15 August, 1996*, edited by Joe Hale (Ashville, NC: World Methodist Conference, 1997), p. 217.

[468] Todays New International Version (TNIV).

Luke 4: 8-19 - "The Spirit of the Lord is on me, because he has anointed me to proclaim good news to the poor. He has sent me to proclaim freedom for the prisoners and recovery of sight for the blind, to set the oppressed free, to proclaim the year of the Lord's favour"[469] were the backbone of his biblical conviction that human beings as God's creation, must know that they are his making. This is only possible through educating humanity to understand themselves and thereby their maker. With this conviction, Wesley made use of every street corner, pulpits and gatherings to share his views to bring about transformation and change. To a great extent he did achieve this as English history speaks for itself as was discussed in the previous chapter.

The primary objective of Methodist policy in the matter of elementary education is the establishment of publicly controlled schools in every district, and the placing of a Christian un-sectarian school within reasonable distance of every family. In pursuance of this policy of a Christian un-sectarian school within reasonable distance of every family, the Methodist Church, while appreciating the steps already taken, expresses its anxiety for the improvement, where necessary, of the syllabi of Biblical and religious instruction/Christian education, daily worship in the schools including the use of appropriate hymns.[470]

B. Board of Education Ministry of the Methodist Church in Karnataka

1. Sunday Schools
2. Methodist Youth Fellowships
3. Women's Christian Fellowship
4. Christian Boarding Schools

The Methodist Church from its very beginning is involved in the educational ministry as its history claims. Illiteracy and spiritual ignorance of the people of the lower income groups including the Dalits and marginalized communities had attracted the attention of the early missionaries in India. The Great Commission and Nazareth manifesto of our Lord to preach and teach, to heal and liberate has been the motivational force despite socio-religious and political odds. The Methodist Educational ministry in India began in 1871 at Lucknow under the leadership of Isabella Thoburn for the orphans at Lalbagh area. From there the educational network has grown across the country from primary to degree level. In many cases education was the point of contact for evangelism and Church planting. Education was a bridge between evangelism and Church planting for Methodist missionaries. Most of the schools were an extension of the Church ministry till the early seventies since schools were managed by their mission

[469] TNIV, the Bible.

[470] Alfred H. Body, *John Wesley and Education* (London: The Epworth Press, 1936), Appendix D, p. 164.

funds. Unfortunately, the Methodist Church and its leadership could not sustain the financial support; as a result many schools were allowed to seek government aid, thereby forfeiting their right to teach Christian education in those schools. This development has led to many unforeseen difficulties affecting their primary objective of education. The Government education department began to dictate its terms and conditions particularly in appointing teachers and providing state syllabus. Christian teachers' hold in these schools came to an end, and the educational ministry of the Church suffered because of this.[471]

1. Sunday Schools

The Sunday Schools of the Methodist Church in India is under the supervision of Education and Christian Nurture board. Sunday school is a strong arm of the Methodist ministry in India. One of the spiritual concerns of the Church is the care and nurture of children of the community. This was carried through boarding homes and Sunday schools. Therefore, the churches were asked to organize Sunday schools for children of their congregation to carry out the ministry of transformative and liberative education. The pastor was given the responsibility to carry out this ministry with the help of qualified persons in his congregation. This ministry continues because the Methodists believe that today's children are the future leaders of the Church.[472]

2. Methodist Youth Fellowships

The Church's constitutional preamble states 'The Methodist Youth fellowship seeks to aid in establishing Christ's Kingdom among all people and in all areas of life, especially within and through the agency of the Church, to share the abundant life in Christ with Youth through evangelism, education, and social work; to enlist all the youth of the church in some form of Christian service and to seek with the youth of all fellowships and mutual help in the building of Christian world order.'[473] With the formation of the Methodist Church in India 1981 (earlier it was known as Methodist Church in South Asia- MCSA), Youth council was carved out of Council of Christian education. This council framed a broad programme based on the preamble including training, counselling, sports ministry and exposure to ecumenical bodies such as National Christian Council of India (NCCI) and Student Christian Movement in India (SCMI).[474] The Methodist Youth Fellowships have contributed substantial number of leaders as pastors, teachers, principals, doctors, medical workers and social workers to

[471] Monica Aruna Samuel, *A Brief History of Methodism in India* (Lucknow: Published by the Methodist Church in India 2006), pp. 171-173.

[472] *Ibid.*, p. 162.

[473] The Editors, *The Book of Discipline of the Methodist Church in India* (Lucknow: Published by the Methodist Church in India, 2004), pp. 325-326.

[474] Monica Aruna Samuel, *A Brief History of Methodism In India* (Lucknow: Published by the Methodist Church in India, 2006), pp. 299-301.

the ministry. Unfortunately, modern youth have got their aims and objectives elsewhere, which has very little to do with the ministry of the Church. Unless, there is a sustained drive for recruitment, training and suitable employment of these young people, the Church will continue to fall short of committed leadership in all walks of ministerial life. The whole Church must wakeup to this urgent need and make amends to attract youth towards the ministry.[475]

3. Women's Christian Fellowship

Women's ministry in the Methodist church goes back to 1870s when two women missionaries came to India with a vision of educational and medical ministry. Women's Society of Christian Service (WSCS) was organized in course of time and it rendered a great service to the Church. Their services were a great help to pastors and local churches. Their activities included, adult literacy work, prayer vigil, sacrificial collection through the 'mite box', thank offering, visiting the sick in the hospitals and homes, making useful things out of scrap materials to raise funds for village pastors, celebrating women's Sunday were some of their important activities to supplement the ministry of the Church. Young women who volunteered to work for the church were given basic theological training to work as women evangelists, deaconesses, principals of Church-managed schools, hostel superintendents, social workers, etc.

4. Christian Boarding Schools

The objectives of these boarding homes were similar to that of Wesley in the eighteenth century: to reach out to the poor and needy in the surrounding villages. Its basic idea was to educate them to be good Christians and social human beings. Christian education was the main focus of these homes but the loss of missionary presence as hostel superintendents and managers resulted in the loss of academic and spiritual concern of the boarders. The lack of concern by the Church for boarding homes resulted ultimately in the loss of leadership for the Church. Almost 90% leadership both ministerial and lay, men and women of the Church came from the boarding schools. As with the older Methodists, this loss is acutely felt today by all. Boarding homes were like pre-seminaries preparing learners for future ministry. Though not everyone responded to the ministerial call, many ended up with Church-related ministry and social service. After 1980s, the Methodist Church lost hold on most of the boarding homes due to other funding agencies financing the boarding homes. Things have changed dramatically ever since in their objectivity and service to the church. After the private funding agencies took over the boarding homes, the Church failed to find right kind of leaders for the boarding homes to lead children to be worthy citizens and good Church members. The author is aware of the present plight of these boarding schools and has a personal experience with the boarding homes as a boarder and

---

[475] Monica Aruna Samuel, *A Brief History of Methodism In India,* pp. 160-161.

now as a minister. In both, educational institutions and boarding schools financial crises seem to have played a major role in hampering the liberative ministry of Christian Education.

C. Analysis and Assessment of Christian Education Programmes based on Empirical study

The empirical research presented here includes select Methodist churches in Karnataka, i.e., nine district central churches, and seven city churches, their Sunday schools, Youth, and Women's fellowships and the boarding schools managed by the Methodist Church. Data was collected through questionnaires and interviews with ordained Ministers, Sunday school teachers and leaders of various fellowships, distributing 400 sets of questionnaires containing nearly 100 questions each. The area covered represents both urban and sub-urban churches of Bidar, Chitguppa, Gulbarga, Shorapur, Yadgir, Raichur, Belgaum, Kolar, and Bangalore. A sample survey was conducted earlier to assess the responses in general. Interviews were candid and informative. The following tabulation, analysis and interpretation of the responses will reveal the ground realities to make possible suggestion and recommendation if any.

It is assumed that the findings that emerge out of the empirical study will help to find the relevance of Wesley's Christian educational emphasis today. A note of caution here however needs to be kept in mind as there could be a stereotyped answer to the questionnaire.[476]

General profile of the Respondents

Table One: Respondents, Sex, and Age Group

Respondents	Male		Female		Total	%	Age Group				Total
	Nos	%	Nos	%			20+	30+	45+	60+	
Teachers	12	6%	53	26.5%	65	32.5%	5	30	25	5	65
Pastors	28	14%	0	0%	28	14%	3	12	11	2	28
Students	10	5%	12	6%	22	11%	22	0	0	0	22
Members	57	28.5%	28	14%	85	42.5%	18	34	25	8	85
Total	107	53.5%	93	46.5%	200	100%	48	76	61	15	200

The above table reveals the general profile of the candidates who responded by completing the questionnaires. Out of 200 plus respondents, only 200 samples are taken into account for better percentile. The respondents are divided into four categories teachers, pastors, students and members. Educators are placed at

[476] The reason being that the author has noted certain answers to the multiple choice have been conventional not convictional. For instance, there was a question about church attendance; almost every respondent has circled regular. Imagine every member attending every Sunday morning, place of worship will be overflowing with worshippers, it is obvious that ground reality is not so. However, there are quite a few respondents who have been honest in answering the questionnaires.

the top as the area of research here concerns Christian education. Rest of them are placed in an order as is shown in the table; the same order is maintained throughout this work. The following tables show the details of the respondents' educational, demographical and church background. The present table informs the percentage of male and female respondents and their age group. A majority of the teachers are female (53) as compared to male (12) teachers. It is to be noted here, that even Wesley entrusted the responsibility of educating children to the women folks in his days. Invariably teaching vocation has more female educators than male at the grass root level. It is no surprise then that this trend is obvious even today. Nearly 1/3 respondents are teachers, though questionnaires were sent to respective churches without specifying the categories. A majority of the teachers, i.e., fifty five members fall under middle age group, only five are below 30 years and other five are retired teachers from teaching world. It seemed a good combination to analyse different view points from all the four age groups about Christian education programmes in their respective churches.

Retired and middle-aged respondents' responses would reveal a clear view of how Church activities and Christian education programmes have seen changes over the years. It is interesting to note that a majority of the respondents are middle-aged apart from the student respondents.

Pastors are transferable in the Methodist Church; therefore they have a variety of experiences from different churches and their Christian education activities. Thus their information is important to assess the ministry of the Church as a whole. As one can notice that there are no female pastors among the respondents. This is one area where Methodists need to improve to be more gender conscious and keep pace with the changing trends in Christendom. Though, student respondents are small, they are important to analyse their views concerning Christian education activities since they are the recipients and learners.

As a large number of respondents, i.e., eighty five are the key members of different churches, some of them are pastorate committee members, others are active participants of the church programmes. Their responses come from their active participation in the concerned ministry and will have specific bearing on the research findings.

Table Two: Educational Qualifications of Respondents

Sl. No.	Respondents	Educational qualification						Total	%
		Undergraduate		Graduate		Postgraduate			
1	Teachers	11	5.50%	25	12.50%	29	14.50%	65	32.50%
2	Pastors	1	0.50%	6	3%	21	10.50%	28	14%
3	Students	15	7.50%	0	0%	7	3.50%	22	11%
4	Members	17	8.50%	43	21.50%	25	12.50%	85	42.50%
	Total	44	22%	74	37%	82	41%	200	100%

As far as educational qualifications of the respondents are concerned, 41% are postgraduates, 37% are graduates and the least, i.e., 22% among the respondents are undergraduates. However, most of the undergraduates are either diploma holders or final year degree students. In other words, every respondent is an educated person. Their views are important for the assessment of Christian education related issues in the Church ministry. A majority of the teachers are postgraduates and graduates while most of the pastors are Bachelor of Divinity (B. D.) and Master of Theology (M.Th.) degree holders as per their profile. Among the 42.50% members, most of them, i.e., 21.50% are graduates and 12.50% postgraduates; only 8.50% are the undergraduates as the table two details it.

Table Three: Urban[477] and Rural Respondents

Sl. No.	Respondents	Urban		Rural		Total	%
		Male	Female	Male	Female		
1	Teachers	7	25	5	28	65	32.50%
2	Pastors	15	0	13	0	28	14%
3	Students	10	12	0	0	22	11%
4	Members	37	15	20	13	85	42.50%
	Total	69	52	38	41	200	100%

The responses among urban and rural sampling is equally spread. Teaching respondents are almost equal from both the urban and rural areas. The ministerial sampling too is evenly spread as one can see from The Table Three.

Rural respondents are mainly from sub-urban areas and townships. Urban category is limited to city and district central church members only. Most of the township and sub-urban members are drawn from nearby villages and rural areas; therefore, they are categorized as rural respondents.

In a strict sense, only the present younger generation could be termed as city people, as most of the older members of the city churches are either from rural or sub-urban, drawn into the city in search of job or better life, or eventually settled down in cities. As it was mentioned earlier pastors are transferable; as a result they keep moving from township to city, from city to towns and villages according to regional conference's appointments. The reason for not covering village churches is that they do not have Sunday schools and youth fellowships due to their involvement in farming and daily labour. They do have regular Sunday worship convenient to their timeframe. Secondly, as questionnaires were in English only the educated group was selected for random sampling.

---

[477] Urban respondents refer to those living in Bangalore and District central church members from Bidar, Gulbarga, Belgaum, Raichur and Kolar. Remaining respondents are categorized under rural, though they live in township but congregants are basically drawn from villages.

Table four: Age of the (Respondents') Church

Sl. No.	Age of the Church	Respondents	
1	100 years and above	94	47%
2	75 years and above	34	17%
3	50 years and above	0	0%
4	25 years and above	33	16.50%
5	Less than 25 years	39	19.50%
	Total	200	100%

The American Methodist ministry came to India in 1856, to Karnataka in around 1880s. The British Methodists were already there in South India much before the American Methodists came on the scene. Many respondents therefore have ticked the 100 years above column referring to the Methodist church's Ministry as a whole in Karnataka rather than their specific Church in which they ministered/worshipped particularly referring to pastors who served in most of these churches. Largest, i.e., 47% respondents are from century old churches such as the Richmond Town Methodist Church (RTMC), Bangalore, Belgaum, Gulbarga, Bidar, Kolar, Yadgiri, Shorapur and Raichur Central Churches. These Churches have already celebrated a century of their service. Chitguppa of Bidar district and Wilson Garden Methodist Churches fall under the 75 years group. Koramangala Methodist Church (KMC) and Indira Nagar Methodist Church (IMC) come under more than 25 years old. St. Paul's Methodist Church, Grace Methodist, Jayanagara Methodist, L. R. Nagara, in Bangalore, Emmanuel Methodist Church (EMC), Raichur, Humnabad, Kalyan nagar in Bidar district constitute the last category of Churches. Questionnaires were administered to all the Churches mentioned in table four and more than 50% of them who were administered questionnaires have responded; for the sake of tabulation a random sampling of 200 respondents have been selected.

Questionnaire I: Information about the Church/Ministry

Table Five: Church has grown in all aspects

Sl. No.	Description	Yes	%	No	%
1	Church has improved in socio-economic and spiritual areas	164	82%	36	18%

Questions were aimed at finding out whether the respondent's church was involved in educational projects, rehabilitation projects of both short term and long term, such as victims of natural calamities, street children, destitute and orphan homes, old age homes, medical projects to serve HIV/AIDS, terminally ill patients etc. How sound was their Church financially? What are the activities which strengthen and nourish their spiritual growth and how do they rate their spiritual status were sub- questions. Overwhelming numbers of 82% respondents have said that their Church has improved in socio-economic and spiritual spheres referring to worship and social services. The choirs and youth take active participation in singing and leading the worship services more now than earlier years. Therefore, many have affirmed that their Church is evangelical and they are involved in various services through educational institutions. Especially to those who are deprived of basic education due to poverty and socio-economic factors. Methodist schools have had boarding homes attached as was the original thought of their founder John Wesley. A few have expressed the need of old age homes and boarding homes for the poor; others have mentioned their Church's involvement in helping the victims of flood, communal violence, cyclone, and orphanages by means of providing materials as well as financial assistance through Non-government organizations (NGOs) and government agencies. The improvement in these areas referred to is probably due to changing times, well-qualified ministers, proactive youth and an exposure to televised worship services etc. It is a positive indication that Methodists are open to change/transformation from their traditional/monotonous mode of worships. There seems to be more of congregational involvement in praise and worship than it used to be three decades ago.

Of course, Methodists have an outstanding record of educational and medical services to their communities as was their founder John Wesley's ultimate aim was to educate people to recognise their relationship with God and humanity as well as to enjoy good health. Unfortunately, medical service centres have not been doing well these days due to non availability of committed doctors and nurses. There seems to be a poor understanding amongst the modern medical and Para-medical professionals that healing ministry is part of the ministry of Jesus Christ and his church. There is a need to revive this noble idea so as to make the local Church, service-oriented and relevant to society in which it exists.

Education projects are doing very well and of course they are more commercialized now than their intended objective that – '**education is a right of every child**' and it is to liberate individuals to see God as their creator and discover their human dignity in their given society.

Table Six: Church Services

Sl. No.	Description	Yes	%	No	%
1	Church Services help character formation & Transformation	184	92%	16	8%

To the question- Does your church service promote behavioural and character transformation? 90% respondents have affirmed by ticking yes. Their answer seems to be genuine; it is believed that every preacher/teacher intends to bring about some desired change in their audience. However, it is the choice of the hearers whether to internalise those changes proposed in preaching and try to live as Christ expects each of his followers or not, depends on each individual. The ministers are only instruments in God's hand leading people towards change. On the other hand, it is the Spirit of God that works in those lives to bring about transformation/change. It is noticeable in those who attend regular church services as they are better behaved than others; however, it depends on each individual. It is difficult to generalize that every member that attends church is transformed or well-behaved. It all depends on how serious a person is in practicing what is being said and done in the church service. Therefore, a counter question could be raised, if the church believes that its service promotes character formation and transformation, why then, there is so much perceived unchristian practice and behaviour both inside and outside the Christian community? There could be many answers for this but the age- old allegation that Church leaders have failed to practice what they preach; they have failed to live up to people's expectations, many have failed in their ministerial vocations sending poor message across to younger generations. This may have hurt the life and growth of the Church. A couple of decades ago preachers and teachers were a revered lot; unfortunately many of them seem to have lost credibility due to questionable spiritual and moral behaviours. This indeed has been one of the reasons for the nominal attitude among the Christian community. The author remembers as a young boy in 1960s and early 1970s that the Church Pastors were treated as God's representatives and *Dharma gurus*; teachers were looked up to as wise sages. The trend is altogether different today. However, God is working through the churches reviving God's people not withstanding the obvious weaknesses in the system. Many younger generations today vouch that their achievements are due to godly up-bringing in both homes and churches. It is indeed a healthy sign to those who are committed to the ministry of the Church. The Church of Christ and Christian education programmes continues to play the transformative and liberative role despite human failures. On the other hand, 10% are unsure of Church service promoting character formation and behavioural change. Though small in number, they seem to have not seen any activities of the Church as promoting such changes in the lives of its people. They are probably non players in the Church activities; therefore they are unaware of transformative effects of the Church services.

'Do you enjoy worship service in your church,' was the closed ended question and to that overwhelming majority of 100% respondents have said they enjoy worship services by ticking 'yes' as their answer. Though surprising, yet that is what the responses are.

It could be a stereotyped answer to avoid further probing. However, it is not fair to doubt their answers in any case. The following table shows what specific part of the worship they liked most.

Table Seven: Enjoy Worship Services.

Sl. No.	Specific areas of worship service you enjoy	Respondents	%
1	Singing	79	39.5%
2	Praying	40	20%
3	Preaching	95	47.5%
4	Whole Service	140	70%

To a specific question, 'Which part of the service people enjoyed most' – singing, praying, preaching or whole service, many ticked more than one answer. 70% said they enjoy the whole service, a conventional answer. Going by their response, it is indeed a consolation for those ministers who make sincere efforts every Sunday after Sunday to reach out to each member through worship service. Though preachers cannot satisfy every member yet it is a very positive assessment of their given Church and it shows the right attitude of the members. 95 respondents have specifically mentioned preaching, i.e., 47.5% worshippers seemed to appreciate preaching, and of course a majority of the pastors have invariably ticked 'preaching along with singing' and whole service. However, there is a need to improve the sermon as part of the ministry, as only 47.5% felt they enjoyed sermons. Wesley caught the imagination of both the rich and the poor, young and old through his preaching while travelling on the horseback. He must have been a powerful preacher. It is recorded that he preached about 45,000[478] sermons. It is unfortunate that today's preachers take their congregations for granted, even though members are well informed and carefully listen to what is being said from the pulpit. Audiences are the best critics and do know whether the preacher has done his homework in preparing his sermon or not. Sermon is the key to educate people of the issues that matter life on earth. Every sermon has to be apt and applied to practical living. Theologizing or philosophizing sermons will not impress people, though some may like it once in a while but everyone may not appreciate such talks. Preachers must touch the inner soul of the congregants through their well-prepared and prayerful sermons. It is noted in the table concerning the respondents' profile that, ministers/pastors are well qualified yet there is a need to improvise their preaching style to impress their members. It seems to be a general trend amongst the preachers to think they know the Bible

[478] Gary M. Best, "John Wesley and Christian Education," unpublished paper, 2003 in possession of the author.

better than the members/congregation, which probably is a wrong presumption. If Wesley had brought in transformation and change in his Anglican Church and its members, it was due to his hard work and waiting on God in sincerity. The Methodist pastor will have to work hard to reach out to his members effectively through sermons. Well-prepared and well-communicated sermon will yield its result without fail.

39.5% respondents have said they enjoy the singing part of the worship. In other words many respondents have marked clearly indicating their love for singing and worship through songs and hymns. John Wesley used his brother Charles Wesley's hymns in his services. Hymns have been the backbone of Christian worship. Wesley brothers have left behind a legacy of preaching and singing to the world of Christian believers. Hymns and preaching is the mainstay and the strength of Methodists unlike the Anglican Church's emphasis on written liturgy and the order of worship.

20% respondents have said 'prayers,' revealing a very poor character of the Church prayer life. Prayer is the key to spiritual transformation, and necessary vibrant Christian living. The reason for only 20% of the respondents ticking prayer could be for ineffective and impersonal long prayers. For instance, the author recalls that as young boys, they did not like those long pastoral prayers which went on for 15-20 minutes putting many boarders to sleep, and it may have not appealed to the members as well. The trend is changing, yet it must be improved further. Prayers must carry the worshipping members along. Prayers must be personal, issue based, must cover current concerns of the families, young people's problems and the ministries of the Church. Prayers must not be pharisaic but well thought-out or well written, to the point. Prayers are meant to encourage, strengthen the weak and comfort the sorrowing among the members. Prayers can move members and prepare their hearts to hear God's word and be blessed. Prayers have been the foundations of mighty miracles and revivals in the history of Christendom.

After asking them to specify their preferential areas of worship, the next question that followed was describing their Church service. The following table shows the details.

Table Eight: Describe your Church Service

Sl. No.	**Description**	**Respondents**	**%**
1	Inspirational	130	65%
2	Ok	54	27%
3	Boring	16	8%
	Total	200	100%

As shown in the above table, 65% ticked saying their Church service was inspirational. That is an interesting development in these churches. There is an element of truth in their answer because many churches have adopted 'praise and worship' as a preparation for the main worship service. This is usually done by the youth of the Church or the choir as the case may be. Indeed this 'praise and worship' has changed the very outlook of the worship pattern in the Methodist churches of Karnataka. In an informal talk some of them expressed they feel good and at peace with themselves when they attend worship service and there is always some encouraging and motivating note that reaches our heart in course of the worship. A majority seem to feel good about attending and worshiping in the Church. Of course, community life will be insipid, if there are no conflicting views from dissenting voices. So is true of the Church services. 27% of the respondents said 'it is Ok,' which is an indication of the casual approach to the Church service. Attending Church is one of life's chores that an individual is required to perform if and when possible. There could be many more in this category but people are not willing to be candid and open about their comments. They probably are more concerned about safeguarding their pastor's image and their worship leaders. Interpretation and assessment may sound judgemental but there is an element of truth. A very small number of respondents, 8% did express that the Church services are boring; all these respondents happened to be young people from the city. It is understandable to share their views because some of the pastors can really be boring. Despite the insipid approach by the pastors many people go to the Church service; they feel good visiting the Church and meeting people once in a week. In addition to the above question there was a sub-question 'who do you credit for the inspirational services in your Church.' The next table has the details.

Table Nine: Who Contributes to the Inspirational Services?

Sl. No.	Description	Respondents	%
1	Pastors	104	52
2	Choir leaders and worship leaders	110	55%
3	Traditions/rituals	45	22.5%
4	Congregations	83	41.5%

A majority of the respondents, i.e., 55% felt it is the choir and worship leaders who inspire the congregation through their music and soul-lifting songs and choruses. Interestingly 52% of the respondents feel that the pastors are the next team of people who contribute to the inspirational services. If pastors fail to encourage these choirs and worship leaders, they cannot independently achieve what they desire to do. The credit must go to ministers who try by all means to infuse inspiration in their respective congregation. Of course the co-operation and the regular participation of the members too has a role in any inspirational service, therefore, 41.5% have given credit to themselves as inspirational factors. Traditions and rituals in the Church life also have their role in inspiring the older generation. Though the younger generation may not understand much of it, older members are attached to traditional values of the Church services. However, a majority of the respondents said, first the choir and worship leaders, next the pastors, members and traditions as those which contribute to the inspirational aspect of the services.

Table Ten: Ministry of the Church is Edifying

Sl. No.	Description	Respondents	%
1	Edifying	145	72.5%
2	Discouraging	23	11.5%
3	Can't say	32	16%
	Total	200	100%

A majority of the respondents agreed to the fact that their Church ministry is edifying. This answer goes well with other given responses. They are very positive about the ministry of the Church in general but in private when probed during interviews they are not as forthcoming as they have in the questionnaires. Since it is a written record and the researcher is a minister himself, the respondents have chosen their responses carefully as it was indicated by the interviewees. However, there is a general feeling that the respondents have carefully responded safeguarding the reputation of Church ministry. Thus self-restrained answers are quite evident from some Church members. 72.5% have said that their Church ministry is edifying. The main objective of the ministry and the minister is to edify people of God through their preaching and teaching the Word of God. If it fails, then the very purpose and existence of the ministry is questionable. Though 27.5% disagree with the general view of the respondents, they are either candid in their assessment of the condition of the ministry of their Church or anti-ministry kind of people. They probably fall under the category of critiques of the ministry in general sense of the churches. 11.5% are straightforward in stating that the ministry of the Church is discouraging. Ministers must take such people into confidence and encourage them.

16% of persons are quite diplomatic in their reply saying "can't say." In their assessment, the ministry is not edifying and they are not willing to be honest in their answers as well. They prefer to be neutral, which is not helpful in the empirical interpretations. A general view is that the ministry is edifying but open to improvement in the light of critical views expressed by 27.5% plus 16% respondents.

Table Eleven: Church Leaders/Pastor – a general opinion of the members/ministers

Sl. No	Description	Yes	%	Don't Know	%
1	Educationally: Well-qualified	172	86%	28	14%
2	Spiritually: Believer	133	66.5%	67	33.5%
3	Socially: Good leader	155	77.5%	45	22.5%
4	Emotionally: Loving and Caring	104	52%	96	48%
5	Leadership-wise: Commands Respect	107	53.5%	93	46.5%

One of the intentions was to know the peoples' opinion about their pastors/ministers and how they esteemed them. Their views are clearly indicated as shown in the above table. 86% know their ministers and their qualifications. It is very much in line with what their ministers' profile shows in table no. two. Out of 28 pastors 27 are qualified and most of them are postgraduates. It indicates that the respondents have given intellectual replies to the questionnaires though some replies may indicate otherwise. This is indeed a true picture of their ministers' qualification. On the other hand, 14% members are not aware of their leaders' educational qualifications. It shows either they have not bothered to know the person ministering to them or they have no idea of what exactly his degrees are while filling up these questionnaires. To be safe, they seem to have marked as "don't know." As many as, 66.5% say that their minister is a believer and 33.5% don't seem to know who he is. It is of course difficult to judge whether he is a believer or not. Because, these answers are in a way subjective and at times conventional. Large numbers of respondents, that is, 77.5% have recognised that their minister is a good person as far as sociability is concerned. It reflects ministers' free movement and friendly nature with their congregants. Many of these pastors are not local people; therefore, to find this kind of appreciative opinion is very encouraging and supportive to the ministry. It also reveals the magnanimity of the respondents to acknowledge the true characteristics of their pastors. As always, no one is above people's criticisms, so are pastors. 22.5% seem to say "don't know."

There are people in the congregations who attend services once in awhile, some even regular to maintain their membership but do not involve in any Church activities. It is but natural for such members to mark neutral answers. It is heartening to find that 52% of the respondents have affirmed that their ministers are loveable and caring. This should encourage Church ministers to work hard to reach-out to the other 48% of their members to win over their goodwill. It is part of the ministry to win the hearts of people to Christ as well as their respect towards the office of the minister/Pastor. Only 53.5% have said that their minister commands respect and 46.5% seem to think otherwise. Many ministers demand respect because they hold that office and few command respect for what they are and what they stand for. The committed and principled life will always be recognised at some point of time though not always. That is a kind of testimony one must strive to maintain in order to keep up their high calling from the Lord and further the wonderful legacy of John Wesley the founder of Methodism.

Table Twelve: John Wesley's Theological and Spiritual Teachings

Sl. No.	Description	Yes	%	No	%
1	Wesley's teachings are imbibed in the ministry of the Church	178	89%	22	11%

As noted in table no. two, every respondent is an educated member of the respective churches. Invariably almost all the respondents have said that John Wesley's teaching is imbibed or followed in their teaching ministry of the Church. Preaching and teaching ministry is given utmost priority over against ritualistic practices of Anglican churches. Methodists are methodical in many ways but are spontaneous in many of their litanies unlike Anglicans who have written litanies for most of the important occasions. They believe that the Spirit of God will lead and intercede as they utter words in prayers. Wesley discarded almost all the written litany as a protest against Anglicanism and passed on the same legacy to his followers. After nearly three centuries the Methodists still acknowledge that their practices are derived from the teachings of their founder. Though there are some changes made with general consensus but basic teachings are still intact. Few did not seem to know what his teachings are. These may be floating members attending the services because of convenience. There are members belonging to other denominations attending the services because of transfers on account of their profession. Such members may not know since the history and teachings of Wesley are imparted in the confirmation classes, Sunday schools and in youth meetings. Those who have answered otherwise may fall into floating member category of respondents.

Table Thirteen: Founders Day Celebration

Sl. No.	Description	Yes	%	No	%
1	Does your Church celebrate the founders Day	130	65%	70	35%

John Wesley was born on June 17, 1703[479] to Samuel and Susannah Wesley. This day is celebrated as the Founder's Day. As many as, 65% respondents have recognized or are aware of the Founder's Day. Such events are a means to perpetuate the legacy of Wesley and his thoughts to the younger generation. The history of Methodist movement should be kept alive by celebrating Wesley's birthday on 17th June every year. It is on that day, his life history should be brought alive to the memory of his followers. 35% are unaware of the Founder's Day celebration, including the author, a Methodist born. It may be a good idea to pass a resolution at the general and regional conferences to see that, this day is kept aside and marked as an important day in the life of the Methodists. In an era where all kinds of Sundays are celebrated in churches all over like for instance Mother's Sunday, Women's Sunday, Father's Day, Youth Sunday, Children's Sunday, Elders Sunday, Hospital Sunday, etc., Founder's Day celebration will not be out of place in the Church service.

Questionnaire II: Ministerial Activities of the Church

Table Fourteen: Educational and Boarding Institutions

Sl. No.	Description	Yes	%	No	%
1	Educational Institutions & Boarding Schools are wings of the Church Ministry	168	84%	32	16%

An overwhelming number of respondents have said that educational institutions and boarding schools are part of the extended ministry of the Church. These institutions form the means of contact with the so-called outside world to spread Christian faith and principles. Boarding schools were training ground for those willing young people preparing themselves to involve in various departments of Church ministries such as working for Christian schools, hospitals, boarding homes, mission and evangelism etc. Wesley used educational institutions and boarding schools to spread his thoughts on education, mission and evangelism. The same legacy continues till date. Christian witness of the Methodists has gone out into the world much more strongly through these institutions than pulpit ministry. Wesley was an amazing preacher and teacher of the word of God. Discipline in boarding homes and standard of education have changed to keep pace with the changing trend. However, the basic functional principles and patterns remain intact. These institutions are indeed the arm of the Methodist ministry in India particularly in Karnataka.

[479] J. Telford, *The Popular Life of John Wesley* (London: Charles H. Kelly, 1900), p. 12.

Table Fifteen: Sunday school Materials used in the Church

Sl. No.	Description	Respondents	%
1	India Sunday School Union (ISSU)	32	16%
2	CEEF[480]	48	24%
3	Vacation Bible School (VBS)	75	37.5%
4	Church's own publication/materials	45	22.5%
5	Any other	0	0%
	Total	200	100%

It is heartening to know that every Church that responded to the questionnaire said they have regular Sunday schools except during the summer vacation break. Most of these churches have boarding homes, attached with and it is compulsory for boarders to attend these activities. 37.5% of respondents say that they use Vacation Bible School materials (VBS). It is understandable that VBS materials are more evangelically inclined in content than the other materials such as India Sunday School Union (ISSU). They also use their materials for 10 days. The Vacation Bible School is held almost every year in most of these churches before they close Sunday school activities for summer holidays. It is probably easier for them to build on the yearly lessons with closing programmes like VBS. 24% of the respondents said their churches use Christian Education department of Evangelical Fellowship of India (CEEFI) materials. 22.5% said they use their own materials; it refers to the combination of the Bible stories, Children's books etc. That means they probably do not have the organised Sunday school materials depending on the teachers. Teachers pick up stories from the Bible and teach the children, that is what is meant when they say they use their own materials. Some use other materials reprinted by their churches beside their own. Many do not seem to know the value of ISSU materials which are carefully prepared keeping the students' age groups in view, with graded lessons and are developed into a proper course accordingly, so that by the time the students leave the Sunday school, they have a fair knowledge of the Bible. VBS and CEEFI too have the same pattern but differ in emphasis. VBS and CEEFI material lay great stress on the born-again experience, and ISSU focuses more on child's holistic development.

John Wesley stressed more on salvation of the soul while teaching children and others as well. Since the Methodists are ardent followers of Wesley's practices, it obvious that their preferred sources are VBS and CEEFI books. It could probably be the reason why a majority of them use Bible-based materials rather than ecumenically sounding materials like ISSU.

---

[480] Christian Education Department of Evangelical Fellowship of India (CEEFI).

Table Sixteen: Sunday school Materials promote Transformation

Sl.No.	Description	Yes	%	No	%
1	Sunday School materials promote discipline & good behaviour	172	86%	28	14%

A complete unanimity exists among the respondents about the use of Sunday school materials. It is impressive as they consider that those materials do promote Christian discipline and behavioural change. Whether that happens among those studying or not is debatable. However, the materials used intend to do so as their aims and objectives make clear. Further it is subject to how effectively these materials are used to bring about its aims and intents. Also how effectively this material is communicated and how it is being understood by the learners is again a debatable issue. The course material is apt according to the age group and its aim is clear. Therefore, many have agreed with the statement. Few others have said that they have no idea because they are not involved in either Sunday school ministry or have sent their children to study those courses. It is obvious that their answers have to be so. The fact remains that many have acknowledged that the available material promotes both discipline and behavioural change which every Church and family expects in their children.

Table Seventeen: Describe your Sunday school

Sl. No	Description	Respondents	%
1	Well organised	98	49%
2	Planned Sunday school syllabus	104	52%
3	Graded lessons	80	40%
4	Lessons are thoroughly Bible based	179	89.5%
5	Sunday School is a strong teaching wing of the Church's Ministry	160	80%
6	Student participation in SS activities is more than teachers	120	60%
7	There is a lot of interactive learning	135	67.5%
8	SS is a pressure-free learning course	175	87.5%
9	SS is a source of spiritual nurture for the growing Children	188	94%
10	Objective of lessons is salvation and character formation	185	92.5%
11	Sunday school is like an elementary seminary training	157	78.5%
12	Sunday school helps shape one's spiritual journey in life	162	81%
13	SS is a forum where students are taught socialization and sharing	140	70%

It is in line with Wesley's philosophy that every child should be saved from all ills; it is also reflected in modern Methodists' views as is clearly indicated in the above table. 94% have said that Sunday school is a source of Spiritual nurture for growing children and the objective of Christian education lessons is to lead every student to the knowledge of Christ and thereby bringing about transformation in their character and behaviour.

89% have also been categorical in indicating that their Sunday school lessons are thoroughly Bible-based. No wonder then, their preferred materials is VBS and CEEFI books. It was noted earlier, that these materials are more evangelical in nature than that of ISSU materials. 87.5% have said that Sunday school learning is pressure-free unlike regular learning in schools where much is expected from the students. Though there are examination and certification in Sunday school yet the course is made to be more pleasurable than pressure oriented. It is indeed a very positive approach to teaching and learning. Students do look forward to attending Sunday schools week after week because there are so many exciting activities such as colouring the work books, writing short answers, puzzles, games, enactments and storytelling. In other words there is a variety of learning. It is indeed an opportunity to impress upon these young lives about Christ and his free gift of salvation, eternal life, and better future that Jesus Christ offers.

81% believe that Sunday school is a place where one's spiritual life's journey is shaped and moulded. It is up to each individual to sustain this positive impact throughout or violate by indulging in misadventures in life. It opens up an opportunity to every Sunday school teacher to see that such damage is forewarned and the learner is prepared to face such life's challenges without falling prey to misadventures. 80% of the respondents feel that Sunday school is a strong teaching wing of the church ministry. Sunday schools along with pulpit and youth wing form the complete training ground for holistic Christian living. The Sunday school gives them a basic information about Christian faith and practice; youth fellowships help them to internalize those doctrinal teaching by open discussion and debate; pulpit ministry of weekly Sunday services play the role of encouraging one's faith and practice to be Christ's witnesses in the world. This is in agreement with the following statement that Sunday school is like an elementary seminary. As many as, 78.5% think that well-organised Sunday schools are like elementary seminary training. What they mean to say is that the learners have a basic knowledge of the Bible. The author vouches for this view from his personal experience. Sunday schools and youth fellowships prepared him to make clear decision in life to be a Christian minister over against the available opportunity of studying professional courses.

70% believe that Sunday schools teach children socialization and sharing and more than 67.5% think that there is a lot of interactive or dialogical learning that is probably a source of socialization and sharing. However 60% believe that it not as much as desired and they disapprove the dialogical method of teaching for reasons known to them. On the other hand, interaction almost always dominated by the teachers in class rooms than with and among students. While other description of their Sunday school is encouraging, the organizational part of the Sunday school needs to be strengthened. Only 49% say that their Sunday schools are organized but 51% disagree with this view. 52% respondents say their Sunday school syllabus is planned but 48% disagree with that opinion. It is clear in the following statement where only 40% believe that lessons are graded while 60% disagree. If the Church wishes their Sunday school to act as elementary training ground then lessons have to be linked well and to be built one upon the other basing on the theory of 'known to unknown.' This is an important area that both pastors and Church leaders must give careful attention in order to strengthen the faith and the practice of their respective churches. Sunday schools are the backbone of growing churches and spiritual development. They need to be carefully guided and backed by all possible assistance to reap maximum results. It is indeed a strong teaching wing of the Church's ministry and must be strengthened by all means.

Table Eighteen: Sunday school Leaders/Teachers

Sl. No.	Description	Respondents	%
1	School teachers who are members of the local Church	174	87%
2	Mature and spiritually minded volunteers	169	84.5%
3	Locally trained leaders	155	77.5%
4	Pastors and their spouses	134	67%
5	Pastorate committee members	145	72.5%
6	Any other	0	0%

Since a majority of the Sunday school teachers seems to be drawn from the teaching fraternity belonging to the local Church as is indicated in table by 87% respondents, they are supposed to have an understanding of educational and child psychology to deal with the subjects as well as the students. As per the above table, not necessarily that every teacher belonging to a particular Church is engaged in teaching but those spiritually minded and mature candidates who volunteer (not necessarily members but worshipers in that particular Church) are appointed to teach Sunday school classes. The author is aware of his days that only God-fearing and sincere individuals were requested to take care of the classes. He himself was involved in teaching Sunday schools for a couple of years. Usually pastors identify them with the help of existing teachers and request those willing to involve themselves in Sunday school programmes. Some of the teachers were sent to the Summer School of Evangelism at Bangarapet, 70 km away from

Bangalore for short term courses in Christian education. Others were trained by those involved in Sunday school ministries at local churches. Pastors and their spouses who have basic Christian education training at Leonard Theological College, Jabalpur and CEEFI head quarters at Hyderabad prepare those voluntary teachers conducting three days to a week retreat at their churches. Thus, as is revealed by the respondents in the above table, Sunday school teachers and leaders are qualified and capable people. Pastorate committee members seem to be active as the table indicates that 72.5% are involved in the teaching ministry of the Church. It is a very encouraging picture but it need not to be an indication of the ground reality. Though there is a lot of change in members' attitude towards the Church ministry, one must accept their opinion as is indicated in their responses. Wesley would have taken great pride looking at such an improvement in his followers as he too entrusted the teaching ministry to those committed women and men in his days, recognising the importance of this ministry for the growth of the organization and the Church.

Table Nineteen: Methods of teaching used in Sunday schools

Sl. No	Description	Respondents	%
1	Formal and lecture Method	123	61.5%
2	Dialogical and discussion method	95	47.5%
3	Interaction and informal Method	158	79%
4	Story Telling method	188	94%
5	Any other	0	0%

As noted in the above section, teachers were carefully chosen from among the Church members with some sort of Christian education training background and others who were spiritually minded were given a basic training to handle Sunday school classes. Since most of them are regular school teachers and other members who volunteer to teaching in Sunday schools are selected, they are usually briefed about the basic methods of teaching. According to the survey, 94% reveal that teachers use story telling method which is commonly adapted in Sunday schools. Probably primary and junior teachers use it most. 79% teachers seem to be using informal and interaction method to get the best out from these energetic young students. Seniors who have graduated from other approaches/methods to education would be comfortable with formal and lecture method. 61.5% have affirmed that the formal and lecture method is being used in senior classes. Only 47.5% have said that they use dialogical and discussion method. The probable reason could be that many churches do not have adults attending Sunday schools, however, there are quite a few city churches where adults do attend and that is where dialogical and discussion methods take place. It will be meaningless with younger children, though one cannot ignore their mental quotient.

A majority of Sunday school members are from the age group of 5-15 years. Only a few Sunday schools have students of 16-21 age group attending classes. Since majority are younger children, the method of teaching too is story-telling. It is not the method that one is concerned about but the message has to reach the minds of the children; to that level of cognition one must choose the appropriate method to win over the learner to Christ. Reaching out to the student/learner should be the key focus and accordingly a wise teacher adapts a method to get across the Christian message to them.

Table Twenty: Major activities of the Youth

Sl. No.	Description	Respondents	%
1	Bible study intending to lead people to Christ	125	62.5%
2	Debates on relevant issues to strengthen Christian faith	143	71.5%
3	Discussion on panel of experts to know of values in life	85	42.5%
4	Games and sports to strengthen fellowships within & outside	167	83.5%
5	Social activities/community services and awareness program	156	78%
6	Any other	47	23.5%

Once the Sunday school student joins a junior college or degree programme they graduate to youth fellowship of their Church. Unlike in Western countries (where every individual member attends Sunday school, no matter what age group they belong) where senior members attend the Sunday school, a well planned course is taught by qualified members of the Church. Here in our context except in the north eastern provinces there is no Sunday school for senior members. Instead they are divided as youth fellowships, young men's fellowship where seniors meet for proper Bible study and discussion, and women's fellowships where a host of activities to strengthen the ministry of the Church take place. Thus, every member is involved at different level and each member is ministered to apart from the pulpit ministry. It is in a way good to group people in their own age groups to have free and open discussion to strengthen each one's faith and practice. This is what the respondents said when asked what are the major activities of the youth in their respective churches.

The Respondents have chosen multiple responses. 83.5% seems to think that games and sports is the major activity that takes place to strengthen relationship and fellowship among the young people. As many as 78%, believe that their youth are involved in awareness programmes and social and community services. This is indeed a positive activity of the Church youth. Jesus himself was involved in helping the poor and healing the sick etc. Christianity is a faith movement that exists for the service of humanity. 71.5% think that their activity includes discussion and debate on current and relevant issues that strengthen one's faith and practice. Youth need to be informed of their faith and the issues that challenge their faith and practice. Young people want a laboratory proven facts to authenticate their faith. These discussions will help clarify such doubts and misinterpretations if any. A Bible study in any Church is very difficult for any member to get involved because it is thought to be uninteresting. However, 62.5% have said Bible study is one of their activities helping those youth know Jesus Christ more personally and accept Jesus as their personal saviour. If the intention is good, how effective is their Bible study is any body's guess. Bible study is a key to nurture and consolidate young people's faith which is taught at Sunday schools. Christian education becomes very crucial in strengthening their vacillating faith during the turbulent period of their youthful life. Temptations of the worldly and fleshly desires are at its peak therefore; these fellowships, meetings, discussions and debate on such issues are very helpful to face these pressing challenges. 42.5% have said that discussion with panel of experts do take place as part of youth activity and 23.5% have marked any other indicating that often youth are used to do manual work, and menial jobs. At times, these are not helpful in encouraging them to attend youth meetings. There must be a planned programme for the year, so that youth will know what to expect. Unfortunately, many youth meetings do not have a planned agenda therefore; quite a few think that it is a waste of time hanging around there every week. This must be corrected by the concerned ministers and youth leaders and advisors.

It is heartening to note what Frank Baker thinks about the aim of youth department: "In life- devoted, in Church- a family, in person- fit, in faith- equipped, in service- world citizen."[481] Youth ought to lead a devoted life, in Church they act as the members of one big God's family, as far as their personhood is concerned, they must like fit soldiers, regarding their faith they must exhibit that they are well equipped to face the challenges of life, and their service is not limited to a certain groups of people but everyone that is in world.

Table Twenty One: Role of the Youth in main Church Services

Sl. No	Description	Respondents	%
1	Major role in worship services	89	44.5%
2	They are not used as much as they should be	140	70%
3	No role at all for the youth in the main services	136	68%
4	Any other	87	43.5%

[481] Frank Baker, *A Charge to Keep: An Introduction to People Called Methodists* (London: The Epworth Press, 1954), p. 142.

Unfortunately 70% of the respondents expressed that youth are not being used as much as they should be in the main service on Sundays. 68% say that youth have no role whatsoever in Sunday service, affirming with those who said youth are not utilized in the Church services. However, 44.5% think that youth are being used and they play an important role. This is probably true of those young churches such as Koramangala, Indira Nagar and others. Youth have been given importance in leading worship services, choir along with other responsibilities in these younger churches. Almost an equal number of respondents seem to think that youth are being used for activities other than spiritual activities. They are used for cleaning, setting up stages, dismantling certain things etc. In other words; they are used as helpers and manual labourers not as future leaders of their churches. This attitude must be corrected and youth must be respected and given responsibilities to lead the Church activities. Young people are the pillars of the growing churches, if they are not trained and trusted with responsibilities the future of the Church is not bright. Younger churches are growing because, younger generation is revitalising the members' faith and practice by appropriate music and soul-soothing songs during the worship services.

Table Twenty Two: Fellowships are training ground for Leadership

Sl.No.	Description	Yes	%	No	%
1	Youth Fellowships are training ground for future leaders	154	78%	44	22%

A majority of the respondents affirmed that youth fellowships are indeed the training ground for future leadership of the Church. Young people are able to discuss issues related to spiritual growth, societal concerns and youth problems whenever they come to meet with one another. They also observe both the strengths and the weaknesses of the existing leadership of the Church which will enable them to correct weaknesses and envisage the strengths in their lives. Many young people graduate from this forum to take up other leadership responsibilities in the Church. Therefore, it is natural for the members to think that youth are the future leaders as they are trained in those youth meetings and fellowships. In fact this is a proper forum where biblical, social and emotional issues are debated and discussed. Thus, they become aware of the issues and concerns their Church community faces. With this information they are able to shoulder any given responsibility in the Church.

Table Twenty Three: Activities of Women's Fellowship

Sl. No.	Description	Respondents	%
1	Bible Study for spiritual nurture	156	78%
2	Prayer meetings for various needs of the church/ community	127	63.5%
3	Visitation of weak and the sick of the church	166	83%
4	To strengthen one another in Christian faith	123	61.5%
5	Any Other	97	48.5%

Another important Church wing in the teaching ministry is the Women's Fellowship. In some churches it is the backbone of spiritual and financial resources. Its members raise lots of money for the Church projects and pray for the ministers and the ministry as a whole on a regular basis. They share in the pastoral ministry of visiting those members who are unable to attend church services and other members as well. Keeping this important role in mind, as many as 83% respondents have identified Women's Fellowships' major activities as visitation to the sick and the weak of the Church. It indicates the real concern and the commitment of this group for those incapacitated members as well as those weak in faith to make them feel that they are part of the fellowship and the community. In addition to their commitment to the members, 78% say they actively participate in Bible study for their spiritual nurture so that they will be able to minister to others. If one is not strong in one's own faith and practice, how can they be able to serve others in the ministry of encouragement and sharing? They are strengthened first; thereafter they go out following the Lord's command to be his witnesses among their people. As mentioned above, the Women's Fellowship is a praying group and it is affirmed by 63.5% respondents. Thus, they strengthen one another in Christian faith as 61.5% agreed with it. Apart from what is being stated above, as many as 48.5% have said that they are involved in other services as well as vocational training, art work and fund raising activities to help the poor and needy of the Church. Such involvement in the ministry of the Church by the women's group is a practical experience and it is more fulfilling to know that they are part of ministerial team of the Church.

Questionnaire III: John Wesley and his thoughts on Christian Education

Table Twenty Four: John Wesley - his educational thoughts & practices

Sl. No	Description	Yes	%	No	%
1	Wesley was a pioneer of education & noted reformer: Is his educational approach relevant to our context?	186	93%	14	7%
2	Salvation is the cure for all sinful activities	125	62.50%	75	37.50%
3	Play has no role in the process of education	23	11.50%	177	88.50%
4	Present boarding schools are similar to Wesley's discipline	169	84.50%	31	15.50%
5	Boarding homes are conducive for imparting Christian education	157	78.50%	43	21.50%
6	Boarders have time to play along with their daily routine	150	75%	50	25%
7	Boarders are exposed to spiritual activity more than other children	166	83%	34	17%
8	Boarding schools keep children away from mischief & distraction	148	74%	52	26%
9	Christian education is an answer to the ills of growing children	118	59%	82	41%

This is a comprehensive table showing a synopsis of Wesley's educational thoughts and practices. Each one was an independent closed-ended question. The first question was concerned with how Wesley used education as a tool to bring about socio-spiritual reformation both inside his Anglican Church as well as outside with colliers, marginalised labourers, and poor farmers, and so he was credited to be the pioneer of education in United Kingdom and as much regarded as reformer. In fact the question was, do you think his educational thoughts and approaches are relevant to our context? There was an overwhelming response to this, 93% saying 'yes.' It is notable how much the Methodists believe that his thoughts and approaches to education and Christian education are very much relevant even after 218 (1791-2009) years. Wesley believed that teaching the truth from the Holy Scriptures will liberate those who are oppressed and marginalized by the exploitative systems and powers that be. As Jesus said, 'truth shall set you free.' Education enlightens people to see their plight and to recognise the exploitative forces around them. Paulo Freire called this as 'naming the world.' Negligible number of respondents did not know whether Wesley's educational thoughts are relevant or not. It probably indicates that they are not aware of his contribution towards education in the eighteenth century. Most of the respondents being teachers, pastors and pastorate committee members they do know the founder's contribution to education which is indeed the strength of Wesleyans today. Many seem to believe that his approach to education will bring back the lost glory of Methodist educational institutions today. Teaching, preaching and healing ministries have been the basis of Methodists growth in the country/world particularly in Karnataka. Wesley set up schools to transform the society by educating colliers and farmers' children. This change in children transformed their parents' lifestyle and thereby the society in which they lived. It seemed to have spread like a contagious virus in transforming and liberating people in that century. No wonder then, more than the Methodist educators, others have recognised Wesley as the pioneer of education and the use of education effectively to set the reformation in. What is needed today is to change the mind-set of the people who treat education as a mere means of earning better salary and positions in life competing with so-called successful rich and powerful people. Instead education must become a transformative and a liberative instrument to establish a just and an egalitarian society.

Wesley spoke boldly against the ills of the day and used the Bible as his authority saying 'Salvation is the cure for all sinful activities'- will this approach work in your Church to bring about reformation was the second question. Interestingly 62.5% say it will work. However, some have written a note saying that if preachers and teachers of the Word can have that clean and holy image like that of Wesley, there is no question why they cannot exercise that spiritual authority to transform their Churches. This then, raises a question of personal transformation first before embarking on God's mission. The preacher-teacher must practice what he wants his congregants to be. His life and actions must bear witness to his calling and mission more than words. Such a committed life of the pastor can surely have an impact on the lives of his congregation. Therefore, one must not have a false image that Wesley was wielding a magic wand to change people's lives during the eighteenth century. The hearer must see that the saved people are different in behaviour and conduct and must witness the power of the spoken word of God transforming the Church. A true salvation experience can transform and change activities and attitudes of a person. As Apostle Paul says in 2 Corinthians 5:17, "if anyone is in Christ, the new creation has come; the old has gone, the new is here!" (TNIV).[482] Probably Wesley rephrased this verse, saying that salvation/new life in Christ is an answer to evil/sinful activities. Therefore, the grand end of preaching and teaching is about saving grace and salvation is to cure the diseases of human nature.

The third question was regarding Wesley's aversion to 'play'; he quotes a wise German proverb to support his stand on the issue of play: 'he that plays when

[482] Today's New International Version.

he is a boy will play when he is a man.'[483] But 88.5% of the respondents rejected Wesley's view about the 'play.' There is an overwhelming respect and agreement with other views of his educational thoughts but the respondents did not buy his argument regarding the play. It is probably because the play is an integral part of educational system and modern educators promote that children must have physical exercises to give vent to their physical energy and emotional feelings. Today, sports and games have become career-oriented fields at the national and international levels. Talented children have made it as their profession to pursue it in life. Not allowing children to play keeping his century's view may have been true during Wesley's time but with changing trends and philosophy of education, play has come to stay as part of the education curriculum. Though small in number yet 11.5% seem to believe Wesley's views about play. They probably have their own reason/understanding to answer so. However, educational fraternity and parents in general will not agree with Wesley on this issue which is very clearly indicated by 88.5%, a majority of the respondents.

A military kind of rigid discipline was followed by Wesley in boarding schools - Kingswood timing: 4 am, Rising, reading, prayer and meditation, 5 am, All met together. 6 am, worked till breakfast, 7-11 am school; Noon, till lunch worked or walked, 1-5 pm. School, private prayer till 6 pm. 6-7 pm walked or worked till supper; 7 pm public service; 8pm bed, the youngest going first.[484] And in the kind of food - Breakfast: milk-porridge and water-gruel, by turns. Supper: bread and butter or cheese, and milk, by turns. Dinner: Sunday – cold roast beef, Monday –hashed meat and apple dumplings, Tuesday- boiled mutton, Wednesday- vegetables and dumplings, Thursday- boiled mutton or beef, Friday- vegetables and dumplings, And so in lent. Saturday- Bacon and greens, apple dumplings[485] that was served, with a heavily loaded time table for study and prayers, sleeping and rising hours, keeping the surrounding clean by themselves, and with no holidays etc., almost similar to Methodist boarding homes. A majority, i.e., 84.5% respondents have affirmed this by marking 'yes.' It sounds familiar to the researcher for he was a boarder himself in 1970s, where boys were asked to rise up as early as 4:00 am to cook breakfast, clean the surroundings and class rooms, then wash up and be ready for morning prayers, breakfast (limited quantity of porridge) and for study till school time. From 9:00 am till 4:30 pm at school, with half an hour break for frugal lunch. From 4:30 till 6:00, it was time for sweeping, cleaning, washing etc. From 6:00 pm till 9:00 pm it was time for prayer, dinner and study, while by 10pm lights would be off. This used to be the heavy schedule. However, times have changed since then without continuing a regimental schedule. Since child psychologists, private funding agencies and educational

---

[483] John W. Prince, *Wesley on Religious Education* (New York: The Methodist Book Concern, 1926), p. 145.

[484] Alfred H. Body, *John Wesley and Education* (London: The Epworth Press, 1936), p. 53.

[485] *Ibid.*, p. 96.

systems have played a greater role in changing that system. Keeping that kind of a life in mind as many as 84.5% have agreed to the kind of discipline that Wesley clamped on his residential students. Though there has been a qualitative change in the boarding homes, many things remain unchanged. Boarding schools need all round development and modernization with committed leaders at the helm of affairs.

Discipline was the foundation of those boarding schools in 1960s and 1970s. Unfortunately, it does not seem to be the same today. It is very evident from the kind of leaders that the Church is getting from these institutions today. 15.5% respondents, though very small in number has disagreed with that view because two Bangalore based boarding schools do not have such rigid rules since they cater to upper class children of the society and they are not expected to do manual duties as other rural and town boarding school children do. A majority of respondents who have agreed with Wesleyan discipline being followed in the boarding schools were boarders at some time or the other in life. That is a true experience.

78.5% of the respondents believe that boarding children have a better chance of being exposed to Christian education although at times it is forced on them. Despite this, many affirm the good things taught there. At times, one might feel whatever is done in boarding schools is by force without any choice. Everything seems imposed on you at that moment in life but looking back in time it seems right in a given situation. One thing is sure that the boarders have plenty of opportunity and exposure to the teaching of Christian education on a daily basis as compared to other school children. It is the best way to expose the students/learners to Christian values – love, truth, and justice; peace, sharing, caring, forgiving and accepting others as God's creation. Therefore 78.5% have expressed that boarding homes are better places to impart Christian education. Of course 21.5% of the respondents seem to believe otherwise because forced or imposed teaching will not last long and may be counter-productive in the outcome. Though they have a point, giving an opportunity either to respond positively or negatively is not a bad idea. Even Wesley was criticised for imposing too much too soon upon the children.

75% of the respondents said that boarders do have time to play along with their daily routine. Yes there is some time during the school time as well as in the evening before vesper. Boarders have more time for play and relaxation on Saturdays. That probably is the reason for 75% respondents to say that boarders do have enough time for play. Boarding schools are like training institutions preparing students for all round development and life. They are not mere academic institutions. By and large students who are educated in boarding schools become more independent to lead their normal life in society. Initially, it appears harsh and tough to go through boarding home education but it yields desired results preparing learners to be independent individuals in a given society.

83% of the respondents feel that the boarders are exposed to spiritual activity more than other children. It is true that the boarders have three times corporate prayers at the boarding homes, individual meditations apart from school chapel in the mornings. On the other hand, day scholars have no other exposure except morning school chapel and family prayers if any. There is no systematic teaching as it happens in the boarding homes for the learners. There is a planned programme under the guidance of an appointed Methodist minister. There is enough exposure to spiritual activities for the boarders, apart from daily programme; they have to attend Sunday schools, Sunday service, youth fellowships and evening service on Sundays. At times, it seems they are exposed to spiritual activities more than other academic and social activities. 17% of the respondents seem to feel otherwise. The reasons could be that modern boarding homes seem to have devalued discipline and spiritual activities as was during missionary days. There is a lot more freedom, no doubt, but commitment to Christian education activities is growing cold among those appointed to superintend the boarding schools. Wesley too had this problem in his time but he knew how to take timely action against such errant teachers and leaders to stem the rot and redeem the situation. Probably there is a lesson or two in what Wesley did in his time for today's leaders to right the wrongs before it is too late for correction.

74% of the respondents feel that boarding schools keep children away from mischief and distraction. The reason is that there is a person(s) constantly supervising. Secondly, mischief mongers are punished. Thirdly, they are (within the four walls) watched by fellow students. Fourthly, they are forced to live a focused life under given circumstances. Therefore, boarders live a controlled life under the multitude of advisers and leaders. Boarding schools have their strengths in imparting spiritual and social values vigorously than mere academic schools. 26% seems to think otherwise, because forced values and discipline may not do all that good to the learners. Education must be pleasurable and enable them to be liberated from so called uncivilised behaviours. But one must recognise that most Indians learn certain things under pressure and imposition, probably it has to do with our culture and upbringing.

The last question under this section shown in the above table was, do you think Christian education is an answer to the ills of growing children? 59% of the respondents think it is so and 41% think otherwise. A majority of the respondents do think that Christian education could be a powerful means in bringing about a tangible transformation in the behavioural patterns of the growing children, because children are taught what is right and wrong with illustrations. The practical lessons with enactment and dramatization will enable learners to see the consequences of both good and the bad behaviours. Again one must realize that it is the teacher who plays the key role in helping children recognise the seriousness of their action be it good or bad. The teacher has an important role in reducing the ills of the growing children and thereby the society at large. Others think that parents and society itself can help reduce ills of growing children, not necessarily Christian education. In other words, moral and spiritual upbringing is not a person's responsibility rather it is a collective responsibility of the given community. Together, growing children could get help to transform their characteristics and be responsible citizens.

An overwhelming response affirms the relevancy of Wesley's education policy. Whether the respondents are aware of its implications and contexts, one doesn't know. As with the Churches and institutions everywhere, anything biblical is wholly acceptable without probing into the texts, interpretation, and relevance to the contexts of the day. There is a need to ground biblical teaching into context and interpret in terms of contextual relevance.

Christian Education is seen as the solution to societal ills. Does it work outside the Church/mission compound? What about people of other faith where corruption, exploitation, bonded labour still exists?

Questionnaire IV: Christian Education as understood by Respondents

Table Twenty Five: Meaning of Christian Education

Sl. No.	Description	Respondents	%
1	Christian Education (CE) is a process where persons are confronted with God and transformed by the Gospel[486]	20	10%
2	CE is a planned educational action to develop self consciousness to realize one's own stand in relation to God and humankind	101	50.5%
3	CE helps in the process of developing positive personality	10	05%
4	CE teaches values like truth, justice, peace, equality, honesty, and respect for other lives etc.	40	20%
5	CE is a character-formation course	21	10.5%
6	CE teaches to maintain socio-cultural and religio-political values	10	05%
7	Any other	0	0%
	Total	200	100%

The respondents were given multiple meanings of Christian education as shown in the above table and they were asked to choose the best meaning of Christian education as they understood accordingly. A majority of the respondents agreed that 'Christian education is a planned educational action to develop self

[486] Christian education is a process in which persons are confronted with God and transformed by the Christian Gospel, and led into and nurtured within the Church, quoted from "The Objectives of Christian Education: A Study Document" (New York: National Council of Churches, 1958), p. 4.

consciousness to realize one's own stand in relation to God and humankind.' They feel that Christian education planned programme with definite objective to develop consciousness within the learner in other words' conscientize the student to understand their relationship with God and with the fellow human beings consciously. No one is forcing upon the learner, instead helping them to realize their stand. If their stand is incorrect then Christian education helps them ratify their stand in relation to God and humankind. Both vertical and horizontal relationships of the learners are developed with the help of Christian education courses. The definition of Christian education appears comprehensive in nature. The ultimate expectation from the Christian education is that the children know their creator and their duty towards humanity. In other words, teach children to understand God and connect themselves as the children to the father; then realize that every human being, no matter what he/she is known by name in a given society; but they are all God's creation, therefore, they are to be treated as brothers and sisters. This is a simple summary of what God teaches through the Holy Scriptures. 50.5% believe that this is a good meaning of Christian education in comparison to other meanings given in the table. 20% of the respondents feel that meaning of Christian education is that – it is a course that teaches Biblical and universal values such as truth, justice, peace, equality, honesty and respect for others. Though this meaning appears clear and simple yet it is inclusive in the above meaning where a majority have accepted. If one's relation to God and humankind is understood by the learner, he or she is enabled to avoid consciously all that hurts either God or human beings. That means the learner has to abide by the Biblical or universal values to be a moderate human being and a good Christian in his/her conduct. These 20% respondents probably looked at those values that are under severe attack these days and hoped that Christian education will help restore these values in the lives of young people to be good witnesses to Christ and be a considerate citizen in the world. These values emerge depending on one's relationship with God and are recognized in their practical dealings with other people in the world. 10.5% respondents believe that of Christian education is a course that helps children in their character-formation. 21 persons out of the total respondents feel that this course shapes children's conduct and attitudes. Character formation is a desired hope of every parent, and even teachers. One of the objectives of Christian education course is character formation. This meaning too is inclusive of what 50.5% have said to be the meaning of Christian education. In helping children to realize one's relation to God and humankind is to shape their behaviour, thereby their destiny. Other 20 persons out of 200, i.e., 10% of the respondents say that 'Christian education is a process in which persons are confronted with God and transformed by the Christian Gospel, and led into and nurtured within the Church.' Compared with the majority's choice, it is more Church oriented and exclusive and not inclusive in meaning. Preferred definition by the majority is broad and inclusive in nature, the reason being, that many who have answered this questionnaire are Pastors, educators and seasoned members of the Methodist churches in Karnataka. Those who have chosen different answers than the majority are students and junior teachers and floating members. 05% and 04% respondents felt that Christian education should help in personality development and teach socio-cultural and religio-political values respectively. Of course these issues/concerns are part of the course and are inclusive in core meaning of what Christian education is to achieve at the end of the day. It is interesting to note that a variety of meanings are ascribed to Christian education and it is expected that the course achieves the stated objective.

Interestingly, in principle majority of the respondents know the meaning of Christian education but in its application to practical life it is difficult to agree with, said many in personal interview with the author. They said it is their personal opinion not necessarily general view.

Table Twenty Six: Objectives of Christian Education

Sl. No.	Description	Respondents	%
1	Christian character formation	185	92.5%
2	To perpetuate traditional values of the church	96	48%
3	To build a moral & vibrant society thro' religious education	121	60.5%
4	To prepare good human beings and responsible citizens	102	51%
5	Any Other	0	0%

92.5% believe that the aim and objective of Christian education through various wings of the Church is to help each member in their character formation in accordance with scriptural teaching. Whether one achieves this objective in practicality or not is a different issue altogether but the intention is Christian character formation of every young and old members of their community. This leads then to believe that the ultimate purpose of this objective is to build a moral and vibrant society. 60.5% of the respondents believe that Christian religious education should result in training them to be responsible citizens. That is a valuable service that any Christian community or a church can render to the society at large. This will be indeed the greatest witness to Christ Jesus who said 'you are the light of the world and salt of the earth.' 51% said that another objective of Christian religious education is to prepare good human beings and responsible citizens. In other words, four statements above explain the purpose of Christian religious education alluding to one major purpose, that is, to be a good Christian in word and deed not merely in profession, thereby to be a practical witnessing Christian. The respondents have agreed to the universal explanation of Christian education objectives.

Table Twenty Seven: Available Sources for Children to make a Moral/Ethical Decision

Sl. No	Description	Respondents	%
1	Sunday Schools	160	80%
2	Parents and family	189	94.5%
3	Sunday Services	153	76.5%
4	Teachers and peers	145	72.5%
5	Any Other	95	47.5%

Once again, it is proved beyond words that the available source for children to help make moral and ethical decision is parents and family. Indian culture lays such a responsibility on parents and family to play an important role of spiritual guides to their young and growing children. Hebrew families too were exhorted by God to teach their children all the time, while walking, talking, sleeping (evening) and getting up, (morning) as is recorded in Deuteronomy 6:7. Family and parents become God's medium to impart His commandments to those that are part of the family. 94.5% agreed to this fact that parents and the family are the first available source of help for children to take moral and ethical decisions. The next important source which the respondents feel is the Sunday school. 80% have mentioned it as another important source for growing children to make moral and ethical decisions. 76.5% feel Sunday services too are a source of help in making moral and ethical decisions. 72.5% say teachers and peers play their role in helping young people to make important decisions in life. It is to be understood that there are many who do not take either families or church seriously but they do have some respect for their peers and teachers. In this context, teachers have to play the role of spiritual guide apart from being subject teachers.

Young people go through certain disturbed and rebellious phase in life and at times they need outside help to cope with adolescent issues in life. Apart from these conventional sources for the young to make moral decisions, there are other mediums such as television programmes, extra-curricular activities and cinema world. This might enable or help them to resolve these issues constructively or positively. 47.5% of the respondents have indicated these sources. Whether these are enabling or not, one cannot say. Only their lives will reveal the effects of such influences. However, the fact remains, that with all these sources available, it is up to the growing children to utilise these sources for their character formation. No one can force them, but an opportunity must be given to the learners to make their choices in life based on the available sources.

Table Twenty Eight: Most Cherished Family Values

Sl. No.	Description	Respondents	%
1	Friendliness	101	50.5%
2	Openness	87	43.5%
3	Mutual respect	112	56%
4	Meal time together	156	78%
5	Family outing	149	74.5%
6	Any other	91	45.5%

A majority of the respondents have affirmed that they value family meal time and outing together as is shown in the above table. More than 56% and 50.5% seem to say, that they cherish mutual respect and friendliness. The researcher has known a few families where each one respects the other. Of course it is typical of Asian culture. On the other hand, there are families that are extremely westernized. This may be an extreme type of modernism or western culture. 45.5% of the respondents cherished family values while playing together indoor games, watching television programmes and working together on special occasions, where ones temperaments, patience and acceptance is put to test and trained in most cases. In other words, each one's strength and weakness is also understood in such occasions where the family members are at play or watching TV. Family values are a great strength in times of difficulties.

Table Twenty Nine: Influences on Your Character Formation

Sl. No	Description	Respondents	%
1	Parents	182	91%
2	Teachers	177	88.5%
3	Friends	113	56.5
4	Society	86	43%
5	Church/Sunday school	180	90%
6	Books/Biographies	118	59%
7	Any other	0	0%

It is obvious how much the respondents laid the responsibility on parents as having the greatest influence on growing children by their responses. 91% have emphatically affirmed this view. As mentioned above, Sunday school is another source of help in guiding young people in making moral decisions. Sunday school and the Church are the second largest force that influences the growing young people. 88.5% believe that teachers influence the young minds as they spend greater times together apart from parents. 59% of the respondents feel that, biographies and books too, have great influence on growing children. Many young people do come from broken and difficult families. For them, the above stated biographies and books become a very important source of influence. Friends also play an important role in influencing young people; therefore, there must be parental advice to these young people to choose the right kind of friends. They either help you become somebody in the society or renegade you no body in the world. 43% of the respondents said that they believe society and its surroundings have their influence as the children grow up to be adults. At times, people and happenings could influence young people intentionally or not, directly or indirectly. The individual has to be careful in allowing oneself to what kind of influence he/she is coming under. At times bad influences are more forceful and powerful than the positive ones in life. Many people in this table as shown above seem to believe that parents, Church and teachers have an open opportunity to impact these growing people (before they go astray in life). It is a God-given responsibility and privilege; one must make full use of it in blessing some one's living. It is because of such godly men and women who influence people around them with their saintly life style the researcher himself would not have come to be what he is today.

Table Thirty: General Survey of Educational System in India

Sl.No.	Description	Response	%
1	Present education system is domesticating	168	84%
2	Does not encourage critical faculty, creativity of the learner	124	62%
3	Socio-cultural values are not imparted candidly	112	56%
4	Religious & social values are taught in the class room	139	69.5%
5	Education maintains status quo and imposes biased values	146	73%
6	Education is a means to earn better salary & position in life	173	86.5%
7	Problem solving approach motivates and it's a practice of freedom	164	82%
8	Educated wants to serve the society	124	62%
9	Education must be relevant and contextual	180	90%
10	Education is liberation from exploitation and oppression	180	90%
11	Today's education system is not relevant to the learners	134	67%
12	Curriculum is academic oriented not service oriented	166	83%
13	Educational institution could become agents of social change	176	88%

14	Institutions must stress on universal value or basic values[487]	185	92.5%
15	Educators & course contents are key to socio-cultural change	170	85%
16	Can education be answer to socio-cultural, values' decline?	129	64.5%
17	Can non-formal education be a tool to transforming society[488]	162	81%
18	Is it catering to meet the IT requirements only	122	61%
19	education does change people's ideas/values and future	183	91.5%
20	Present education system dose not encourage dialogue	165	82.5%
21	Present education system follows 'banking method'	175	87.5%

An overwhelming majority seems to disagree with the general definition/ view of the present education system as shown in the above table. Though many have marked otherwise, 84% of the respondents have said 'yes,' meaning that our education system is domesticating. In other words, what they are expressing is that, it is time the present kind of system is changed. 62% of the respondents said that the present education system does not encourage creativity and develop a critical faculty in the learners. 54% people have said that socio-cultural values are not imparted candidly in the class rooms. It is interesting to note that 69.5% seem to believe that religious and social values are taught in the class room but not candidly imparted to the learners (according to point no.4).

73% feel that our education system (teaches to) maintains the status quo and does impose biased values depending on the teacher's conviction and belief. Unfortunately 86.5% believe our education system prepares people for better salary and seeking better position in life rather than preparing students as good human beings and responsible citizens. 82% of the respondents feel that Paulo Freire's problem-posing approach to education motivates the learner and develops a confidence, and such education means 'practice of freedom.' Only 62% agreed that educated people desire serving the society and 38% do believe it to be so. The objective of education is to draw the full potentiality of the educatee so that he/she will transform the society as they themselves have been liberated from ignorance and oppression. An overwhelming majority of 90% agree that education must be relevant to meet the needs of the learner and it must be contextual taking the learners' surroundings into account, so that the learner is able to relate what is being taught and learnt in the class rooms. 90% believe that education ought to be liberative and must help the educatee to see oppressive and exploitative forces and free themselves as they will have been conscientized by education.

487 Universal Values refers to – Truth, Justice, Peace, Faith, Honesty, Equality, Discipline and respect for the elderly & gurus/teachers.

488 Non-formal education refers to Sunday schools, pulpit preaching, youth debates/meetings to create awareness to socio-political issues etc.

67% seem to agree that today's education system is not relevant, in other words it is out-dated, as much of the information passed on is rather irrelevant to the learners. 83% have a strong opinion that our education is basically academic-oriented and not service-oriented. Therefore, modern students do care for what they are learning; do not bother to practice what is being taught. They are happy by rote learning to score best grade possible to get a professional job to earn a big pay package and enjoy life. He/she has the least concern to serve the society. Their aim in life seems to amass wealth and join the rich club of the nation. The question that remains unanswered is this, what next after reaching the end of the ladder? What use is one's education to common people and the country? It is good to note that 88% of the respondents believe that educational institutions could become agents of social change. These institutions can be trend-setters for a better society if they are based on universal values such as truth, justice, peace, honesty, equality, discipline, respect for the elderly and teachers who have shaped one's present status. 92.5% strongly believe that institutions must lay greater emphasis on the universal values mentioned above. That is where the future of the given society and community lies. A society without credibility has no respect in the world. It is heartening to know that 85% believe that the socio-cultural change depends on educators and the content of the course they teach in the class rooms. That lays a greater responsibility on the teaching community to strive hard to meet that expectation. Education alone cannot rid society's ills but a collective effort can be an answer to the decline of socio-cultural values. Educated people must take the lead as models of value keepers and education must continue to create awareness about the socio-cultural values and its enduring benefits. Though 64.5% of the respondents said that education is an answer to value-decline, 33.5% feel otherwise. Interestingly 81% believe non formal education that goes on in Sunday schools, pulpit preaching, youth debates/meetings as creating awareness of socio-political issues etc., could be instrumental in bringing about transformation and change in the society. This then, calls for the Church in the world to be more pro-active in playing its role as 'salt of the earth' and 'the light of the world.' In other words, it can be a moral and spiritual watch dog. 61% of the respondents say that education caters to the needs of the information technology world. It is financially sound and it attracts younger generation. Earlier it was noted that many students go in for professional courses by paying a huge fee. This may enable them to enjoy life later, but not necessarily preparing them to serve the society. A majority, i.e., 91.5% seem to believe that education does change educatee's world view, value system and his/her future in course of learning. If changed for the better then, the objective is accomplished, if not, it is a failure. 82.5% agree that the present education system does not engage students in dialogue and still believes learners as the dumping ground. That is to say as 87.5% believe that our system still follows the banking method of education which Paulo Freire fought against in his life-time and revolutionized the education system to make it learners'- centered.

Some of the Inferences from the Empirical Study

The Scripture seems to hold sway in their Sunday school activities like their founder John Wesley.

No satisfactory answers to the following questions are found. How is Sunday school related to Church service? Does it act as an auxiliary of the Church's education ministry? Do Sunday school children get to know the happenings in the main service?

The Sunday school timings, its suitability for teachers and children, organization and structures seems to be immaterial for the Methodist leadership.

Bible stories are geared to derive morals for life – is there enough opportunity given to the learner to distinguish between right and wrong? Teachers seem to have taken very narrow approach to Christian education like their founder.

Most of their lessons seem the 'other- worldly,' in other words, the lessons are heaven bound, no earthly good. It is time that the Methodists should go beyond 'saving souls' theory and be inclusive in their approach to Christian education taking the contextual realities of the learners.

Only 70% have said that students are taught socialization and sharing. Compared to the other issues in the table seventeen does not indicate their openness to pluralistic context and much less of socialization and sharing. They seem to be narrow in their objectives of Christian education like Wesley. There must be room for growing children to develop a broader perspective of their faith and practice. Learners must be trained to be inclusive and accommodative of others in their thinking and practice.

The question is: do Sunday school teachers need proper training to cater to spiritual, cognitive and contextual needs of the learners? If the teachers' view of Christian education is so narrow, obviously they need an ecumenical exposure as well as training in holistic approach to Christian education. That is to say, those teachers must be given a training which gives them a basic theological, psychological and sociological grounding to understand the students as well as contextual realities of the day.

Sunday school lessons needs to include more interactive and dialogical methods. Lecture method may have lot of information to be passed to the learners though, there must be an opportunity given to informal discussion and interaction clarify their doubts and difficulties with an issue or issues. In other words, dialogical and participatory methods must be adopted to involve students actively.

Summary

The analysis and interpretation of 30 tables do reveal the ground reality of Christian Education in the Methodist Churches of Karnataka. Though the responses are on expected line, they could have been more expressive and revealing. The respondents have been careful in their answers in many cases since questionnaires were administered by the senior Pastors and the author himself an ordained minister. Therefore, they may not have been forthright in answering the questions. There were some critical questions about the pastors' life style and their commitment to their calling. Many respondents including pastors have been general and have given conventional answers. The main objective of this exercise was to see what is happening in the Sunday schools, youth fellowships and pulpit ministry of the Methodists. The answers have been reasonable and do reveal the present status of Christian education activities in their respective congregations. Each table does reveal a room for improvement keeping John Wesley's Christian education thoughts. Findings will be discussed in the last chapter. This empirical analysis leads to re-examination of Wesley's thoughts on Christian education from the perspectives of empirical findings and from Paulo Freire's understanding of education for suggesting a relevant Christian education model or a programme.

Chapter 4

A Critique of John Wesley's Theory and Practice of Christian Education from the Perspective of Freirean Education Theory of Liberation

A. Paulo Freire's Educational Theory and Approach - A Brief Sketch 155

1. A Brief Background of Paulo Freire – The Educator 156
2. The Process of Education - Conscientization 159
    a. Assumptions of Conscientization 160
    b. Stages of Critical Consciousness/Thought 162
    c. Qualities of Critical Consciousness 164
    d. Agenda of Critical Consciousness 165
3. Purpose of Education- Liberation/Humanization 166
4. Alternative Method of Education – Problem-posing, not "Banking system" 168
5. An Alternate approach to Education- Participatory or Dialogical 170
6. A Critics of Paulo Freire's Theory and Approach 172

B. Re-reading Wesley's Thoughts on Christian Education, and his Pedagogical Approach from the Perspective of Freirean Liberatory Pedagogical Paradigm 178

1. Wesley and Freire: Commonalities in their thoughts and concerns 178
2. The Process of Christian Education - Conscientization 180
3. Pedagogical Approach - Contextual relevance/rephrased 183
4. Liberation and Humanization- Wesley's understanding 185
5. Role of Dialogue in the Process of Education 186

6. Analysis of Wesley's Educational Views, Convictions and Practices Concerning Education 186
7. Framework of Freire: Its Implications for Wesleyan thoughts on Christian Education and Contemporary Methodists Education Ministry 192

Chapter 4

A Critique of John Wesley's Theory and Practice of Christian Education from the Perspective of Freirean Education Theory of Liberation

A. Paulo Freire's Educational Theory and Approach - A Brief Sketch

This Chapter re-examines Wesley's Christian education thoughts from the perspective of both the empirical studies and Freirean approach to education. It also endeavours to highlight the relevant educational features of John Wesley and Paulo Freire. This chapter does not however commit itself to deal with a comparative study of the two: the eighteenth century John Wesley and the twentieth century Paulo Freire in terms of their personalities, profession or life, except for their views concerning education. It is to be noted that these leaders came from different backgrounds, different epochs belonging to different continents, time and history. To compare John Wesley with Paulo Freire or with any other will be unfair for they belong to different contexts. Wesley was an educational practitioner, while Freire was an educational revolutionary. Therefore, it is interesting to discover the strengths and weaknesses in their approaches to education and to appraise the present Christian Religious education programmes in Methodist Churches drawing insights from both Wesley's educational theory and that of Paulo Freire, the famous Brazilian educator. Still, Wesley and Freire have a contrasting understanding and definition of the Gospel, the self and dialogue. For Freire the self is not given; it is a process of formation, it changes in different contexts. Truth cannot be finalized; it is to be discovered in the process of learning. The nature of pedagogy is also different. For Wesley the pulpit is a pedagogical tool, for Freire, the oppressive socio-political context becomes a pedagogical tool. For Wesley, gospel truth was *a prior;* for Paulo Freire it is not. Education for Freire is an opening up of the self to discover the *unfinalizable* truth. Education is a process of formation of the self. For Freire, the teacher is a cultural worker and a transformative intellectual. [489] For Wesley, the teacher is a picture/role model of a parent and a true Christian in life and practice. However, in the midst of contrasting views there are certain commonalities in their concern for human liberation and for their well being.

1. A Brief Background of Paulo Freire – The Educator

This section highlights the background, life, work, theory and approach, strengths and weakness of Freire's revolutionary educational programme. Particularly, it highlights his educational pedagogy and approach which have similar overtones with the Christian education methods and approaches of the eighteenth century John Wesley.

Paulo Regulus Neves Friere was born in Recife, Pernambuco, Brazil on September 19, 1921.[490] Recife, the capital of Brazil's north-eastern province is known to be one of the most impoverished parts of the Latin American nation.[491] His father was a military police officer and he had a Catholic mother. His parents were not so well-to-do financially, and the 1929 Great Depression[492] worsened their condition. During that phase in life Freire learnt what it means to be hungry, poor, and deprived.[493] These experiences seem to have shaped his concerns for the poor and to construct his particular educational theory – pedagogy of the oppressed.

Due to economic constraints in the family, Freire's early education was interrupted on several occasions. With all these odds at hand he was able to complete his studies in high school. Later he studied Law, Philosophy and Sociology of language and finally earned his Ph.D. in 1959[494] at the age of 38. Later he taught Portuguese at a Secondary school from 1944-45. In addition, Freire worked as a trade union lawyer where he got interested in literacy training.[495] In 1944, he married Elza Maia Costa de Oliveira, a fellow teacher. The two worked together for the rest of their lives and had five children.[496]

Elza being an educator herself, stood firm like a pillar of support when Paulo Freire endeavoured to understand the uniqueness of human beings, and

---

[489] Midwives do not deliver but enable others to do – so do the educator. Insights drawn from the meeting with Dr. Christopher Duraisingh on 15th May 2008 at UTC.

[490] Nicholas Lossky et.al., (ed), *Dictionary of the Ecumenical Movement,* 2nd edition (Geneva: World Council of Churches, Publication 2002), p. 480.

[491] Akheto Sumi, *Understanding the Nature and Purpose of Christian Religious Education*, (Jorhat, Assam: Barkataki and Company Private Ltd, 2005), p. 218.

[492] *Ibid.*, pp. 218-219.

[493] Denis E. Collins, *Paulo Freire: His Life, Works and Thought* (New York: Paulist Press, 1971), p. 5.

[494] Akheto Sumi, *Understanding the Nature and Purpose of Christian Religious Education*, pp. 218-219.

[495] *Ibid.*

[496] *http:/www.google/Paulo_Freire. A Biographical Sketch of Paulo Freire,* p.1.

helped him in his educational thought formation.[497] Freire's personal testimony about her supports to the fact that, "Elza was a fantastic educator"[498] and she shaped my career.[499] Freire's contribution to pedagogy continued throughout his career, in various capacities and positions till he died of heart failure on 2nd May, 1997 at the age of 75.[500] He had a series of colourful experiences in life. First his revolutionary work began to bear fruit but in 1964, a military coup thwarted that effort; Freire was imprisoned as a traitor for 70 days. After a brief exile in Bolivia, Freire worked in Chile for five years for the Christian Democratic Agrarian Reform Movement and the Food and Agriculture Organization of the United Nations. In 1967, Freire published his first book, *Education as the Practice of Freedom* (*Educacao Como pratica Liberdade*).[501] He followed this with his most famous book, *Pedagogia do oprimido*, first published in Portuguese in 1968[502] and the first English translation *Pedagogy of the Oppressed* was published in 1970. The book examines the struggle for justice and equity within the educational system and proposes a new pedagogy.[503] The importance of his work was widely recognized. He worked with the World Council of Churches in Geneva, extending his literacy services to African countries, visited United States of America as a seminar speaker to many universities. He was invited by the Ecumenical Christian Centre, Whitefield near Bangalore in May 1973 to deliver a lecture on 'Education – Oppression or Liberation.'[504]

When a Political amnesty in Brazil was declared in 1979, Paulo Freire returned home along with many political exilee ending 16 years of exile in March, 1980 as the process of liberalization in Brazil set in.[505] On his return to Brazil, Freire was kept busy travelling throughout the country, lecturing, engaging in dialogues with students and teachers, publishing etc.[506]

---

497 Akheto Sumi, *Understanding the Nature and Purpose of Christian Religious Education*, p. 219.

498 William B. Kennedy (ed), "Conversation with Paulo Freire," in *Religious Education*, Vol. 79, No.4, (Fall 1984), p. 512. Cf. Sumi, *Understanding the Nature and Purpose of Christian Religious Education,* p. 219.

499 Paulo Freire, *Conscientization* (Bagota: Association of Educational Publishers, 1972), p. 17. Cf. Sumi, *Understanding the Nature and Purpose of Christian Religious Education,* pp. 219 & 281.

500 Akheto Sumi, *Understanding the Nature and Purpose of Christian Religious Education,* p. 219.

501 Paulo Freire, *Pedagogy of the Oppressed,* translated by Myra Bergman Ramos (New York: Herder and Herder, 1972), p. 12.

502 *http://www.google/paulo_Freire. A Biographical Sketch of Paulo Freire,* p.2.

503 *Ibid.,* p. 5.

504 Ninan Koshy & Vinayak Purohit, *Education for Liberation: Addresses by Paulo Freire and Critical Reflections on Indian Education* (Whitefield, Bangalore: Ecumenical Christian Centre Publication, 1983), p. 7.

505 Peter MacLaren and Peter Leonard, *Paulo Freire: A Critical Encounter* (London: Routledge, 1993), p. 2. Cf. Akheto Sumi, *Understanding the Nature and Purpose of Christian Religious Education,* p. 229.

506 Akheto Sumi, *Understanding the Nature and Purpose of Christian Religious Education,* p. 135.

Paulo Freire is termed the exemplary organic thinker/revolutionary of our times by Antonio Gramsci.[507] He is an educator par excellence for revolutionizing the educational system of our times. As Freire asserts, education is either for domestication or for freedom. It is though customarily conceived as a conditioning process, it can equally be effective as an instrument of de-conditioning or liberation. The choice is left open depending on the educator.[508]

Education can be de-conditioning because the human has essentially become a conditioned being, barely capable of knowing what 'conditions' him/her. But, as a human being he/she is capable of reflecting on his/her action and in behaviour, and in perceiving his/her hidden reality which is called "problematization."[509] Problematization is both asking questions and calling into question the domesticating and subversive or exploitative authority. A revolutionary educator's task is to challenge both the students and the reality which is to be studied.[510]

Paulo Freire's educational theory and practice were developed in a society characterized by rigid hierarchical social structure, neo-colonial exploitation, a precarious and selective educational system where schools were instruments of maintaining the status quo, high percentage of illiteracy, prevalence of poverty etc.[511] these issues are very similar to the social situation at the time of Wesley in United Kingdom.

Rather than going into details of the philosophical aspects of Freire's theory and practice, this section provides an overview of insights from his established theory and approach to education.

Paulo Freire propounded a philosophy of education that came not only from the more classical approaches stemming from Plato, but also from the modern Marxist and anti-colonialist thinkers. In fact, in many ways his *Pedagogy of the Oppressed* could be best read as an extension of, or reply to, Frantz Fanon's *The Wretched of the Earth*, which emphasized the need to provide native populations with an education which was simultaneously new and modern (rather than traditional) and anti-colonial (not simply an extension of the culture of the colonizer).[512]

---

[507] Peter MacLaren and Peter Leonard, *Paulo Freire: A Critical Encounter*, p. xiii.

[508] Paulo Freire, *Cultural Action for Freedom*, (Middlesex, England: Penguin Books Ltd., 1974), p. 9.

[509] Problematization is to reflect on issues rationally, raise questions for better clarity, and to choose which is relevant with necessary modification and leave the irrelevant.

[510] Paulo Freire, *Cultural Action for Freedom* (Middlesex, England: Penguin Books Ltd., 1974), p. 9.

[511] Ninan Koshy & Vinayak Purohit (ed) *Education for Liberation: Addresses by Paulo Freire and Critical Reflections on Indian Education* (Whitefield, Bangalore: Ecumenical Christian Centre Publication, 1983), p. 9.

[512] *http://www.google/paulo_Freire/bio. A Biographical Sketch of Paulo Freire,* pp. 2-3.

2. The Process of Education - Conscientization

Conscientization is a word that is used by Freire (distorted by many thinks Moacir Gadotti) to show the relationship that should exist between thinking and acting. A person (or better a group of people) who become conscientized (without forgetting that no one conscientizes anyone else, but that people are conscientized mutually, through their daily work) is able to discover the reason why things are the way they are. This discovery should be accompanied by transforming action as a proof of conscientization. [513]

Freire's vision of education is rooted in his native Brazilian and later Africa's Guinea-Bissau context. Therefore, the coining of the term 'conscientizing method' is born out of such a social context says Moore.[514] One of the most important developments in educational method in this century is the method described by Freire as conscientization. Through conscientizing, people name the agents of oppressions and re-form social reality. Education is thus the means of liberation - 'leading out into a more just social reality,' a better world. The concerns are of transformation. The methods begin by looking for oppressive social structures – anything that destroys life – and they move toward reforming those structures in order to create, support, and preserve life.[515]

Conscientization therefore, refers to the process in which human beings, not as recipients, but as knowing subjects, achieve a deepening awareness both of the socio-cultural reality which shapes their lives and of their capacity to transform that given reality.[516] Conscientization represents the development of the awakening of critical awareness,[517] when the oppressed people become aware of their own potentialities.[518]

Peter Berger, a renowned contemporary sociologist however, points to the dangers of misuse of Freire's methodology.

Freire called his method 'concientizacao' literally, 'making conscious.'[519] This name has caught on as...'consciousness-raising' in the United States.... The concept of 'consciousness-raising,' as currently used, implies some highly questionable assumptions. It implies philosophical error and political irony.... 'Consciousness-raising' is a project of higher-class individuals directed at a lower-

---

[513] Moacir Gadotti, *Reading Paulo Freire: His Life and Work,* translated by John Milton (Albany, New York: State University of New York Press, 1994), Notes, p. 166.

[514] Mary Elizabeth Mullino Moore, is a professor of Theology and Christian Education at the School of Theology at Claremont Graduate School and author also of (Education for Continuity and Change); *Teaching from the Heart: Theology and Educational Method* (Minneapolis: Fortress Press, 1991), p. 166.

[515] *Ibid.*, p. 164.

[516] Paulo Freire, *Cultural Action for Freedom* (Middlesex, England: Penguin Education, A division of Penguin Books Ltd., 1974), p, 51.

[517] Paulo Freire, *Education for Critical Consciousness* (New York: Continuum, 1994), p. 19.

[518] *Ibid.*, p. 13.

[519] Berger, Peter L. *Pyramids of Sacrifice: Political Ethics and Social Change* (New York: Basic Books, Inc., Publishers & Anchor Books edition, 1974 & 1976), p. 112.

class population....[520] Coupled with this arrogance is a recurrent irritation with 'those people' who stubbornly refuse the salvation that is so benevolently offered to them: 'How can they be so blind?'[521]

> If the hierarchical view of consciousness simply referred to levels of information on specific topics, there would be no need to quarrel with it.... If one wishes to extend this superiority to information and perspectives in general, plausibility disappears, for peasants very clearly have far superior information on other topics such as plant and animal life, soil conditions, the weather, and a multitude of manual skills and material artifacts.[522]

Therefore, to consider peasants otherwise would be poor assumption on the part of educators; for their world of information in a given context is superior to the intellectuals.

a. Assumptions of Conscientization

There are several basic assumptions of conscientization that needs to be named before one tries to understand the implied worldview in these assumptions regarding social systems and their functions either to oppress or liberate human beings.[523] The first assumption is that education either perpetuates the present social system or brings about transformation. It cannot be neutral. Richard Shaull says while introducing Freire's pedagogy of the oppressed:

> There is no such thing as a neutral educational process. Education either functions as an instrument which is used to facilitate the integration of the younger generation into the logic of the present system and bring about conformity to it, or it becomes "the practice of freedom,' the means by which men and women deal critically and creatively with reality and discover how to participate in the transformation of their world.[524]

The second assumption is that humanization is the human vocation, but the corrupt nature of human instead opts to indulge in the activities of

---

520 Berger, Peter L. *Pyramids of Sacrifice: Political Ethics and Social Change* (New York: Basic Books, Inc., Publishers & Anchor Books edition, 1974 & 1976), p. 113.

521 *Ibid.*, p. 114.

522 *Ibid.*, pp. 114-115.

523 Mary Elizabeth Mullino Moore, *Teaching from the Heart: Theology and Educational Method,* p. 169.

524 Paulo Freire, *Pedagogy of the Oppressed* (New York: Herder and Herder, 1972), p. 15.Cf. Mary Elizabeth Mullino Moore, *Teaching from the Heart: Theology and Educational Method,* p. 169.

dehumanization.[525] Humanization[526] is a calling, and we choose whether we will participate in humanizing the world or in dehumanizing it. Those who choose the latter steal the humanity of others and, in the process, dehumanize themselves as well. Though this is a real option, it is a distortion of the vocation of becoming more fully human.[527] Doing good to all and treating others better than oneself is what the Bible teaches, while indulging in activities other than these amounts to distorting ones vocation or calling.

A third assumption is that **oppressors are not capable of liberating the oppressed: the task of the oppressed is to liberate both themselves and their oppressors.**[528] Any attempt by the oppressors to liberate the oppressed will be experienced by the oppressed as a **false generosity**. This means, that a certain suspicion attends any effort by persons in power to give up their power for others.[529]

A fourth assumption is that **education needs the pedagogy of the oppressed**. Sometimes Freire describes this education as the practice of freedom. Such pedagogy is created with the oppressed individuals and peoples, and it is aimed at humanization. Oppressed persons thus are subjects in the process, not objects.[530] Pedagogy of the oppressed is also pedagogy of questioning, both in school and in the societal struggle.[531] Thus, "Attempting to liberate the oppressed without their reflective participation in the act of liberation is to treat them as objects which must be saved from a burning building."[532]

A fifth assumption is that **a pedagogy of the oppressed leads to action**. It is concerned not only with absorbing knowledge but also more importantly with identifying social realities and responding to them through liberative action. In addition, the action itself is subject to continuing re-examination and revision.[533]

---

525 Paulo Freire, *Pedagogy of the Oppressed* (New York: Herder and Herder, 1972), p. 28. Cf. Mary Elizabeth Mullino Moore, *Teaching from the Heart: Theology and Educational Method*, p. 169.

526 Humanization is the way in which men and women can become aware of themselves, their way of behaving and thinking, when they develop all their capacities by thinking not just of themselves but of the needs of everyone. Moacir Gadotti, *Reading Paulo Freire: His Life and Work,* translated by John Milton (Albany, New York: State University of New York Press, 1994), Notes, p. 164.

527 *Ibid.*

528 *Ibid.*, pp. 28-29.

529 Mary Elizabeth Mullino Moore, *Teaching from the Heart: Theology and Educational Method*, p. 170.

530 *Ibid.*

531 Moacir Gadotti, *Reading Paulo Freire: His life and Work* (New York: State University of New York press, 1994), p. 60.

532 Paulo Freire, *Pedagogy of the Oppressed*, p. 52.

533 Mary Elizabeth Mullino Moore, *Teaching from the Heart: Theology and Educational Method*, p. 170.

In one stage, pedagogy serves to unveil the world of oppression, and in the other it serves to transform that world.[534] Conscientization is therefore quite different from 'banking' education in which the teacher stores information in students. Freire sees banking education as problematic because it attempts to control thinking and action, and leads people to adjust to the world and inhibits their creative power.[535]

This view eventually led to the formation of a project called – the Movement of Popular Culture and it motivated Freire to launch a new institution christened as 'culture circle' - The Culture Circle is a teaching unit that replaces the traditional school. It is formed by a group of people who get together to discuss their work, local and national realities, their family life, etc. There is no place for the traditional (banking) teacher – the one who knows everything – nor is there for the pupil who knows nothing. The cultural circle allows the pupil at the same time as he/she becomes literate; to learn to *read*, that is, analyze his/her practice and act upon it.[536] This concept was to counter the term school which traditionally stood for a passive concept. The Institution of Popular Culture de-codified popular terms such as teacher with coordinator, lectures with dialogue, pupils with participants, syllabus with learning units.[537] Thus, Freire, proposed an alternative method of educating the learners.

b. Stages of Critical Consciousness/Thought

Freire's pedagogy includes the goal of critical consciousness. Freire categorizes consciousness into three stages of growth which culminate in critical thought.[538] They are critical, magical and naïve consciousness. He believed that **critical/**[539]**critical transitivity** – [suggests the dynamism between critical thought and critical action. Here, the individual sees herself or himself making the changes needed. A critically transitive thinker feels empowered to think and to act on the conditions around her or him, and relates those conditions to the larger contexts of power in society].[540] The Critically transitive consciousness is characterized by depth in the interpretation of problems; by the substitution of causal principles for magical explanations; by the testing of one's findings and by openness to revision; by the attempt to avoid distortion when perceiving problems and to avoid preconceived notions when analysing them; by refusing to transfer

---

[534] Paulo Freire, *Pedagogy of the Oppressed,* p. 40. Cf. Mary Elizabeth Mullino Moore, *Teaching from the Heart: Theology and Educational Method,* p.171.

[535] *Ibid.,* p. 64. Cf. Mary Elizabeth Mullino Moore, *Teaching from the Heart: Theology and Educational Method,* p. 171.

[536] Moacir Gadotti, *Reading Paulo Freire: His Life and Work,* translated by John Milton, (Albany, New York: State University of New York Press, 1994), Notes, p. 165.

[537] Paulo Freire, *Education for Critical Consciousness,* p. 42.

[538] Peter MacLaren and Peter Leonard, *Paulo Freire: A Critical Encounter,* p. 32.

[539] Paulo Freire, *Education for Critical Consciousness,* p. 44.

[540] Critical transitivity, Peter MacLaren and Peter Leonard, *Paulo Freire: A Critical Encounter,* p. 32.

responsibility; by rejecting passive positions; by soundness of argumentation; by the practice of dialogue rather than polemics; by receptivity to the new for reasons beyond mere novelty and by the good sense not to reject the old just because it is old, by accepting what is valid in both old and new[541]. consciousness always submits traditional practices to analysis; for a critical mind, what is true today may not be so tomorrow. Thus, critical consciousness represents things and facts as they exist empirically, in their practical and circumstantial correlations. Critical consciousness is thus integrated with reality. **Magic/intransitive**[542] consciousness, in contrast, simply apprehends facts and attributes to them a superior power by which it is controlled and to which it must therefore submit. Magical consciousness is characterized by fatalism which makes human beings resigned to the impossibility of resisting the power of facts. **Naïve** - the state of consciousness, is characterised by an over-simplification of problems; by a nostalgia for the past; by underestimation of the common people; by a strong tendency to gregariousness; by a lack of interest in investigation, accompanied by an accentuated taste for fanciful explanations; by fragility of argument; by a strongly emotional style; by the practice of polemics rather than dialogue. In short, naïve transitive consciousness can evolve toward critical transitivity, characteristic of a legitimately democratic mentality, or it can be deflected toward the debased, clearly dehumanized, fanaticized consciousness characteristic of going along the mass.[543] **Semi-transitive** - where people exercise their thought and action for change. Partly empowered, they act to change things and make a difference, but they relate to problems one at a time in isolation, rather than seeing the whole system underlying any single issue. Semi-transitive people may also naively follow strong leaders with populist rhetoric, in the hope that one strong man can set the world right rather than they themselves having to make the changes needed [544] consciousness sees traditional practice as a static, established fact, and thus is deceived in its perception. It considers itself superior to facts, in control of facts, and thus free to understand them as it pleases and super imposes itself on reality.[545] Only education can facilitate the passage from naïve to critical transitivity, increasing learners' ability to resist the emotional power of the transition.[546]

---

[541] Paulo Freire, *Education for Critical Consciousness*, p. 18.

[542] **Intransitive thought** - where people live fatalistically, thinking that their fate is out of their hands. Only luck or God can influence their lives. They do not think their action can change their conditions. Disempowered, they are stuck in time, under the thumb level of the dominant elite now and forever, as far as they can tell. Peter MacLaren and Peter Leonard, *Paulo Freire: A Critical Encounter*, p. 32.

[543] Naïve transitivity, Paulo Freire, *Education for Critical Consciousness*, pp. 18 & 20.

[544] Semi-transitive - *Paulo Freire: A Critical Encounter*, p. 32.

[545] Paulo Freire, *Education for Critical Consciousness*, p. 44.

[546] Paulo Freire, *Education for Critical Consciousness*, p. 32.

However, critical understanding leads to critical action; magical understanding to magical response. Freire, wanted people to transcend/supersede their magical and naïve perception of reality to that of critical consciousness. He proposed that this transition could be achieved through active dialogical method; changing the programme content of education; by the use of techniques like thematic 'breakdown' - a splitting of themes into their fundamental nuclei. The entire programme is a totality made up of interrelated units which in themselves are also totalities. The thematic breakdown splits the total themes in search of their fundamental nuclei, which are partial elements[547] and 'codification' - process attempts to re-totalize the disjoined theme in the representation of existential situations. In decoding, individuals split the codification to apprehend its implicit themes.[548] The transcendence in this context signifies the capacity of human consciousness to surpass the limitations of the objective configuration.[549]

c. Qualities of Critical Consciousness

Critical consciousness could be described as having four qualities: Power awareness, critical literacy, de-socialization, and self-education.[550]

i. Power Awareness. Knowing that society and history can be made and remade by human action and by organized groups; knowing who exercises dominant power in society for what ends and how power is currently organized and used in society.
ii. Critical Literacy. Analytic habits of thinking, reading, writing, speaking or discussing which go beneath surface impressions, traditional myths, mere opinions, and routine clichés; understanding the social contexts and consequences of any subject matter; discovering the deep meaning of any event, text, technique, process, object, statement, image or situation; applying that meaning to one's own contexts.
iii. De-socialization. Recognizing and challenging the myths, values, behaviours, and language learned in mass culture; critically examining the regressive values operating in society, which are internalized into consciousness – such as racism, sexism, class bias, homo-phobia, a fascination with the rich and powerful, hero-worship, excess consumerism, runaway individualism, militarism, and national chauvinism.
iv. Self-Organization/Self-education. Taking the initiative to transform school and society away from authoritarian relations and the undemocratic, unequal distribution of power; taking part in and

---

[547] "Breakdown": Paulo Freire, *Pedagogy of the Oppressed*, translated by Myra Bergman Ramos (New York: Herder and Herder), pp. 113-115.

[548] "Codification" *ibid.*, pp. 106-108.

[549] Paulo Freire, *Cultural Action for Freedom,* p. 52.

[550] Peter MacLaren and Peter Leonard, *Paulo Freire: A Critical Encounter,* pp. 32-33.

initiating social change projects; overcoming the induced anti-intellectualism of mass education.

d. Agenda of Critical Consciousness

The Freirean pedagogy which tries to develop this critical consciousness is a student-centered dialogue which problematizes generative themes from everyday life as well as topical issues from society and academic subject matter from specific disciplines. An agenda of values for that pedagogy could describe it as:[551]

i. Participatory. From the first hour of class, students are asked to participate in making their education by decoding thematic problems. The learning process is interactive and co-operative so that students do a lot of discussing and writing instead of listening to teacher-talk.
ii. Situated. The course material is situated in student thought and language, beginning from their words and understandings of the material, relating the material to their conditions.
iii. Critical. The class discussion encourages self-reflection and social reflection in terms of how we talk about issues, how we know, and how the learning process itself is working or not working. The students reflect critically on their own knowledge and language as well as on the subject matter, the quality of their learning process, and the relation of knowledge to society.
iv. Democratic. The classroom discourse is democratic in so far as it is constructed mutually by students and the teacher. Students have equal speaking rights in the dialogue as well as the right to negotiate the curriculum. They are asked to co-develop and evaluate the curriculum.
v. Dialogic. The basic format of the class is dialogue around problems posed by teacher and students. The teacher initiates this process and guides it into deeper phases. By frontloading questions and back-loading lectures, the teacher invites students to assert their ownership of their education, building the dialogue with their words. They are doing education and making it, not having education done to them or made for them.
vi. De-socialization. Freirean dialogue de-socializes students from passivity in the classroom. It challenges their learned anti-intellectualism and authority-dependence (waiting to be told what to do and what things mean). It interferes with the students' silence, submission, and sabotage which they learn in traditional classrooms. Freirean education also de-socializes teachers from the dull and domineering teacher-talk they are

551 Peter MacLaren and Peter Leonard, *Paulo Freire: A Critical Encounter*, pp. 33-34.

socialized into, transforming them into problem-posers and dialogue-leaders instead.

vii. Multicultural. The class recognizes the various racial, ethnic, regional, age-based, and sexual cultures in society. It takes a critical attitude towards discrimination and inequality. It examines the cultures of dominant and non-dominant groups. The curriculum is balanced for gender, class, and race.

viii. Research-oriented. This critical pedagogy is based on classroom and community research by the teacher into speech, behaviours, and conditions of the students, as well as into their levels of cognitive and affective development. It also expects students to be researchers inquiring into problems posed about daily experience, society, and academic material.

ix. Activist. The classroom itself is active and interactive thanks to problem-posing, co-operative learning, and participatory formats. The critical dialogue also seeks action outcomes from the inquiry wherever feasible. Is knowledge power? How do people act on knowledge and from knowledge to gain power, to change things?

x. Affective. The critical, democratic classroom is interested in the broadest development of human feeling as well as the development of social inquiry and conceptual habits of mind. The problem-posing, dialogic method includes a range of emotions from humor to compassion to indignation.

To be critical, the empowering educator needs to be,(what Henry Giroux termed a teacher as), a 'transformative intellectual.' Teachers are to be change agents in both school and society.[552] However, one should be mindful of his/her conditions and contexts, that which will teach both limits and scopes for bringing about transformation. Therefore, teaching methods and language depends on these given situations.

Freire has opened frontiers for education to be liberative which will have to be developed in one's own context based on local languages and common terminologies. On the other hand, Conscientization is a process towards achieving liberation.

3. Purpose of Education- Liberation/Humanization

The true vocation of humanization is to liberate humanity, including the oppressed and the oppressors, and those, like teachers, who are frequently recruited from among the elite classes to work with the oppressed, but who unwittingly perpetuate domination through teaching.[553]

---

552 Peter MacLaren and Peter Leonard, *Paulo Freire: A Critical Encounter*, pp. 29, 34.

553 *Ibid.*, p. 13

A true liberation is the process of humanization however, is not another deposit to be made in the person. Liberation is praxis: the action and reflection of people, upon their world in order to transform it.[554] Education for Freire is a moment of the transformation of a person mediated by the transformation of the world, particularly the society in which one lives.[555]

Teachers must, therefore, abandon the educational goal of deposit-making and replace it with the posing of the problems of learners in their relations with the world. "Problem-posing" education is responding to the essence of consciousness intentionally.[556]

> Liberating education consists in acts of cognition, and transferrals of information. It is a learning situation in which the cognizable object intermediates the cognitive actors, i.e., teacher on the one hand and students on the other. Accordingly, the practice of problem-posing education entails at the outset that the teacher-student contradiction be resolved. Dialogical relations-indispensable to the capacity of cognitive actors to co-operate in perceiving the same cognizable object – are otherwise impossible.[557]

The problem-posing method does not polarise the activity of the teacher-student: the teacher is not 'cognitive' at one point and "narrative" at another. He/she is always "cognitive," whether preparing a project or engaging in dialogue with the students. The teacher does not regard cognizable objects as his private property, but as the object of reflection by oneself and the students.[558] In this way, the problem-posing educator constantly reforms his/her reflections in the reflections of the learners. The students no longer are docile listeners; they are now critical co-investigators in dialogue with the teacher. The teacher presents the material to the students for their consideration, and re-considers his earlier considerations as the students express their own. The role of the problem-posing educator is to create, together with the students, the conditions under which knowledge at the level of the traditional is superseded by true knowledge.[559]

How does one distinguish the banking and problem-posing approach to education? Banking education then, anesthetizes (numbing of creative faculties) and inhibits creative power, whereas, problem-posing education involves a constant unveiling of reality. The former attempts to maintain the submersion

---

[554] Paulo Freire, *Pedagogy of the Oppressed*, p. 66.

[555] Moacir Gadotti, *Reading Paulo Freire: His life and Work* (New York: State University of New York press, 1994), p. 60.

[556] Moacir Gadotti, *Reading Paulo Freire: His life and Work,* p. 60.

[557] Paulo Freire, *Pedagogy of the Oppressed*, p. 67.

[558] *Ibid.*, p. 68

[559] *Ibid.*

of consciousness; the latter strives for the emergence of consciousness and critical intervention in reality.[560]

Therefore, education according to Paulo Freire is the practice of freedom- as opposed to education as the practice of domination – it denies that human being is abstract, isolated, independent, and unattached to the world; it also denies that the world exists as a reality apart from people.[561] But critical reflections consider neither the abstract human being nor the world without people, instead people as humans in relations, in their relations with the world. Liberation is not a human phenomenon alone but God's initiative too. The story of Israelites tells the liberative nature of God and He does liberate them from their Egyptian oppressors and exploiters. Therefore, what is important to liberation is the belief that God is an active force in the creation of justice; God is not simply the creator of idea of justice or the motivator for people to act justly, but God also acts to bring about justice.[562] God offers liberation to the whole creation and to every part of it[563] – the oppressed, exploited, and the marginalized, where the oppressors too are part of His redemptive/liberative passion.

4. Alternative Method of Education – Problem-posing, not "Banking system"

Paulo Freire feels strongly that the present education suffers from narration sickness, where teachers are the narrators; students are to learn by rote the narrated content.[564] Learners become thus the 'containers' into receptacles to be filled by the teachers. Education thus becomes an act of depositing, in which learners are the depositories and teachers are the depositors. Freire terms this kind of an education as a 'banking system.'[565] In the banking concept of education, knowledge is a gift bestowed by those who consider themselves knowledgeable upon those whom they consider to know nothing. Projecting an absolute ignorance onto others, a characteristic of ideology of oppression, negates education and knowledge as process of inquiry. Banking education maintains and even stimulates the contradiction through the following attitudes and practices, which mirror oppressive society as a whole: a) the teacher teaches and the students are taught; b) the teacher knows everything and students know nothing; c) the teacher thinks and the students are thought about; d) the teacher talks and students listen – meekly; e) the teacher disciplines and students are disciplined; f) the teacher chooses and enforces his choice, and the students comply; g) the teacher acts and the students have the illusion of acting through the action of the teacher; h) the teacher chooses the programme content,

---

560 Paulo Freire, *Pedagogy of the Oppressed*, p. 68.

561 *Ibid.*, p. 69.

562 Mary Elizabeth Mullino Moore, *Teaching from the Heart: Theology and Educational Method*, p. 176.

563 *Ibid.*, p. 178.

564 Paulo Freire, *Pedagogy of the Oppressed*, p. 57.

565 *Ibid.*, p. 58.

and the students adapt to it; i) the teacher confuses the authority of knowledge with his own professional authority, which he sets in opposition to the freedom of the students; j) the teacher is the subject of the learning process, while the pupils are mere objects.[566] In this concept the scope of action allowed to the students extends only as far as receiving, filing, and storing the deposits. This approach does not encourage learners to critically consider their reality. It makes them mere spectators and not re-creators of their present world.[567] Whereas the alternate active educational method helps a person to become consciously aware of his/her context and condition as a human being and empowers him/her to transform it where education then, becomes an instrument of choice for liberation.[568]

Following these principles, Freire suggests four different steps in teaching method to achieve the desired result:

The first step is to *name the world.* In naming the world, learners not only to name the world as they experience it but also to hear how others experience and name it. They need to recognise not only the aspects of a situation that are obvious to them but also the aspects that might be invisible. In naming the world, the learners comprehend the world and its oppressors and oppressive forces as a whole, holistically, with its intentions and impediments. A comprehensive and holistic approach can enable a revolution to happen in transforming the world. Thus, revolutions are not caused by one or two precipitating incidents; but are provoked by inequities, oppression, ambitions, ideological difference, and human needs of all kinds. If one has to name the world, he/she needs to take all these factors into consideration.[569] To speak a true word is to engage in *praxis*: to transform the world in accordance with reflection; and to name the world. These are interchangeable terms for Freire. It is the act of humans engaging together in *praxis*. In such acts humans live humanly: expressing, developing, re-creating, and affirming their humanity.[570]

The second step is *to discern the meaning in those words.* Learners need to be encouraged to discern the meanings in the many different perspectives and to discern what each perspective reveals about the vast social structures that include every dimension of the planet. This requires an ability to move back and forth between particular perspectives and a larger, global picture.[571]

The third step is to *define the problems in the social structures.* The challenge from a larger perspective is to define the problems in a way that is sufficiently

---

[566] Paulo Freire, *Pedagogy of the Oppressed*, p. 59. Cf. Moacir Gadotti, *Reading Paulo Freire: His Life and Work* (New York: State University of New York press, 1994), p. 52.

[567] Paulo Freire, *Pedagogy of the Oppressed*, pp. 61-62.

[568] *Ibid.*, p. 56.

[569] Mary Elizabeth Mullino Moore, *Teaching from the Heart: Theology and Educational Method*, p. 187.

[570] Peter MacLaren and Peter Leonard, *Paulo Freire: A Critical Encounter*, p. 96.

[571] Mary Elizabeth Mullino Moore, *Teaching from the Heart: Theology and Educational Method*, p. 187.

complex to take account of the many interrelated aspects of a situation and the ever-changing nature of the social structures. In other words, the analysis needs to take account of the many perspectives discussed above, to allow for complexity, and to recognize the tentativeness of any definition of the problems. Tentativeness is especially important because no one can possibly know and include every aspect of a problem in analysis and/also, situations do actually change.[572]

The fourth step is to *formulate strategies of action and to act.*[573] The final step in Freire's Conscientization is to formulate strategies of action and to act. Here again, the challenge offered by theology is to formulate and participate in multiple strategies of action as a response to the multiple factors in any situation. If only one definition of the problems and one strategy of action are put forth, the likely result is inadequate as a response to the problems. Also, some persons will be excluded from the solutions and their oppression will be perpetuated.[574] Perhaps, Freire stands as the most influential thinker about education in the late twentieth century. With these innovative ideas Paulo Freire has been particularly popular with informal educators with his emphasis on dialogue and his concern for the oppressed. However, Freire is best-known for his attack on what he called the "banking" concept of education, in which the student was viewed as an empty account to be filled by the teacher. He was not the inventor of this concept. He was however able to draw upon, and weave together, a number of strands of thinking about educational practice and liberation. For instance, Rousseau's conception of the child as an active learner was already a step away from *tabula rasa* (which is basically the same as the "banking concept"), and thinkers like John Dewey and Alfred North Whitehead were strongly critical of the transmission of mere "facts" as the goal of education. But, Freire certainly made a number of important theoretical innovation that have had a considerable impact on the development of educational practice laying the foundation for what is now called critical pedagogy[575]

5. An Alternate approach to Education- Participatory or Dialogical

The concept of dialogue for Freire is a horizontal relationship. It is characterized by love, humility, hope, faith and confidence which create a space for critical inquiry.[576] Dialogue is the loving encounter of people, who mediated by the world, 'proclaim' that world. They transform the world and in transforming it, humanize it for all people.[577] On the contrary, dialogue proposed by the elites is vertical; in

---

[572] Mary Elizabeth Mullino Moore, *Teaching from the Heart: Theology and Educational Method*, p. 188.

[573] Mary Elizabeth Mullino Moore, *Teaching from the Heart: Theology and Educational*, p. 172.

[574] *Ibid.*, p. 189.

[575] http://www.infed.org/biblio/b-poped.htm.

[576] Paulo Freire, *Education for Critical Consciousness* (New York: Continuum Publishing Company, 1994), p. 45.

[577] *Ibid.*, p.115.

this kind of dialogue, a person who is being educated needs only to listen and obey. Therefore, the first virtue of dialogue consists of respect for those who are being educated as people not as containers.[578] The essence of dialogue is 'the true word.' True words are units of reflection and action. It is an encounter between humans mediated by the world, in order to name the world.[579] Hence, dialogue cannot occur between those who want to name the world and those who do not wish this naming – between those who deny other people the right to speak their word and those whose right to speak has been denied to them. Those who have been denied their primordial right to speak their word must first reclaim and prevent the continuation of this dehumanizing aggression.[580]

> Dialogue cannot exist ...in the absence of a profound love for the world and for [human beings]. The naming of the world, which is an act of creating and re-creation, is not possible if it is not infused with love ....It is necessarily the task of responsible subjects and cannot exist in a relation of domination.....The naming of the world, through which [people] constantly re-create that world, cannot be an act of arrogance. Dialogue... is broken if the parties (or one of them) lack humility. How can I enter into a dialogue if I always project ignorance onto others and never perceive my own ... if I consider myself a member of the in-group of 'pure' (persons), the owners of truth and knowledge, for whom all non-members are 'those people' or 'the great unwashed'? ...Dialogue further requires an intense faith in (humanity), faith in their power to make and remake, to create and recreate, faith in their vocation to be more fully human (which is not a privilege of an elite, but the birthright of all).....Founding itself upon love, humility and faith, dialogue is a horizontal relationship of which mutual trust between the participants is the logical consequence.[581]

True dialogue cannot exist unless it involves critical thinking – thinking which discerns an indivisible solidarity between the world and (humans) admitting of no dichotomy between them – thinking which perceives reality as process and transformation, rather than as a static entity – thinking which does not separate itself from action, but constantly immerses itself in temporality without fear of the risks involved. Critical thinking contrasts with naïve thinking, which sees 'historical time as a weight, a stratification of the acquisitions and experiences of the past,' from which the present should emerge as normalized and 'well behaved.' For the naïve thinker, the important thing is accommodation to this normalized

---

[578] Moacir Gadotti, *Reading Paulo Freire: His life and Work* (New York: State University of New York press, 1994), p. 50.

[579] Peter MacLaren and Peter Leonard, *Paulo Freire: A Critical Encounter,* p. 96

[580] *Ibid.*, p. 17.

[581] *Ibid.*, p. 101.

'today.' For the critic, the important thing is the continuing humanization of the people.[582]

True humanism, which serves human beings, cannot accept manipulation under any name whatsoever. For humanism there is no other way than dialogue. To engage in it is to be genuine, and committed. Humanism is to make dialogue live. It is not to invade, manipulate not even to make 'slogans.' It is to devote oneself to the constant transformation of reality.[583]

Dialogue and problem-posing never bore anyone to sleep. It awakens awareness. Within dialogue and problem - posing, educator - educand and educand - educator go forward together to develop a critical attitude. The result of this is the perception of the interplay of knowledge and all its adjuncts. This knowledge reflects the world; reflects human beings in and with the world explaining the world. To reject problem-posing method of education at any level is to maintain an unjustifiable pessimism towards human beings and to life.[584]

This then is why Freire calls it "education as the practice of freedom." It is not mere transfer or transmission of knowledge. It is not the act of depositing reports or facts in the educand. It is not the perpetuation of the values of a given culture, it is not an attempt to adapt the educand to the existing environment.[585] Thus, the content of education springs from the learners themselves and their relations with the world, and transforms and broadens itself as the world becomes revealed to them.[586] Therefore, Freire felt, traditional curriculum is disconnected from life, centred around words, and void of reality.[587] In this context, Conscientization methods are significant because they enhance people's consciousness of their environment and its impact. In today's perspective, this consciousness is urgent because people are free to shape their world. They are free to become agents of humanization.[588]

6. A Critics of Paulo Freire's Theory and Approach

Freire's work has been subject to criticism as much as he has been appreciated for his theory and approach to education. Many feel that there is incoherence in his linguistic and practical approach to educational theory and the people involved. "His words are curiously unmoving. We really never get close to these oppressed. Who are they? Freire's definition seems to be 'anyone who is not an oppressor.' Vagueness, redundancies, tautologies, endless repetitions provoke boredom, not action. Freire's organization is so chaotic that the oppressor, presumably the

---

[582] Peter MacLaren and Peter Leonard, *Paulo Freire,* p. 101.

[583] Paulo Freire, *Education for Critical Consciousness*, pp. 114-15.

[584] *Ibid.*, pp. 126-127.

[585] *Ibid.*, p. 149.

[586] *Ibid.*, p. 59.

[587] *Ibid.*, p. 37.

[588] Mary Elizabeth Mullino Moore, *Teaching from the Heart: Theology and Educational Method*, p. 175.

intended reader, will find the going difficult." [589] Many modern educators seem to describe Freire as an eclectic thinker, so was Wesley called by his contemporaries. Cited here are a few select observations to severe criticisms of his style and originality.

John Egerton comments, "it has become fashionable among romantic radicals in this country (refers to the United States of America) to read and talk about Illich and Freire. But, Freire is no more radical than most of us. There is no originality in what he says; it is the same old rap. He has lectured us, criticized our narrow focus on small problems, but his alternative, the global perspective is *stale rhetoric*. He is a political and ideological theoretician, not an educator. There is nothing concrete and specific in what he says."[590]

Paul V. Taylor, in his "Texts of Paulo Freire," comes close to calling Freire a plagiarist, while Gibson notes that Freire borrows heavily from Hegel's "Phenomenology." Gibson's dissertation which examines Freire's theory, practice, and history in a Marxist context is the sharpest critique of Freire to date.[591]

According to **Thomas Groome**, however, one shortcoming in his writings so far is that nowhere does Freire explain clearly what he means by *praxis*.

> As a result, it is not at all clear how one might attempt to construct an intentional pedagogical activity by a praxis approach in something other than a literacy program. I also criticize him of placing undue emphasis on the present and future, to the almost total neglect of the past. He sounds at times, as Habermas does, as if nothing from the past is to be made available again to people in the present. I attempt to correct this in the shared praxis approach by insisting that the Story of the faith community be constantly remembered. It certainly cannot be imposed upon the present as a final word. Rather, it is to be placed in dialectic with the present. If the past is forgotten and left unreclaimed, it will determine and control our present, if it is critically appropriated, it can be emancipatory.[592]

---

589 Rozanne Knudson, "Review of Pedagogy of the Oppressed." *Library Journal*, April 1, 1971. "Freire's work can seem abstract and overly intellectual to readers unfamiliar with the language of dialectical argument or theological debate." Herbert Kohl, "The Making of History." *Hungry Mind Review*, March 1990. "Freire's books, often laden with dense jargon and Marxist terminology, can be heavy going." Frances Rafferty, "Literacy Man's Utopias." *Times Educational Supplement*, October 29, 1993. A number of people who have worked on the Freire model are beginning to understand that Freire's methods make it possible to be critical about nearly everything except those methods themselves." Bruce O Boston, "Paulo Freire." In *Paulo Freire*, Stanley Grabowski, ed. Syracuse University Publications in Continuing Education, 1972.

590 Egerton, John. "Searching for Freire." *Saturday Review of Education*, April 1973, quoted from http://www.google/paulo_Freire.

591 http://www.google/paulo_Freire.

592 Thomas H. Groome, *Christian Religious education: Sharing Our Story and Vision*, (San Francisco: Harper & Row Publishers, 1980), pp. 176-177.

Commenting on Freire's style of writing, - Tom F. Balke says, "Freire's text may lose certain readers who are unable to invest the time and effort to navigate his philosophical-linguistic discourse. Certain sections of the text may be accessible only to those educators and theoreticians of the progressive left who are comfortable with Freire's language of liberation. Feminist readers may experience difficulty in dealing with the masculine language used throughout the text. Some readers may also yearn for examples of women's initiatives in the fields of cultural action, education, Conscientization, and social change."[593] M. David doubts the work of freire in his book saying, "His discussion of peasant literacy is written in a language replete with academic abstractions and newly coined expressions that speak only to an elite male intelligentsia. He also leaves basic questions unanswered. Could not 'Conscientization' be another means of anesthetizing and manipulating the masses? What new social controls, beyond simple verbalisms, will be used to implement his social policy? How is Freire's humanistic and liberating ideology reconciled with the logical conclusion of his pedagogy -- the physical violence of revolutionary change?"[594] Bruce Boston says, " it ill behooves an educator for liberation to present himself to interested readers cloaked in such an obscure, convoluted (complex and difficult to understand), dull, overly metaphysical style, devoid of the real human experience which generated such provocative ideas."[595] According to Edgar Z. Friedenberg, "There is certainly no honor to be gained by putting down a work so well intentioned and generally well-received. This is a truly bad book. The pedantic style, the consistent understatement of the opposition and the very peculiar avoidance of Freire's own extensive experience as a source of illustrative material, in preference for fragments of published work.[596]

Paulo Freire's concept of *conscientization,* according to **David Millwood** is "almost as a new religion with Freire as its high priest. Others see it as just so much hot air with Freire as chief windbag."[597] Though Freire, in his literacy work was involved with real men and women,

> Freire produces only abstraction when he writes about the human person. In his writings the person lives often in no historical time; has no body, passions, and emotions. Since the concept of oppression is an important concept in Freire's social philosophy, it is unfortunate that he does not give a more adequate treatment of it. No criteria are given

[593] Tom F. Balke, "Review of The Politics of Education." *Studies in the Education of Adults,* April 1986.

[594] M. David, "Review of The Politics of Education." *American Anthropologist,* March 1986.

[595] Bruce O Boston, "Paulo Freire." In *Paulo Freire.* Stanley Grabowski, ed. Syracuse University Publications in Continuing Education, 1972, quoted from http://www.google/paulo_Freire.

[596] Edgar Z. Friedenberg, Review of Pedagogy of the Oppressed. *Comparative Education Review,* Oct 1971.

[597] David Millwood, "Conscientization and What It's All About." *New Internationalist,* June 1974, quoted from http://www.google/paulo_Freire.

> for judging what objective exploitation would be or what a responsible person would do. Though Freire's theory of conscientization is impressive, it still suffers from a number of weaknesses. Freire has valiantly attempted to avoid the idealist position, but it appears that he does not succeed. His theory of conscientization depends on some sort of transcendent view of reality through which individuals come to see what is real and authentic. There appears to be little room in his view for the painful struggling with different views and opposing viewpoints. It all comes down to the dominant classes with their distorted view of reality and conscientized individuals with their view of the reality that really is. Casting social reality in black and white terms is more characteristic of the simplistic religious preacher than the critical philosopher of knowledge and education.[598]

Mathew Zachariah says Conscientization appears to be a movement that has seen its heyday.

> Conscientization may be criticized for not proposing concrete measures for improving the standard of living of the people. Conscientization may also be criticized for being patronizing in its own way. Do ordinary men and women need to be conscientized before they recognize that they lead desperate, oppressed lives marked by hunger, disease, and the denial of dignity? They know the score and do not need middle class do-gooders to tell them. They acquiesce in their oppression because they have no other choice. To offer them hope through Conscientization is worse than deceitful. What they need is for people to fight on their side, so they can overthrow the oppressors. Conscientization has been criticized for evading or worse, camouflaging the issue of leadership. No amount of talk about 'educator-educatees' and 'educatee-educators' can get around the fact that there are teachers and students in Conscientization. It is a short step from that criticism to characterize the leaders of culture circles[599] not benevolently as 'teachers' but as meddlesome, outside agitators.[600]

Ivan Illich says, the term Conscientization has been coined in Brazil to label a kind of political self-help adult education organized mostly by clergymen popularizing Marxist categories to help the poor discover that they are 'humans.'

---

[598] John L. Elias., & Sharan Merriam. *Philosophical Foundations of Adult Education.* Krieger Publishing, 1980, quoted from http://www.google/paulo_Freire.

[599] A distinctive learning environment, called the 'culture circle.' Peter MacLaren and Peter Leonard, *Paulo Freire: A Critical Encounter,* p. 111.

[600] Matthew Zachariah, *Revolution through Reform.* Praeger, 1986, quoted from http://www.google/paulo_Freire.

It could be used by the historian to describe an enterprise that was decisively shaped by the Church through the institutionalization of the sacrament of Penance in the 12th century, an enterprise that since then has been followed by other techniques. "I would call Conscientization all professionally planned and administered rituals that have as their purpose the internalization of a religious or secular ideology. Conscientization consists of the colonization and standardization of vernacular probity and honour through some universal set of institutional rules."[601] After hearing reactions from different quarters about his new found concept – Conscientization, Freire responded, "I am trying to forget the word 'Conscientization,' but not the process. For the last seven years I never used the word. That word is too much corrupted."[602]

The overall impression is that Freire is being asked to provide a universal answer to all the educational problems of our societies. It is as though he were regarded as a *guru* whose message offers a solution to problems of which he is not even aware. What is happening is that Freire is being turned into a kind of fetish, as a witness to the interest in his 'method,' his 'Conscientization,' his 'system,' as though he were offering a universal panacea (remedy for all maladies).[603]

John Elias comments about Freire's treatment of the concept of *Oppression*. The problem with Freire's social criticism is its simplistic nature. Freire deals only in vague generalities. Oppression is never clearly defined. Freire concentrates on the oppression of the poor and fails to deal realistically with oppression as it is found at all levels of society. It is a mistake to see only the poor as oppressed and all others as oppressors.[604] In an interview with Freire, Gary quotes as saying, "For years I have been searching for an instance in which peasants have broken out of their oppression, even at a local level, but have found none. When I asked Freire, he admitted that neither has he."[605]

Freire's *anthropology* does not take consistently into account the diverse sources of limitations to human freedom. Consequently, it tends to present a too simplistic and optimistic view of the actual possibilities of socio-political transformation. Further, this radical change is referred to often as if it were merely a matter of perceiving its necessity and then willing its occurrence. The Marxist influence certainly does not help to correct these appreciations, which fail to take

[601] Ivan Illich, *Gender*. (Pantheon, 1982), p. 158, quoted from http://www.google/paulo_Freire.

[602] George Mathew, ed. *A Day with Paulo Freire* (Delhi: Indian Society for Promoting Christian Knowledge, 1980), p. 68.

[603] Pierre Furter, "Profiles of Educators." *Prospects*, Vol. 15, No. 2, 1985, quoted from http://www.google/paulo_Freire.

[604] John L. Elias, Conscientization *and De-schooling* (London: Westminster Press, 1976), quoted from http://www.google/paulo_Freire.

[605] Gary MacEoin, "Conscientization for the Masses." *National Catholic Reporter*, March 17, 1972.

into account the complexity of the problem of the human predicament and the pervasive presence of radical evil in particular."[606]

Many charges have been laid against Paulo Freire particularly about *dialogue* and *originality*.

> Some have seen him as a dangerous and violent revolutionary. Others have seen him as a quaint, rather unoriginal and eclectic philosopher. It is difficult not to feel that he richly deserves the accusation that he is, jackdaw-like, borrowing concepts, which cannot be torn from the detailed material and economic arguments in which they are embedded. One major criticism had been that Freire's concept of dialogue is contradictory. In my view there are considerable grounds for saying he is wrong-headed about material conditions and therefore for calling into question his whole concept of dialogue. Others suggest that Freire's concept of dialogue is 'contradictory' because it involves strong intervention, purpose and structure on the part of 'teacher-learners.' Are his theories about dialogue anything more than an elaborate attempt to bridge the gap between the leaders and the people by blurring their differences? His comprehensive and frequently unclear terminology persistently veils and perhaps also dissipates the thrust of his writing. The reader's expectations are frustrated constantly by the countervailing tensions and paradoxes which pervade his writing.[607]

"On first reading, Freire's eclecticism is refreshing. Considered more carefully, it's a disaster. One may call Freire, existentialist, Marxist, structuralist, and Christian but he fails in his attempt to graft his Christian ethical categories onto his Marxist concept of historicity."[608]

From the above criticisms it seems as though Freire's educational theory addressed those who are oppressed and the oppressors. How about those who were neither oppressed nor oppressors within the same community? His use of terms such as oppression and dialogue has a certain ambiguity which is discussed by his critics in the preceding passage. Freire seems to be silent about such questions. However, this section does not intend to answer Freirean critics rather it shows certain weaknesses in his theory and approach for further study and research.

One philosophy, however, is as groundbreaking now as it was in 1970s. Paulo Freire presents a very strong argument in pedagogy of the oppressed. These ideas challenge the very base of the establishment. Freire attacks many education

---

606 Daniel S. Schipani, *Conscientization and Creativity* (New York: University Press of America, 1984).

607 Tom Leach, "Paulo Freire." *International Journal of Lifelong Education*, Vol. I, No. 3, 1982, quoted from http://www.google/paulo_Freire.

608 David Nasaw "Reconsidering Freire," *Liberation*, Sep/Oct 1974, quoted from http://www.google/paulo_Freire.

systems for avoiding the problems that are so apparent. So, did Wesley challenge the bases of English educational system and attacked the kind of education imparted to students.

B. Re-reading Wesley's thoughts on Christian Education, and his Pedagogical Approach from the Perspective of Freirean Liberatory Pedagogical Paradigm

John Wesley did synthesize a philosophy of education that was an amalgamation of the ideas that he picked and chose from both religious and secular educators. From these educational and theological convictions, he not only challenged the foundations of English education, but called for reformation and re-framing of educational ideals and practices. Wesley showcased his views with the Kingswood School, the laboratory where he experimented with his own educational theory and method. As is noted in this chapter there are certain Wesley's pedagogical approaches which could be reframed drawing insights from Paulo Freire's ideas of liberation, humanization, Conscientization, participation and dialogue. The following points will show how they were in agreement on several educational issues though they belonged to different era in history. However, it is fact that Salvation/liberation cannot be forced upon individuals, it has to be experienced. Wittingly or unwittingly Wesley and Freire seems to indicate such a view.

1. Wesley and Freire: Commonalities in their thoughts and concerns

As was noted earlier, though Wesley and Freire were heroes of two different epochs, and contexts, and expressed their views in vocabularies that were prevalent in their times; yet their thoughts and intents have common strands of concern. The following points will clarify the above statement.

- For both Wesley and Freire issues (of human sufferings) and intents (emancipation) of their labour seemed to be the same but approaches were different. Both worked for the deprived and the marginalized class of the society. In turn they did impact the world of their times to an extent.
- Wesley's educational work was primarily humanitarian; his early schools were established for the poorer classes. He observed the poverty and misery of the poor, and he was moved with compassion to give them a better life/existence.[609]
- Freire worked for the Conscientization of the oppressed lots, to name the world as the world of exploiters, and to find a way of liberation.
- For Wesley internal experience was one of the causes to evolve an educational theory to liberate colliers and the marginalized people of his country whereas for Freire, external experience caused him to evolve

[609] Alfred H. Body, *John Wesley and Education*, p. 133.

an educational theory to liberate the oppressed/exploited people of his country.

- For Wesley the driving force was salvation of human beings from sin and suffering. On the other hand, Freire's basic concern was the freedom of people from their oppressors and the oppressive systems.
- For Wesley irreligious activities and social evils are due to the absence of religious education in the formal education system. Religious convictions compelled Wesley to work towards the liberation of humanity and society. He saw God in Jesus Christ as the only hope for human liberation.
- For Freire, education itself is change which enlightens people to name their situation or the world to recognize the forces behind their present plight, which conscientizes them to fight against oppressive elements, such as socio-political systems and powers. In other words, for him education is the liberative force. Social conditions compelled him to fight against the evil system.
- Wesley fought both spiritual and social evils of his time. Freire however, was more interested in fighting against the social system, and unlike Wesley, he was not compelled by religious convictions. In fact, religion had a very minor role in Freire's revolutionary educational programme.
- "A Religious education can only be successful under the guidance of a teacher in whom is the spirit of true religion."[610] For Wesley, the teacher played an important role in liberative education, as a friend and as a parent as well. Freire too recognised the important qualities of the teacher and the teaching act.[611] Thomas Groome expresses this approach more explicitly: "The heart of religious education is the heart of the religious educator."[612]
- Both Wesley and Freire were concerned with the person of the teacher and the qualitative relationship between teachers and learners. Modern educators such as Thomas Groome, Maria Harris and Daniel Schipani too are in agreement with Wesley's views.[613]
- Like Freire who developed his own course materials to teach Latin American adults so is John Wesley credited to have supplied a course of higher education providing provincial universities in his time.[614]

---

[610] Alfred H. Body, *John Wesley and Education*, p. 67.

[611] Mary Elizabeth Mullino Moore, *Teaching from the Heart: Theology and Educational Method*, p. 173.

[612] *Ibid.*

[613] Mary Elizabeth Mullino Moore, *Teaching from the Heart: Theology and Educational Method*, p. 174.

[614] Elmer L. Towns, *A History of Christian Educators*, pp. 213-214.

- Interestingly, both Wesley and Freire were accused of almost being plagiarists in their writings, which is borrowing ideas from others without acknowledging the original source.
- Wesley seemed to have been the first one to regularize 'evening schools' for adults and 'early morning schools' without affecting their daily work.[615] So, did Freire with Latin American adult education.
- Both of them strived for 'individual' transformation, it was in terms of the individual in the community – for one in the Church, the other is society.
- Both stood for a biblical liberative approach to a holistic living. Both challenged the establishments, one the Church of England and other the political powers of Latin America.
- Wesley and Freire concentrated on the pragmatic spheres of life – re-awakening of the individual, political stance, and against the social evils.

2. The Process of Christian Education - Conscientization

One of the purposes of Christian education is to awaken that which is dormant in the learners which Freire called Conscientization. In other words, stirrup God given gifts in the educatee so as to enable him/her to realize full potentiality of his/her life. The process of Christian education then, is to make the learners aware of their relation to God and humanity not merely saving souls. Examining Freirean pedagogy would mean, Wesley's narrow objectives should replace the all-embracing ones. For instance, humanization must replace saving of souls only, i.e., restoring the whole being in the image of God rather than being concerned with saving souls only. Programmes should be inclusive in nature as exclusivist thinking has no much prospect in the post-modern world, Christian education must go beyond 'saving soul,' as spirituality alone will not suffice to liberate individuals; physical, psychological and faith aspects too constitute all round transformation of the learners which Freire aggressively promoted.

Wesley's overarching objective of Christian education was: "Our design is, with God's assistance, to train up children in every branch of useful learning."[616] Being committed to this conviction, he held that men must be saved by faith, where salvation would help them to become better citizens of their communities.[617] Teaching citizenship is the essential feature of education. Michael Ramsay the Archbishop of Canterbury, once talked of education as not being merely the imparting of knowledge but 'the drawing out of the powers of the mind, spirit and

[615] Alfred H. Body, *John Wesley and Education,* p. 139.

[616] John Wesley, "A Short Account of the School in Kingswood, near Bristol, 1768" *The Works of John Wesley,* 3rd edition, complete and unabridged, Vol.13, edited by Thomas Jackson (Grand Rapids: Michigan: Baker Books, 1998). p. 283.

[617] John Owen Gross, *John Wesley: Christian Educator* (Nashville: Board of Education, the Methodist Church, 1954), p. 15.

body' to transform them as better people.[618] In fact, Freire popularized this idea as part of his revolutionized educational philosophy in the twentieth century.

Wesley was a man of his time who advanced the cause of Christian education to the best of his ability. As Cragg commented, "it is only right to remember that few men in his [Wesley's] period did more to promote the cause of education."[619] The legacy of John Wesley however, does offer some implications for contemporary Christian education. Therefore, it is in this context that one must re-read and reconstruct Wesley's thoughts on Christian education today since a lot has happened and changed between the eighteenth century and the present century. Wesley's own followers have gone through a sea-change in their interpretation and approach to Christian education, particularly his own model school at Kingswood (later relocated to Bath near Bristol in UK). This section will re-examine Wesley's Christian educational thought in the light of Paulo Friere the modern educator and theorist. Though there are many educators, however, he has been considered as one of the most innovative and creative liberation educationist of our times. Re-reading Wesley's theory of education in the light of Freire's insights and the present education practice of the Methodists would help in appealing to the modern day learners and educators. One cannot question Wesley's intentions but some of his methods and approaches are hard pills to swallow. Pluralism, multiculturalism and cosmopolitanism[620] of the author's context compel to deconstruct certain ancient and archaic concepts such as 'will-breaking' and reconstruct Wesley's approaches to make them relevant for the post-modern educators and learners.

Early Wesleyans were ready to do whatever it took to provide Christian education; the question is: was their enthusiasm misguided? Or was it, due to certain circumstances, more important then, than now? The response could be "no" to both questions. Some of Wesley's and his followers' methods may be put to question but, not their motives. Further one could see nothing in the present day that negates the need for thorough Christian education. The details of the situation/context change. The excessive notions and theories in today's changing world of education provoke the same need for thorough Christian education that the vacuum of ideas and opportunities provoked on behalf of the poor of the 18th century England. But suffice it to say that we have not outgrown our need to keep Christian education in the 'primary' category for Methodists.[621]

---

618 Gary M. Best, *Transforming Lives: Christian Education in a Multi-Cultural Society* (Peterborough, Warrington: The Epworth, 2008), p. 11.

619 G. R. Cragg, *The Church in the Age of Reason (1648-1789)* (New York: Penguin books, 1970), p. 149.

620 Peter Pericles Trifonas, (ed), *Revolutionary Pedagogies: Cultural Politics, Instituting Education, and the Discourse of Theory* (London: Routledge Falmer, 2000), pp. 258-259.

621 Wesley Tracy, "Christian Education in the Wesleyan Mode", in *Wesleyan Theological Journal*, Vol. 17, No.1, (Spring 1982), pp. 40-41.

Though Freire did not talk about Christian education as such but while eliciting the nature of dialogue, he talks about Christian characteristics such as love, humility, trust, etc., without naming a religion. On the other hand, as was stated at the beginning, the Gospel forms the starting point for Wesley. Christian education is thus a special form of education because Christianity is a special form of religion. Love is the hallmark of the Christian religion. Loving is a human act, it must express itself in personal relationships. Horizontal relationships of inter-human loving are defined and made possible for humankind by the gift of love to human by God in an act of grace. In personal relationships, it is always the divine first and the inter-human thereafter. It is said, Christian education is far more than instruction, although it may begin there.[622] Murray says, "The centre of Christian education is Christ… the norm of humanity."[623] "All learning without love is but splendid ignorance."[624] Two centuries later Victor Murray echoes almost the same thought that 'love is the characteristic of Christian religion.'[625] "There is a saying that education is not education unless it teaches life's true values."[626]

For Freire (*Favela*),[627] the slum was like a laboratory from where he evolved his educational theory which captured the imagination of the world. Wesley established Kingswood in the vicinity of miners and poor farmers as a model school initially for the exploited poor and the needy children of the area to spread the message of liberative and transformative education. What made Kingswood school radically different from most other schools of its day was the undergirding religious motivation that pervaded every lesson, whatever its subject content. Because, Wesley's view of a good student was not just how clever he became but how transformed in moral and behavioral attitude he was.[628]

Wesley seemed to have admitted selected children in his Kingswood as he was against indiscriminate admission of all sorts of children (with the worst ones tending to corrupt the better).[629] On the contrary, he seemed to have worked mainly for those children from both the socially and economically backward community. Were their parents good? There is a seeming contradiction in his opinion and practice here. Elsewhere he says good parents have had some mischievous children and vice versa. How well did his charge against public

---

622 Wayne R. Rood, *Understanding Christian Education* (Nashville: Abingdon Press, 1970), pp. 338-339.

623 A. Victor Murray, *Education into Religion* (New York: Harper and Row, 1953), quoted by Wayne R. Rood, *Understanding Christian Education* (Nashville: Abingdon Press, 1970). p. 339.

624 Gary M. Best, "John Wesley and Christian Education" unpublished paper, (2003), p. 4.

625 Wayne R. Rood, *Understanding Christian Education* (Nashville: Abingdon Press, 1970). p. 338.

626 Gary M. Best, "Wesley and Education", a paper presented at Lincoln College, Oxford (14 May 2003), p. 18.

627 Paulo Freire, *Education for Critical Consciousness*, p. 82.

628 Gary Best, "Wesley and Education," a paper presented at Lincoln College, Oxford (14 May 2003), p. 8.

629 Elmer L. Towns, (ed). *A History of Religious Educators*, p. 212.

schools stand the test while examining his own model school at Kingswood? By his own admission in his remarks on the state of Kingswood school 1783, "at present the school does not in anywise answer the design of the institution, either with regard to religion or learning... children are not religious... learning is no better than at other schools."[630]

Regarding the facilities at the boarding home that Wesley established, he provided no cushion beds, instead simple food and strict discipline. After nearly three hundred years gap, the Methodist boarding homes in India are no better now than then. The author himself was a boarder in 1970s, substantiating it from personal experience. Though things have improved since then, due to various help coming from different funding agencies and are providing cotton beds. Methodist Schools have changed a lot keeping in mind the national or general curriculum and educational programmes and state policies. Narrow definition and interpretation of Christian education as Wesley thought and taught may not serve modern learners effectively. There is a room to reconstruct his thoughts and ideas to modernize them to be inclusive and effective for the twenty-first century readers.

3. Pedagogical Approach - Contextual relevance/rephrased

Freire does not discuss the issue of discipline as part of the education process, since his programmes were centred on adult literacy. Adults are supposed to be determined, disciplined and mature learners; on the other hand Wesley was dealing with children between 6-14 age groups. The issue of discipline is paramount in this age group. However, Wesley's discipline was so harsh, because he believed education must be "pain to be profitable."[631] Wesley defended the rigidity and strict discipline of his system as being the only way possible by means of which his schools could hope to avoid the vices and the slipshod intellectual activity of the schools of his day.[632] On the contrary, Freire gave lot of freedom to learners as he was working mostly with adults in volunteer non-institutional groups.[633]

Wesley's theology was so orthodox and his methodology so ancient, that for instance, he did not allow parents to visit their children while studying in his boarding school nor were the children allowed to go on vacation till their graduation. He did not allow children to play; instead Wesley let them do manual work in the garden to compensate for physical exercise. This famous rule forbidding Kingswood students to play continues to haunt Methodist educators even today. Therefore, present day Methodists have gracefully overwhelmingly

---

[630] John Wesley, " Remarks on the state of Kingswood School, 1783" *The Works of John Wesley,* 3rd edition, complete and unabridged, Vol.13, edited by Thomas Jackson (Grand Rapids: Michigan: Baker Books, 1998). p. 302.

[631] Wesley Tracy, "Christian Education in the Wesleyan mode," p. 45.

[632] Alfred H. Body, *John Wesley and Education,* p. 135.

[633] Eileen Bellett, "Religious Education for Liberation: A Perspective from Paulo Freire," *British Journal of Religious Education*, Vol. 20, No. 3, (Summer 1998), p. 138.

rejected his views on play which is amply made clear in their response to the questionnaire. This stance may have been resulted from his childhood memories, and as an undersized youth. Wesley was bullied and beaten for sport by his fellow students at Charterhouse and "he had seen enough brutal and debasing forms of fun among adults such as cockfighting and bull baiting."[634] But, more likely the rule reflects the practice of the Herrnhut Moravians[635] and the eighteenth century mindset with regard to play. The following quotation from John Wesley Prince, Professor of Religious Education at the University of Chattanooga, Tennessee, proves the point:

> In Wesley's day the physical, moral and religious values of play had not been discovered. As a matter of fact, play was looked upon as directly hostile to moral and religious development. It was for this reason that August Hermann Francke, a leading eighteenth-century educator, said, "play must be forbidden in all its forms." Wesley probably was influenced and was in agreement with Francke's philosophy.[636]

The author himself a boarder in 1970s, has a personal experience of this, where no parents were allowed to visit them during the school days, echoing Wesley's rule. Unlike Wesley, parents were allowed to see and collect their children/wards whenever school closed for vacation. There was not much time given for play but twice a day manual work was compulsory. It is enlightening to discover the roots of these rules now which were hard to understand then. The packed daily schedule at boarding schools had a lot of positive impact and kept mischievous students at bay. Any one found guilty of violating boarding school rules was expelled just like what Wesley did to those who tried to corrupt the good students. Those days most of the Methodist schools in Karnataka were under management of the Church, most schools had resident teachers involved actively in Church activities, particularly Sunday schools, Christmas programmes and Vacation Bible Schools (VBS) etc. In fact, they were part of the physical and the cognitive developments of the students as well as their spiritual formation. There are fond memories of good old days even today of intimate and holistic relationship between students and teachers. Unfortunately, most of the schools are aided by the state government today, and with that, the familial relationship that existed then between students and teachers has long been forgotten. Spiritual activities are hardly there except at the advent season. The commitment that existed then for teaching is no more a concern today. It is a job to be done and a profession to be improved upon is the attitude of teachers.[637]

---

634 G. M. Best, "John Wesley and A Christian Education," an unpublished paper (2003), p. 4.

635 Elmer L. Towns, (ed). *A History of Religious Educators*, p. 223-224.

636 John W. Prince, *Wesley on Religious Education* (New York: Methodist Book Concern, 1926), p. 145.

637 Interview with Ms. Ammol, Adela, (not real name), a retired Principal of Methodist Schools and the Manager of Baldwin Schools Bangalore, 2 July 2008.

Wesley seemed to have disapproved of the Utilitarian approach to education instead he advocated that education should have lasting impact on the learners and should not be used for short term gain. He believed education to be liberative and transformative of both society and humanity. In other words, he saw education as life-changing and life-enhancing rather than seeing it as simply a process by which one acquires certain information and learns skills.[638] True education produces good citizens and leaders to build a better nation and its future. It probably was the unspoken intention of Freire as well as Wesley when he said: "The grand end of education is to cure the diseases (sufferings/ills) of human nature."[639] Freire too did not believe in utilitarian attitude towards education. In other words, education should not be means for survival or for temporary gain, rather it should work as a change agent to liberate the oppressed and transform the oppressors thereby establishing an egalitarian society.

4. Liberation and Humanization- Wesley's understanding

Freire popularized the pedagogy of liberation, and it is interesting to note that Wesley too believed that Christian education seeks to liberate and humanize peoples, societies and cultures in conformity with scriptural teaching. For him education is liberative. Wesley thus used traditional terminology to express his educational thoughts such as salvation, regeneration, justification and sanctification. In modern language, all these terms meant to make an individual a better person, in faith, and practice. Salvation is a process, in fact, transforming straying or estranged human beings into reformed persons. Redemption of people in modern terminology is liberation, from their struggles and sufferings, be it spiritual or physical. Wesley worked for the liberation and transformation of colliers, and their children's poor conditions. He made an all out effort to liberate exploited and marginalized farmers, labourers and slaves alike. Here, Wesley's views are very similar in intention to that of Freire's liberative education.

In the given circumstances what Wesley wrote in his tract entitled "*Thoughts upon Slavery*"[640] in 1774 is commendable. Naboth Muchopa in his foreword to Wesley's republished article 2007, writes that Wesley "wrote and preached about the evils of slavery" as he was committed to the belief in "human dignity and equal worth before God."[641] His firm belief was that educating the oppressed people in the word of God would result in liberation from both physical and spiritual oppression. It sounds unfair to read too much into his statements from

[638] Gary Best, "John Wesley and Education", p. 2.

[639] Elmer L. Towns, "John Wesley" in *A History of Religious Educators*, p. 218.

[640] John Wesley, *Thoughts Upon Slavery*, First published in 1774. Republished by the Racial Justice office of the Methodist Church for the Bicentenary of the Abolition of Slave Trade Act (1807), (London: Methodist Church House 2006).

[641] *Ibid.*, pp. 2-3. Cf. "Interrogating John Wesley's Thoughts upon Slavery: A Black British and Caribbean Theological perspective," by Michael N. Jagessar, *Bangalore Theological Forum*, Vol. XL, No. 1 (June 2008), p. 71.

21st century's contextual reality. According to Michael Jagessar, Wesley and Wilberforce worked within a conservative Tory mindset and with an evangelical Christian ethos that strongly emphasized human depravity, sin, atonement and conversion among other things. These notions would have certainly influenced their faith and faithfulness. Wesley did teach in his later years that faith not properly nurtured by its fruits might well prove to be vapid. Yet, this does not mean that his understanding of salvation was holistic, to include social, political and economic liberation.[642] Probably not, if one looks at Wesley from a wider perspective, he was concerned with holistic human liberation. However, whatever, Wesley said and done those years had its own impact which history cannot lie, though it might not fit within the frame of Michael's critical thought after the gap of more than two centuries.

5. Role of Dialogue in the Process of Education

Wesley was vertical in his views and Freire was horizontal in his actions. Dialogue was an important part of Freirean education philosophy but Wesley seems to have given no importance to dialogue in teaching and preaching. At times, he appears autocratic and dictatorial in his teaching and preaching. However, there are instances where he seemed to have engaged in interactions with his audience, Kingswood children, and other leaders. As far as his teaching methods are concerned, he seemed to have adapted a monologue, and the banking system, which Paulo Freire disapproved. There is a need to modify certain Wesleyan thoughts in the light of Freirean views as well as present practice of Christian education in the Methodist Churches.

6. Analysis of Wesley's Educational Views, Convictions and Practices Concerning Education

Some of the following points are mentioned under section 'limitations of Wesley's methodology' however, they are discussed here again to restate his views and convictions.

- Is it fair to deal with a child's sinful nature and adult's acts of sin on the same pedagogical parameters? Wesley's view that children are capable of mature religious consciousness is based on his theological convictions and his doctrine of grace.[643] However, it seems unfair to deal with children's sin of omission and adult's sin of commission on the same level. Today his statements have to be re-read in the light of twenty-first century context.

[642] Michael N. Jagessar, "Interrogating John Wesley's Thoughts upon Slavery: A Black British and Caribbean Theological perspective," *Bangalore Theological Forum*, Vol. XL, No. 1, (June 2008), p. 68.

[643] James Riley Estep Jr. "John Wesley's Philosophy of Formal Childhood Education" in *Christian Education Journal*, Vol. INS, No. 2, (Fall 1997), p. 48.

- Is a militant approach to education necessary? For Wesley, the fear of God, holiness and wisdom were cardinal principles of education. Everything else had to be subordinated to these principles, and one had to serve them. First and foremost, he wanted to train soldiers for Jesus Christ, men who could fight and sacrifice, men of the calibre of the early Church. It appears that he had a military mindset; therefore, all his programmes do reveal this thought pattern. Many however, admired his energy but disapproved his theory of 'will-breaking and perpetual supervision.'[644] Probably one of the extreme statements he made was that, 'they, who teach children to love praise, train them up for the devil."[645] Some of these views need deconstruction in order to make his intension relevant for today's readers. His behaviouristic methodology needs transformation. Appreciation and encouragement are integral to the learning process, and recognition of a learner has its place in education.
- Will a puritan approach to education work in today's context? Wesley seems to contradict his own views in many instances. For example, he says, anything that is too much, either freedom or punishment, can adversely affect the young lives.[646] His approach to education in practice appears to be rigid and puritanical.
- While saying no to play, was Wesley oblivious of children's natural instincts? Psychologists would argue then, that, how can a growing child be deprived of natural instinct to play with peers? In this context one could recall, Horace Bushnell who, advocated play "as the symbol and interpreter of Christian Education liberty."[647] To authenticate his argument Wesley quotes a harsh German proverb – "He that plays when he is a boy will play when he is a man."[648] Southey calls this a "sour German proverb" and that Wesley had forgotten the sensible English saying, "All work and no play makes Jack a dull boy."[649] When seen in perspective that play in Eighteenth Century School did not consist of football, cricket or hockey but bestial sports like cockfighting, bearbaiting, and prize fighting. In addition to German influence, Wesley's memories at Charterhouse may have formed his rigid attitude

---

[644] Alfred H. Body, *John Wesley and Education*, p. 143.

[645] Elmer L. Towns, (ed). *A History of Religious Educators*, p. 220.

[646] Alfred H. Body, *John Wesley and Education*, p. 68.

[647] James Riley Estep Jr. "John Wesley's Philosophy of Formal Childhood Education" in *Christian Education Journal*, Vol. INS, No. 2 (Fall 1997), p. 49. Cf. J. E. Reed, and R. Prevost, *A History of Christian Education* (Nashville: Broadman and Holman, 1993), p. 319.

[648] Alfred H. Body, *John Wesley and Education*, p. 60.

[649] John Owen Gross, John Wesley: Christian Educator, (Nashville: Board of Education, The Methodist Church, 1954), p. 14.

towards recreation.[650] However, Wesley is not the only person to have made such a statement. Even August Hermann Francke,[651] a leading German educator of eighteenth century said, "Play must be forbidden in all its forms."[652]

- Wesley proposes too many things too early for young children to learn which is beyond their natural - cognitive and physical development.
- Wesley regarded secular education as equivalent to 'sending children to the devil' and large public schools as nurseries of all matter of wickedness.[653] What did Wesley mean by his over-generalization? It would seem then, apart from his schools and few other private schools, the rest were nurseries of wickedness. It sounds rather subjective and fundamentalistic and an over statement concerning the curriculum of other schools and play.
- "A Religious education can only be successful under the guidance of a teacher in whom is the spirit of true religion."[654] How does one know whether one has the spirit of true religion or not? What were the parameters that Wesley used to judge one's spirit of true religion?
- Some of Wesley's contemporaries objected strongly to the bringing up children too strictly: giving them more of religion than they liked; telling them of it too often; or pressing it upon them whether they liked it or not. His critics thought that the common methods that were used in those religious schools harmed them more, especially if any severity were used; and concluded by saying that those children who had been trained up in this manner, as soon as the restraint was taken off, were commonly worse than others.[655] The author agrees with the above view from his personal experience as a boarder, and many of his co-boarders were repulsive of the spiritual activities in the boarding homes, though they would not dare to rebel openly against the authorities.
- By modern standards, Wesley tried to impose maturity too fast on his Kingswood children. It seemed to contradict his own advice to teachers that if teaching is to bear fruit – you must tell them ten times over or you do nothing.[656] That is to say, repeat yourself, do not impose too much at a time, but wait for them to understand before you proceed

---

[650] John Owen Gross, John Wesley: Christian Educator, (Nashville: Board of Education, The Methodist Church, 1954), pp. 13-14.

[651] Elmer L. Towns, (ed). *A History of Religious Educators,* p. 190ff.

[652] John W. Prince, *Wesley on Religious Education,* (New York: Methodist Book Concern, 1926), p. 145.

[653] John Wesley, Sermon 94, "On family Religion" *The Works of John Wesley,* Vol. 7, p. 83.

[654] Alfred H. Body, *John Wesley and Education,* p. 67.

[655] Ibid.

[656] Elmer L. Towns, *A History of Religious Educators,* p. 222. Cf. *The Works of John Wesley,* Vol. 7, p. 82.

further in teaching. "Beware of that common, and accursed, way of making children parrots."[657]

- W. H. Fitchet wrote that, Wesley tried on a large scale, "to transfigure boys of seven or eight and ten into middle-aged saints."[658] His quick-fix solution to the so called sinful behaviours seems farfetched in today's context.
- The plethora of subjects published in 1768, that included french, latin, greek, hebrew, history, geography, chronology, rhetoric, logic, ethics, geometry, algebra, physics, music, biographies, and other religious material, would seem to an outsider that Wesley was providing a constipating intellectual diet.[659] In the Plain Account of Kingswood School published in 1781, two more subjects had been added - natural philosophy and metaphysics.[660]
- Wesley was the product of the eighteenth century, and he seemed to have shared its blindness to the meaning of childhood.[661] Wesley perceived every child as "bred in sin, apt to evil and altogether as a 'brand to be plucked out of the burning."[662] This perception may have hindered John Wesley to understand the nature of child objectively.
- Salvation by force: Wesley encouraged Kingswood masters to make sure that the pupils were all fully saved. A rather unstable English master by name James Hindmarsh instilled such a fear of damnation in the children that they became hysterical. He delighted in their utmost distress because he believed their screams indicated that the devil was being driven out of their lives. In September 1770, he took them to see a dead body to reinforce the impact of his words about their mortality and it resulted in thirteen days of religious fervour in which the Lord seemed to have rested on them and pierced their hearts with conviction. Wesley seemed to have approved it. On one occasion, Wesley himself placed a child's finger into the flame of a candle to convey a sense of the

---

[657] James Riley Estep Jr. "John Wesley's Philosophy of Formal Childhood Education" in *Christian Education Journal*, Vol. INS, No. 2, (Fall 1997), p. 48.

[658] John Wilkins Sigsworth, *World-Changers: Karl Marx and John Wesley*, p. 189, quoted from W. H. Fitchett, *Wesley and His Century*, Cincinnati: Jennings and Graham, 1966.

[659] John Wesley, "A short Account of the School in Kingswood, near Bristol,1768" *The Works of John Wesley*, 3rd edition, complete and unabridged, Vol.13, edited by Thomas Jackson, (Grand Rapids: Michigan: Baker Books, 1998). p. 283. See also, details of course of Academics at Kingswood school, *John Wesley and Education*, by Alfred H. Body, (London: The Epworth Press, 1936), p. 162.

[660] John Wesley, " A Plain Account of Kingswood School, 1781" *The Works of John Wesley*, 3rd edition, complete and unabridged, Vol.13, edited by Thomas Jackson, (Grand Rapids: Michigan: Baker Books, 1998). p. 295. Cf. John Wesley Prince, *Wesley on Religious Education*, (New York: The Methodist Book Concern, 1926), p. 138.

[661] Elmer L.Towns, *A History of Religious Educators*, p. 225.

[662] James Riley Estep Jr. "John Wesley's Philosophy of Formal Childhood Education" in *Christian Education Journal*, Vol. INS, No. 2 (Fall 1997), p. 47.

pain in hell.[663] This is an extreme and fanatical approach to teaching. Today, such acts are considered outrageous and primitive; of course, modern educators would deplore such methods of education.

- Inconsistency and reactionary elements are evident in Wesley's pedagogy and approach. For instance, he said, "if too harsh measures were adopted, it will not be strange if religion stinks in their nostrils."[664] At the same time, he instructed his teachers to make sure that students were fully saved and the method applied to achieve this objective was cruel (cf. above point). His reaction to Rouseau's *Emile* is noted earlier, and his sharp reaction to public schools of his time is also stated earlier. However, many of his educational views are unquestionably eccentric.[665]
- Will his revival methods/pedagogy work with twenty-first century learners? Wesley's position is that religious education and change/conversion supplement each other. Therefore, he said, 'the goal of all work with learners at home, in the schools, in the Methodist society is to make them pious, to lead to personal religion and ensure salvation/liberation.[666] The purpose of religious education for Wesley was to instill in children true religion, holiness and the love of God and humankind, and to train them in the image of God.[667]
- He was an Ecologist: Wesley had profound and prophetic educational qualities; as an educational leader he was far in advance of his times in which he lived.[668] It is true that one can find an ecologist in John Wesley, concerned with environment far ahead of modern eco-theologians. For instance he set up his school in the woods in order to teach health and environment with practical examples, he encouraged gardening,[669] pulling weeds, hoeing, etc; he exhorted the parents with the concepts of justice and mercy. Do not hurt anything that has life. Do not rob birds' nests; much less kill animals not even snakes for they are like innocent worms or toads.[670]

---

[663] Gary Best, "Wesley and Education," a paper presented at Lincoln College, Oxford on (14 May 2003), p. 9.

[664] Alfred H. Body, *John Wesley and Education*, p. 68.

[665] John Wesley Prince, *Wesley on Religious Education* (New York: Methodist Book Concern, 1926), p. 103

[666] John Wesley Prince, *Wesley on Religious Education*, p. 87. Cf. Elmer L. Towns, *A History of Religious Educators*, p. 218.

[667] John Wesley Prince, *Wesley on Religious Education*, (New York: Methodist Book Concern, 1926), p. 87-88.

[668] John Owen Gross, *John Wesley: Christian Educator* (Nashville: Board of Education, The Methodist Church, 1954), p. 3.

[669] Alfred H. Body, *John Wesley and Education*, p. 142.

[670] John Wesley, *The Works of John Wesley*, Vol. VII, p. Sermon, 95, p. 98.

- His visit with Moravians in Germany after "Aldersgate" experience had left him with a deep admiration of their piety, yet Wesley disapproved their tendency towards spiritual complacency and the personality cult which had grown up around Count Zinzendorf, a Moravian leader.[671] Unfortunately, this thought did not spare either Methodists or its leaders. Sycophancy and spiritual complacency appear to be at its worst among the top leadership especially spiritual leaders today.
- His teacher-student ratio, one master to five students does indicate an extremely advanced perception of the education system.[672]
- Parent-teacher meeting of today at schools seems to owe its origin to Wesley. He instituted a procedure that weekly Wednesday masters-parents meeting to build a better relationship between parents and schools.[673]
- Freire was a revolutionary activist so was Wesley during his time, addressing varied issues that deprived human beings' rightful and happy living.
- Wesley's education system in a way was 'binding' a person to Christian understanding of life, its values apart from social life. Freire's system was in terms of 'liberating' the individual in society.

As noted earlier, Wesley was strongly influenced by what John Locke had said: that the natural human mind, in its original state, would seem to be blank. Its content is drawn from two sources – 'external sensible objects and internal operations.' These are 'the only original from where all ideas take their beginnings.' In other words, "the mind of the child at birth is like a blank sheet of paper."[674] Hence, one must be careful in imprinting values that would have lasting impact.

The goal of education according to Johann Friedrich Herbart is, to produce civilized and cultured human beings.[675] It is not merely saving souls as Wesley thought as part of his education process; instead it should go beyond that. Thus, true education should be challenging, exciting, vibrant and interesting. It should extend one's horizons. It should be life-enhancing not life-restricting.[676]

---

[671] Albert C. Outler, (ed). *John Wesley* (New York: Oxford University Press, 1964), p. 353.

[672] Alfred H. Body, *John Wesley and Education,* p. 140.

[673] *Ibid.*, p. 139.

[674] Wayne R. Rood, *Understanding Christian Education* (Nashville: Abingdon Press, 1970). p. 286.

[675] *Ibid.*, p. 312.

[676] Gary M. Best, Transforming Lives: Christian Education in a Multi-cultural Society (Peterborough, Warrington: The Epworth, 2008), pp. 19-20.

7. Framework of Freire: Its Implications for Wesleyan thoughts on Christian Education and Contemporary Methodists Education Ministry

In order to help assess and analyze the work of both the Methodists in Karnataka and John Wesley the founder of Methodism for objectivity, relevance and application from the perspective of Paulo Freire is considered as suitable in this context. Though Freire has not been considered as a Christian educator *per se*, he has had Christian influence directly from his mother and indirectly from the religion of his country. His perspective on education has been liberative. His objective of education has been to Conscientization people that will help transform human beings for a holistic living. Therefore, one can infer Christian concerns in his writings as well as in his liberative work. God's command to Egyptian Pharaoh "Let my people go" (Exodus 5:1; 7:16,; 8:1, 20; 9:1,13; 10:30) must have been the compelling force for Freire to embark on such a radical liberative education in his own context. In other words, Freire's work has been within the premise of a biblical and a Christian environment, though he does not call it Christian education. Probably, Freire intended his views to have a relevance beyond the 'so called Christian world.' His inner convictions are clear when you analyze his comments on the Christian education teacher. He says, the "Christian education teacher is one who has undergone the 'Easter experience."[677] He continues further saying, good religious education in common with other areas of the curriculum depends, to a large extent, on the attitude of the teacher. Freire goes further, insisting that his coordinators[678] should be willing to die to themselves as experts in order to rise again as 'co-learners' in the education process. This new birth demands the re-orientation of one's attitude. According to him, the coordinators had to recognize that they did not possess all the answers. In education for liberation, there is no complete knowledge. Christian education teachers who seek to develop critical solidarity in their students must die in order to transfer knowledge to ignorant students in order to be born again in the search for knowledge. Christian education teachers need also to recognize the impossibility of neutrality. Freire says, "I have known the problems and the difficulties. I have in my life had to die as this intellectual I have been, in order to be born again as different one."[679]

Christian religious education for liberation, on the other hand does not require the removal of the Agreed Syllabus nor the structures planning. The way forward is in the willingness of the teachers to revolutionize their thinking so that

---

[677] Eileen Bellett, "Religious Education for Liberation: A Perspective from Paulo Freire," *British Journal of Religious Education*, Vol. 20, No. 3, (Summer 1998), p. 139.

[678] Paulo Freire uses this term co-ordinator as synonym for teacher because he perceived that term teacher connotes oppressive structures.

[679] Eileen Bellett, "Religious Education for Liberation: A Perspective from Paulo Freire," *British Journal of Religious Education*, Vol. 20, No. 3, (Summer 1998), p. 140.

through Conscientization, an approach to curriculum development is initiated which is truly liberating.[680]

Of course, Wesley was not a theoretician as such but a practical Christian religious educator, though his approach and methodology were too harsh and primitive. Yet, his main objective was to transform the sinful humanity with the message of salvation or liberation in Christ. Wesley's narrow and vertical understanding of God and his liberative act needs reconstruction today. It is here Freire's framework of liberative approach to education helps in reconstructing Wesleyan thoughts in radicalizing Christian education programme for a liberative praxis. Thoughts on educational methodology such as similar to the 'banking' system of education, over-burdening the learners, with frightening methods and rigid approaches, narrow understanding of sin and salvation etc. Like Freire, one must take the whole gamut of vertical and horizontal relationships between God and humanity into account to build the kingdom of God on earth.

Thus, there are striking similarities with regard to the contextual realities and objectives of Wesley and Freire: both were working among the marginalized, oppressed, poor and the exploited, though Wesley had a large audience spread across in his fifty years of public service and Freire implemented his educational theory on a select people's group but both with the intention of radicalizing the education process towards a liberative and transformative objective. The Methodists too are ministering mainly among the poor and the downtrodden of the society, particularly rural and slum dwellers to empower them with the message of liberation and transformation. Although, there is a paradigm shift within the Methodists, their core concern is not completely abandoned. The Indian Methodists have gone through contextual changes in their theological and practical ministry. Methodism came from Untied States of America to India in 1856. Wesleyan thoughts were americanised in order to be relevant to their context. When the American missionaries came to India, they tried to Indianize/contextualize their views. At the same time, they encountered British Methodists already in India. To shorten the story, the missionaries and local leaders picked up selective ideas from both American and British Methodism and formed their workable agenda for their Church ministry. Therefore, there is considerable difference between what Wesley practiced and the practice of the present Methodists. The message of liberation seems relevant today as it was to Wesley and Freire. There is a need therefore to develop an approach to impart the message of liberation in Christ effectively without disregarding other's religions and faith. The aim and content of the Christian education approach should be rooted in praxis as Wesley the founder of Methodism was a practical man.

---

680 Eileen Bellett, "Religious Education for Liberation: A Perspective from Paulo Freire," *British Journal of Religious Education*, Vol. 20, No. 3, (Summer 1998), p. 141.

Summary

To conclude, John Wesley's and Freire's exclusive language could be seen as an aberration by the modern reader especially feminist readers. Freire was accused of being andocentric in his earlier writings by feminist writers. On the other hand, one must realize that they spoke the language of their days to express their concerns about systemic aberrations and oppressive structures; however, in a given socio-cultural milieu there is room to re-structure the language which is archaic in a sense.

To be fair, one must appraise the eighteenth-century educational endeavour, and not belittle Wesley's works by norms and standards of the modern psychologically-minded educational system and civilization.[681]

Alfred Body, however, opines that one must not overlook Wesley's contribution as the precursor of the great provincial universities of the present day, which have spread knowledge and culture throughout the land, breaking down the barriers of privilege and creed and making learning accessible to all.[682] In a way, there are lots to learn from both the educators, as well as to unlearn certain impractical approaches and difficult methods. Both, Wesley and Freire are not holding out gospel truths but suggestions for our educational system's improvement and implementation of those relevant approaches and methods for the advantage of modern generations/learners. What Wesley said is important: The service of man was a visible manifestation of his service to God.[683] Wesley indeed was the trend setter in a sense. His focused objectives and methods of education were a marked departure from traditional education. He believed that residential education away from towns and cities meant to bring effective change in learners' behaviour and attitudes, leading to transformed/civilized human beings. This is how an individual could move on to be a good human being and a Christian. Therefore, the ultimate aim of Wesley's education was to bring about change and liberate humanity from all that hindered this positive change and transformation. If strictly viewed from the Freirean liberative paradigm, Wesley may not come anywhere closer in comparison. However, if both are analyzed from a broader perspective as is seen in the section that mentions commonalities in their thoughts and views, both were reformers in their own rights; both had concern for the marginalized and exploited humanity. Both hoped to humanize society of their times. Both worked for the well-fare of the society without any strings attached. Both went through immense struggles like Wesley was almost thrown out of the Church of England, Freire was imprisoned and exiled for working in order to bring about liberation to those enslaved to the political and traditional systems.

Wesley helped the marginalized, the oppressed, and the exploited community of farmers and colliers to see what is holding them back from coming up to the

---

[681] Alfred H. Body, *John Wesley and Education*, p. 132.

[682] *Ibid.*, p. 142.

[683] *Ibid.*, p. 134.

levels of others in the society. Thus, conscientizing those through the process of education by way of teaching and preaching to liberate themselves from the forces and systems that blind folded them to experience the full life which God intended for each individual. His work and intention almost appears like that of Freire's without using those technical terms like Conscientization and Liberation.

On the other hand, the use of Paulo Freire's framework in this book does not advocate the wholesale adoption of the Freire's revolutionary theory of education; instead its intention is to serve as a framework to analyse the Wesleyan Christian education thoughts. The present context of the Methodists today seems to be no better than that of people's condition during Wesleyan era and Freire's people in Latin America. Therefore, this research work endeavours to assess the educational thoughts of Wesley and Methodists from the perspective of Freirean liberative approach to education and to propose an approach to Christian education whose aims and contents must be rooted in praxis. It is assumed that such an approach will have the capacity to be truly liberating and transforming.

The next section will highlight the findings and suggestions made towards the formation of a relevant Christian education in the light of insights derived from Wesley and Freire and the empirical research.

Chapter 5

Towards a Relevant Model of Christian Education

A. Theological Reflections, Findings and Recommendations 199

B. Relevance of Wesley's Christian Educational thoughts for Contemporary Christian Education, particularly Methodist Churches in Karnataka 208

Implications of this research 208

Proposals 209

Summary 212

Chapter 5

Towards a Relevant Model of Christian Education

A. Theological Reflections, Findings and Recommendations

It would seem that for Wesley, his reflections, his theological thinking, his thoughts on education, etc., started with his conception of sin in his understanding of the situation. In fact, John Wesley's argument is that human beings have inherited Adam's original sin. The entire human race, including children have inherited Adam's fallen nature and behaviour. They suffered because of Adam's fall, and have ever since suffered the most deplorable effects because of that.[684] He quotes Romans 5:12-20, to substantiate his stand: death through Adam and life through Christ, and "For in Adam all die, so in Christ all will be made alive" (I Corinthians 15:21-22). However, he admitted his uncertainty as to the method by which original sin is transmitted. He is of the opinion, however, that it is handed down by natural generation through the blood unity of the race with Adam.[685] Wesley infers the imputation of Adam's guilt from the fact of the sufferings of the human race. He constantly views the condition of human nature brought about by Adam's sin in terms of disease. All that is there in the world are sick of sin. Wesley says, "The whole world is, indeed, in its present state, only one great infirmary."[686]

Wesley was an eclectic educator, so was his theology. True to his nature he was selective even in his theological understanding of sin and its ill effects on humanity. He seemed to have developed his opinion about original sin and its consequences based on selective views of Augustine of Hippo (354-430),

---

[684] John Wesley Prince, *Wesley on Religious Education* (New York: The Methodist Book Concern, 1926), p. 21, quoted from *Works of Rev. John Wesley* M. A. Vols. II, p. 36 & V , 539-540, 548-549 from 1831 edition,

[685] *Ibid.*, quoted from *Works of Rev. John Wesley* M. A. Vol. V, pp. 539, 549 from 1831 edition.

[686] John Wesley Prince, *Wesley on Religious Education* , p. 23, quoted from, *The Works of Rev. John Wesley* M. A. Vol. II, p. 545.

and reformers like Martin Luther (1483-1546) etc. As Augustine maintains, sin incapacitates humankind from doing good, and because humans are born sinners, they lack the power to do good.[687] Augustine further comments that human nature is biased towards evil as such that an individual is inclined to choose evil rather than good.[688] Therefore, human beings are helpless to do the good until grace falls upon them, and when grace is thus given they are irresistibly moved toward God and the good. John Wesley was thoroughly Augustinian in his view of the scope and destructiveness of sin and in man's inability through his own resources to cope with it.[689] But, Wesley being an optimistic English man, he was not a disciple of either Augustine or Calvin in their teaching of predestination where God seem to be projected as favouring few and condemning the rest for eternity. In other words, Wesley went all the way with Augustine on sin and grace just short of predestination,[690] because Wesley believed that God will not permit any person to be damned unless He damns Himself.[691] His belief was that the prevenient grace of God is like the sunshine which enables everyone to see, the air which every humans breathe, and the water which every one drinks; is everywhere available to everybody and it is entirely free.[692]

John Wesley further affirms that, human beings are sinners who can be saved only by the unmerited grace of God as revealed and conveyed in Jesus Christ. This sinful nature exists in various forms, so sin and its consequences affect one's life and existence in society. Therefore, in modern theology, sin is redefined in terms of social oppression, exploitation, acquiescence to injustice, passivity to evil and negative thinking etc. Therefore, Wesley insisted that the solution to this problem lies in what God has done for humanity in Jesus Christ. Following this logic Reformation theology too insists that Christ saves humanity, not only from the power of sin but also from its consequences.[693]

The truth that Wesley wishes to make clear is that as the individual is estranged from God, he is so, not by his own personal acts of disobedience, but by something deeper and inherent in his nature, that he believes to be original sin. Wesley describes human nature as wholly degraded, and that a considerable portion of the lost image may be regained, although the vessel that contains this will stay nonetheless earthen in its character.[694] Wesley thinks that humankind is under the dispensation of grace, which is universal and efficacious in supplying

---

687 Walter A. Elwell (Ed), *The Concise Evangelical Dictionary of Theology* (Grand Rapids, Michigan: Baker Book House, 1991), p. 467.

688 John Wesley Prince, *Wesley on Religious Education*, pp. 27-28, quoted from, *The Works of Rev. John Wesley* M. A. Vol. V, pp. 548, 562, 586, 593.

689 William R. Cannon, "Salvation in The Theology of John Wesley," p. 4.

690 *Ibid.*

691 John Wesley, *The Works of John Wesley*, 3rd edition, Vol. 6, Sermon 59, sec.14. p. 240.

692 William R. Cannon, "Salvation in the Theology of John Wesley," p. 5 (yes it was then but nothing seems to be entirely free these days, everything is either taxed or priced).

693 Walter A. Elwell (ed). *The Concise Evangelical Dictionary of Theology*, pp. 467-468.

694 John Wesley Prince, *Wesley on Religious Education*, p. 33.

whatever deficiency may be owing to fallen nature. So he explains grace as the big, broad ocean of God's mercy, while faith is the refreshing wave from that ocean that washes up the desolate human shore to quicken it and make it productive and capable of Christian growth.[695] Wesley taught that not only is salvation due to grace, but that the creation of Adam and the life of all people and their strength and everything they possess is due to the same power. Salvation is the very highest blessing in the power of grace to confer.[696] In other words, Wesley's theology affirms God's sovereign will to reverse humankind's sinful, devilish nature by the work of the Holy Spirit, a process he called prevenient, justifying and sanctifying grace (grace being almost synonymous with the work of the Holy Spirit).[697] Salvation is completed by one's repentance and return to the original right relationship with the Creator by the work of the Holy Spirit.[698] The universal efficacy of God's grace is the heart of Wesley's Arminianism. [The Jacobus Arminian was a celebrated Dutch Reformed Theologian (1560-1609). His school of thought is called the Arminianism which insisted that "the divine sovereignty was comparable with real human free will; that Jesus Christ died for all and not only for the elect and unlike two fractions of Calvinistic views of predestination which are unbiblical. Both fractions, like the Supralapsarian- is a doctrine of predestination which maintains that God decreed the election and non election of individual before the fall of Adam and Sublapsarian is also Calvinistic doctrine of predestination which holds that it was only after the fall that God decreed the election or non election of individual to salvation. This teaching has been common among the Calvinists].[699] Arminianism believed that Christ died for all and his free grace is available to all. The individual has the freedom either to accept or to reject Christ. This view was popularized by John Wesley.[700] The teaching of salvation or liberation is the central concern in the theology of John Wesley. He was an evangelistic theologian.[701] His writings indicate the above views aplenty. According to him, sin has no power to affect adversely the behaviour of the true Christian; however, there is a tendency to backslide and a possibility of sinning.[702] Therefore, Wesley writes, that you are to work out your own salvation with fear and trembling; for it is God who works in you both to will and to work to desire the right.[703]

---

695 William R. Cannon, "Salvation in The Theology of John Wesley," p. 6.

696 John Wesley Prince, *Wesley on Religious Education,* p. 34.

697 Walter A. Elwell (Ed). *The Concise Evangelical Dictionary of Theology,* p. 549.

698 *Ibid.*, p. 550.

699 Ref. *The Oxford Dictionary of the Christian Church,* Oxford: Oxford University Press, 1998, pp. 1552, 1560. Also cf. John Wesley Prince, *Wesley on Religious Education,* p. 36.

700 Walter A. Elwell (ed), *The Concise Evangelical Dictionary of Theology* (Grand Rapids, Michigan: Baker Book House, 1991), p. 40.

701 William R. Cannon, "Salvation in The Theology of John Wesley," p. 3.

702 *Ibid.*, p. 7.

703 John Wesley Prince, *Wesley on Religious Education*, p. 38, quoted from *The Works of John Wesley,* Vol. V, p. 574.

According to him, the definition of first "repentance is a conviction of one's utter sinfulness, guiltiness, and helplessness…."[704] In other words, first know yourselves and realize who you are in light of God's holiness. Thus, the individual who is convinced of his original sin passes the porch of repentance, but is not yet born again and cannot be said to have entered the edifice of religion. The person must pass through the door of faith. Surprisingly, it is difficult for the reader to separate which one is prior, repentance or faith, for they merge into each other almost imperceptibly. The point Wesley wants to make is that he who comes to God in faith must fix his/her eyes on all that is bad in themselves and sincerely feel a lack of all that is good.[705] To be more plain, in the thought of Wesley the new birth is not merely an outward change that leads to an exact performance of religious and social duties. But, it is the new disposition, an inward transformation into the mind that was in Christ. The bent of the nature is changed. The carnal nature is changed into holiness, and the disease of nature is arrested. The love of the world gives way to the love of God, pride is replaced with humility, self-will merges in the will of God and sensual tempers are transformed into spiritual. These are the first principles of Christianity, but more is required of the individual for his eternal salvation than these principles. However, the individual should keep working out his/her own salvation and keep moving towards Christian perfection. Faith working by love is the length and breadth, depth and height of Christian perfection or holiness of God. He further clarifies that Christian perfection/ sanctification/holiness,[706] does not guarantee that an individual is free from carnal 'man' but they have to guard constantly against sin, and practice the power of Christ. The liberative grace keeps a person so long as the person keeps it, in other words, so long as he that is born of God keeps himself, the wicked one will not trouble him, but if he keeps not himself, and if he not abide in faith, he may commit sin like any other persons.[707] Thus, the individual's faith-power is received through Christ to overcome and to advance in perfection.[708]

On the other hand, Wesley held a lofty conception of holiness. He never professed to have attained it; he hesitated in believing he possessed it. In reply to an allegation by other Churchmen; he said: "I have told the entire world I am not perfect; I tell you flat, I have not attained the character I draw."[709] However, the Methodists strive forward with God's help that is how they desire to be distinguished from others.

---

[704] John Wesley Prince, *Wesley on Religious Education*, p. 38, quoted from *The Works of John Wesley*, Vol. V, p. 47.

[705] *Ibid.*, p. 50, quoted from *the Works of John Wesley.*

[706] John Wesley Prince, *Wesley on Religious Education*, p. 57. (Wesley uses terms such as piety, real-religion, Christian perfection, holiness, and sanctification interchangeably in his writings)

[707] William R. Cannon, "Salvation in The Theology of John Wesley," p. 8.

[708] John Wesley Prince, *Wesley on Religious Education*, p. 61, quoted from *The Works of John Wesley*, Vol. I, pp. 108, 124.

[709] *Ibid.*, p. 62.

Wesley's position with regard to Christian religious education follows logically from his theology. It was noted that he believed in the depravity of the entire human race including the young ones. According to him, both young and old are alienated from God due to the fall of the first Adam/man. He also believed in the universally efficacious grace of God. He was of the opinion that the whole human race is by nature evil, yet no individual is altogether evil, indicating that there is hope for every repentant sinner of regeneration in Christ. It is also noticed that liberation or salvation from sin is the main purpose in life which begins in repentance and the conviction of one's own despicable condition. Transformation is possible through faith in the redemptive and liberative work of Christ. The result of this work in an individual is inward and outward holiness/sanctification, growing experience in the love of God and humankind, sustained and nourished by the means of grace.[710] These theological views were liberally used in his writings as well as in his preaching to reach out to the common people with the message of liberation/salvation by faith in Christ and in his atoning grace. Wesley's educational theory was that religious experience is possible in childhood; therefore, the goal of all work with children, at home, in the school, and in the Methodist societies is to make them pious, to lead them to personal religion, and insure salvation.[711] The intention is not to familiarize them with Christian rituals; rather the purpose of Christian education is to instill in children the true religion, holiness and love of God and humankind, and to train them in the image of God.[712] Wesley's theology, if closely analyzed then, was largely a theology of reaction to those biased theological views of his time. However, he was quick to borrow those views that were biblically sound and practically understandable by common people. Wesley's eclecticism is no surprise though he was considered to be a man of one book. At times his reasoning is unsound as it was noted in his handling of Children's salvation and Christian perfection. There may not have been essentially any new contribution made either to theology or education as such by Wesley. As Albert Outler put it that Wesley was neither a 'theologians theologian' since he belonged to no single school of theological thought, nor did he establish one.[713] However, the effective uses of those views from others are commendable.

Therefore, the onus of Christian preaching, Christian education and all other ministries of the Church of Christ should be to bring about awareness of people's own spiritual condition leading them to experience God's free grace and healing which is liberation (Salvation) be it from original sin, oppression, exploitation or any other forces that deprive human beings of true happiness and fullness of life.

---

[710] John Wesley Prince, *Wesley on Religious Education*, p. 81.

[711] *Ibid.*, p. 87.

[712] John Wesley Prince, *Wesley on Religious Education*, pp. 87-88.

[713] Albert C. Outler, "The Place of Wesley in Christian Tradition," in *The Wesleyan Theological Heritage*, edited by Thomas C. Oden and Leicester R. Longden (Grand Rapids: Zondervan Publishing House, 1991), p. 77.

Helpful Suggestions and Recommendations:

- One of the findings of this research work is that Wesley was not only a reformer, preacher but an educator too in his own right. The notion of Wesley being identified only as a reformer, preacher, and hymnodist is also now recognized as a pioneer of education. Though some of his thoughts such as 'no play,' military kind of discipline, keeping children in isolation from the society etc., could be reconstructed so as to make these thoughts relevant to the present context, he is an educator apart from being a reformer. Reformation and societal transformation is an outcome of his educational work and preaching.
- Wesley adapted harsh methods to impose a salvation experience on young children at Kingswood school. God in Christ Jesus never imposed His will on humanity; rather an individual has been given freedom to choose either to accept or to reject Christ. Salvation ought to be a personal experience, should not to be thrust upon individuals. Such polemical views should consciously be avoided.
- Wesley was not afraid of borrowing good/healthy thoughts from other scholars and implements them on his own terms. He agreed with the views that were in accordance with his theological convictions and disagreed with those views which he thought were unintelligible. Methodists should review their stand in the light of this finding especially with regards to ecumenical relationships, women's ministry and theological openness.
- Wesley did not shy away from challenging the wrong practices of his time; his challenge was not merely a political rhetoric as he practically proved their fallacy. For instance, he challenged the fundamentals of English education and proved to the world that it could be done better by way of showcasing Kingswood school as a model of both Spiritual and Secular education, the two faces of the same coin. Methodism will do well, if they retrace their present programmes to their founder and follow them earnestly.
- For Wesley sin was a serious issue, no matter who commits it. Therefore, he did not differentiate a child's sin from an adult's sin as both are in need of forgiveness and redemption/liberation. Whether it is fair to deal with a child's sin on par with that of an adult or not is a different issue. If Wesley had been part of twenty-first century thinkers, he would de-construct his eighteenth century thoughts; would advocate the progressive theories and views relevant to the theological and socio-political context of the day.
- Wesley's military approach to education from a puritan perspective to discipline was acceptable then. Now, it may not yield same results. His military mindset and behaviouristic methodology in educational process needs reconstruction.

- Wesley's famous 'sour German proverb'- "He that plays when he is a boy will play when he is a man,"[714] sounds anachronistic today. This attitude was rejected by a majority of the Methodist respondents, and certainly educational psychologists will not approve such a theory as part of the learning process today. As every religion or faith believes in the redemption of a person – in turning over to be a better person, as Wesley himself believed. His attitude towards the transformation of a person lacks consistency.
- Wesley's overstatements about public schools, forcing religion on children and harsh discipline indicate his subjective and fundamentalists' nature of his convictions and the eighteenth century attitude towards the approach of puritan austerity.
- W. H. Fitchet wrote Wesley tried on a large scale, "to transfigure boys of seven or eight and ten into middle-aged saints."[715] His quick-fix solution to the so-called sinful behaviours seems farfetched in today's context. In no way, Christian educators would adapt such a method in their teaching.
- Wesley's curriculum could be described as a constipating intellectual diet. Being an eighteenth century product, he seemed to have shared its blindness to the meaning of childhood.[716] This perception may have hindered John Wesley to understand the psychology of the child objectively. This is an eye-opener for the present educators to avoid extremes of any kind in the educational system.
- Wesley's fanatical approach to teaching such as placing the finger of a child on flame of candle to convey a sense of pain in hell is deplorable. No one should think of repeating such an inhuman approach to learning.
- Inconsistent opinions, reactionary aspects and fundamentalistic elements are evident in Wesley's pedagogy and approach. In other words many of his educational views are unquestionably eccentric.[717]
- Wesley no doubt, had profound and prophetic educational qualities. But, as an educational leader he lacked the means of implementation as under-girded by the needs and demands of learning in the light of education psychology, though he was way ahead of his times.[718] He was indeed an ecologist, concerned with the conservation of

---

714 John Wesley Prince, *Wesley on Religious Education* (New York: The Methodist Book Concern, 1926), p. 145.

715 John Wilkins Sigsworth, *World-Changers: Karl Marx and John Wesley*, p. 189, quoted from W. H. Fitchett, *Wesley and His Century*, Cincinnati: Jennings and Graham, 1966.

716 Elmer L. Towns, *A History of Religious Educators*, p. 225.

717 John Wesley Prince, *Wesley on Religious Education,* p. 103.

718 John Owen Gross, *John Wesley: Christian Educator* (Nashville: Board of Education, The Methodist Church, 1954), p. 3.

the environment, being far ahead of modern eco-theologians. For instance, he set up his school in the woods in order to teach health and environment with practical examples. He encouraged gardening,[719] pulling weeds, hoeing etc. He urged: "Do not hurt anything that has life. Do not rob birds' nests; much less kill animals not even snakes for they are like innocent worms or toads."[720] This is an important instruction and suggestion that every teaching fraternity must inculcate this attitude in their scholars.

- Wesley disapproved personality cult and sycophancy. Unfortunately, his followers particularly American Methodists in India seems to have nurtured the same tendency of personality cult, what was once disapproved by their founder. There is perceived difference between British Methodists' form of worship and Indian Methodists' worship in Karnataka as well as their attitudes towards leadership. This could serve as a wake-up call to the present Methodists to honour their founder's principle rather than man.
- The concern for a healthy teacher-student ratio, one master for five students, and the need for parent–teacher meetings, we owe it to Wesley. In fact, he had instituted a procedure to hold weekly Wednesday masters-parents meeting to build a better relationship between parents and schools.[721] This could be emphasized with a greater degree of urgency today to have a better understanding between teachers and parents to improve the child's learning.
- If the goal of education according to Johann Friedrich Herbart is to produce civilized and cultured human beings,[722] then it is not merely for saving souls as Wesley thought. Thus, true education should be challenging, exciting, vibrant and interesting. It should extend one's horizons. It should be life-enhancing not life-restricting.[723] Wesley did what he could in a given context. However, there is always room for modification to suit it to the present context without devaluing one's convictions.
- Generally, the overarching influence of John Wesley's educational and theological thought is seen in all spheres of Methodist ministry in Karnataka. However, these must be strengthened further to keep the legacy of Wesley alive, and pass on the same to next generation.

[719] Alfred H. Body, *John Wesley and Education*, p. 142.

[720] John Wesley, *The Works of John Wesley*, Vol.VII, p. Sermon, 95, p. 98.

[721] Alfred H. Body, *John Wesley and Education*, p. 139.

[722] Wayne R. Rood, *Understanding Christian Education* (Nashville: Abingdon Press, 1970). p. 312.

[723] Gary M. Best, *Transforming Lives: Christian Education in a Multi-cultural Society* (Peterborough, Warrington: The Epworth, 2008), pp. 19-20.

- Wesley used at times the 'Revival method of education,' to lead people to liberation (Salvation) in Christ; He advised his teachers to adapt the objective methods for effective learning along with the 'Root and Branch' method. Without doubt his curriculum was content centred being true to his traditionalist/essentialist[724] approach to education. Wesley presupposed his methodology based on his notion that a learner is a 'blank sheet of paper'[725] though it is not stated anywhere in his writings, at times his educational methodology vivifies the fact. Friere called this kind of an approach to education as 'banking' method and he disapproved it since it negates the very meaning of 'education.'
- Wesley believed that the service of humanity was only a visible manifestation of his service to God.[726] In that, his educational methods and activity were channels for God's transformative activity.
- Wesley remained an aristocrat[727] in spirit and typically autocratic[728] in dealings with educational and ministerial issues. This type of tendency in leadership is as such incompatible with the modern trends.
- Wesley and Freire are on par with each other in the use of exclusive language, and are accused of being androcentric in their writings, which need to be modified and adapted to suit one's situation today.

The respondents have a good idea of what is meant by Christian education and its aims and objectives as shown in table number seventeen of the third chapter.[729] Their Sunday school materials are in line with their theological convictions. Many agree with the theological and educational thoughts of John Wesley because they are biblically sound and practically viable. His educational thoughts are plain and his theological views are practical. The whole purpose of his preaching and teaching is to lead people to experience liberation in Christ. However, many respondents have rejected his idea of 'no play' theory since it is an outdated view of a one-sided philosophy. On the other hand, some older generation of the Methodist Church in Karnataka think it is a good idea to keep children away from mischief.

---

724 The aim of essentialism is to transmit knowledge, to master the facts. This is what Freire called 'banking' and he opposed such a method of teaching

725 Wesley Tracy, "Christian Education in the Wesleyan mode," p. 43.

726 Alfred H. Body, *John Wesley and Education*, p. 134.

727 *Ibid.*, p. 133.

728 *Ibid.*, p. 140.

729 See page 123 of the present book.

B. Relevance of Wesley's Christian Educational thoughts for Contemporary Christian Education, particularly Methodist Churches in Karnataka

John Wesley's simple theological and broad-based educational theory does offer insights for today's Christian education ministry of the Methodist Churches in Karnataka.

Conscientizing the young learners is a natural function of education, and Christian education in all its forms can encourage that process.[730]

While analogies are not wholly exact either in comparison or in meaning, yet they indicate a message: Christian education without worship is like geography without maps and field studies, science without its experiments, theory of music without singing or playing an instrument, learning to swim without entering the water, and literature without reading books.[731] So, from this, one can draw the following conclusions.

Implications of this research

1. One must learn to take the ideals and practices of others to formulate them to suit one's own context of educational and theological convictions.
2. The leadership of the Church should not be over concerned about the funds and give up their fundamental theological and educational convictions while running the educational institutions. Commercialization of education goes against the Methodist founder's basic conviction.
3. The character and the function of the teacher are paramount to the educational process, and the success of any educational endeavour depends on the quality of the personnel involved. Careful attention should be given to selection and training of the faculty both academically and more importantly spiritual qualities and experiences.
4. Wesley used education as a means to a spiritual end. That is to say, transformation and liberation of the world in Christ needs to be realized and accomplished through Christian education.
5. Christian education must be critical not of its own practices and contents, but it needs to set itself as a model programme to other educational institutions particularly in regard to their well balanced curriculum and academic discipline.
6. Wesley had considerable authority over the educational programmes of his time and the personal involvement in the implementation of his planned curriculum. However, certain practices of modern Methodism reflects a departure from Wesley, namely the freedom of teaching Christian education has been curtailed considerably because the other funding agencies have been allowed to run the show. Indiscipline in boarding schools and Churches too

---

[730] Gary M. Best, *Transforming Lives: Christian Education in a Multi-cultural Society*, p.164.

[731] *Ibid.*, p.156.

is evident. Teacher-student familial relationship is missing since there are no residential tutors any more.

7. Wesley made all possible efforts to improve the quality of education and desired to change it at its fundamental levels. His challenge did help in reinventing educational ideals and practices particularly at the Kingswood school.

In the light of these implications the present Methodist Schools and leaders in Karnataka have a lot to work towards improving the existing schools and boarding homes to keep the legacy of Wesleyan ideals and practices alive. Wesley's thoughts and practices may be ancient. But, his ideals and principles do offer a relevant direction for the present Christian education ministry in the Methodist Churches of Karnataka today. However, 'Problem posing' methodology of Paulo Freire is a corrective suggestion to Wesley's 'banking system' or traditional approach to education as well as Christian education ministry of the Methodist Churches in Karnataka.

Freire's framework will also help to reconstruct Wesleyan fundamentalist approach to discipline and imposition of religious views on the learner.

Wesley's theory of education makes use of almost every element of his theology and is indissolubly associated with it. If his theological premises are agreed upon, the consequent educational principles appear rational and logical; other than this, many of his educational theories and approaches are eccentric and questionable. Therefore, significance of Wesley as an educator should not be judged, however, so much by the particular details of his pedagogy as by the deep-seated conviction which he held that education itself is the most probable method of bringing religion to children and making them Christian. He championed the central idea of Christian education that children are not to be left to grow up in sin but must be carefully disciplined and instructed from their earliest years possible.[732]

Proposals

According to a famous Chinese proverb: "If you are planning for a year, sow rice; if you are planning for a decade, plant trees; and if you are planning for a lifetime, educate a person."[733] Therefore, Christian educational institutions should have the following characteristics;[734] to make Christian education relevant today, and its curriculum should have a systematic progression in making the learner a transformed person. That means the Christian education curriculum needs to be geared towards personality formation and to be a powerful liberative and transformative force.

---

[732] John Wesley Prince, *Wesley on Religious Education*, p. 148.

[733] Gary M. Best, *Transforming Lives: Christian Education in a Multi-cultural Society* , p. 20.

[734] *Ibid.,* pp. 37-38.

- Christian education course should adapt a questioning approach, in Freire's language 'problem posing' approach which searches for the real transformative truth and not just what may be socially, politically or culturally acceptable;
- Christian education programmes should not be treated as merely story telling activities in the Sunday schools instead it ought to have high academic standards because each child deserves the best; in other words, it should be educative and informative at the same time;
- Christian education must strive to impress upon the learners that the affirmation of wisdom and humility as valid objectives of the educational experience;
- Christian education must teach to appreciate the importance of forgiveness leading to liberation, reconciliation leading to transformation, and renewal of relationship with God and humanity; in other words, education must strive to inculcate in the learners the value of tolerance and harmonious living in multi-cultured society like India;
- Christian education programmes must create passion for justice combined with indignation at prejudice and intolerance in whatever form that it appears;
- One of the major focus of the Christian education activities is a recognition of the importance of one's worth and self-knowledge, combined with an equal understanding of the importance of community and environment, so that the needs of the individual are balanced with the needs of society;
- Christian educators should inculcate the values of respect both for oneself and for other people including the nature;
- There must be a space for creativity, and openness; inclusive ideals should be carefully crafted as part of the education and learning process;
- An effort must made to imbibe an understanding of the concept of service and of human responsibility for the welfare of the world that God has created;
- A refusal to accept the traditional views that things have to be the way they are and a belief in larger possibilities for good because education should be an instrument for transforming the society in the interests of justice and freedom;
- Christian education ought to impress upon the learners an attitude of appreciation that the learning is a life-long process and that the more we learn the more is expected from us;
- This research has pointed out that there is huge gap between the work of John Wesley and the ministry of present Methodists. However, it is possible to bridge the gap by the renewed commitment to legacy

and educational thoughts of John Wesley. Therefore, the research recommends that the thoughts of Wesley are as relevant today as much as they were then.

In the light of whole discussion in this research work, the following proposals and objectives for the Methodists Christian education ministry in Karnataka have been framed as recorded below.

They are: first proposal is to lead the learner or individual to know the world that God has created and to participate in it as a responsible citizen. A second is to lead the learner or individual to encounter the world, person to person. This encounter begins with listening, especially listening to the poor and the oppressed, whose voices may be the hardest to hear. A third proposal of Christian education is to lead persons toward social consciousness so that they will know themselves as social beings apart from being Christian connected with other beings in socio-cultural systems.[735] Such social awareness includes an awareness of how the action of one person affects other persons. One other common purpose is a natural outgrowth of the other, that is, to lead individuals to envision how their decisions in this moment will contribute to a better future. Individuals and communities are encouraged to see themselves as participants whose praxis, i.e., performative actions in the world will influence the future shape of the universe.[736]

Therefore, the first objective of a broad based education should be to lead a person to know and participate in the whole world as responsible citizen, including every individual and the eco-natural world. Addressing oppressions in the individual's own situation would expand to include oppressions where culture meets culture, tradition meets tradition, and nation meets nation.[737]

The second objective is to lead a person into encounter with the world, Individual to individual; this includes listening to one another and to the physical world – its groans and needs – and to those excluded, i.e., marginalized, and oppressed individuals from social participation for any reason including reasons other than economic oppression. These persons may be children, women, the aged, individuals with disabilities or any other socially outcastes. Encountering the world also includes listening to those who are more oppressors than the oppressed, for even their voices are heard very little at the deeper level.[738]

The third objective is to lead persons to social consciousness so that they will know themselves as social beings connected with others in a web of social relationships, including all elements of the world as part of the social matrix. Social consciousness is important if individuals are to know themselves within a matrix of social relationships. Methodists cannot afford to live in isolation and be

---

735 Mary Elizabeth Mullino Moore, *Teaching from the Heart: Theology and Educational Method*, p.181.

736 *Ibid.*, p. 181.

737 *Ibid.*, pp. 181-182.

738 Mullino Moore, *Teaching from the Heart: Theology and Educational Method*, p. 183.

oblivious of the society in which they live. They have a responsibility to live both as witnesses to kingdom values as well as social beings. This is essential to both liberative and transformative teaching in a fragmented world such as the twenty-first century.[739]

The last objective flows from the others mentioned above. Educational intention is to lead persons to envision how their decisions in this moment will contribute to the future of the whole planet earth. The key to Conscientization is acknowledging that all of the earth is affected by what we study and do not learn, and what we intend to do and do not do.[740]

Summary

Wesley and Freire were educators in their own right. But for the linguistic differences and times, there are striking similarities in their convictions, approaches and purposes of their educational activities. They were reformers in a sense, radicals at times in action, and spoke against wrong practices such as slavery, exploitation and oppression. The ultimate end of their dream was the liberation of humanity and transformation of the society. Wesley talked about spiritual redemption leading to total liberation and Freire talked about political liberation leading to humanization and transformation.

Some of the educational theories and methods of Wesley and Freire may be questioned but not their motives. Particularly Wesley believed in the primacy of Christian education and he strove to provide Christian education no matter what others thought of him. Further nothing among the twenty-first century Christians that negates the need for thorough Christian education instead there is an urgency and felt need amongst the parents to inculcate Christian values either through formal (Christian education) or informal teaching (family/Church worship). Even the world provokes every human being that there is a need for egalitarian values such as equality, justice and peace today as the vacuum of ideas and opportunities provoked on behalf of the poor of the eighteenth century England of Wesley's day. But, suffice it to say that Methodists of today have not outgrown the need to keep Christian education as a primary course to impart Christian and moral values. According to the questionnaire data something seems strangely out of joint when you see the poor state of affairs in practice of Christian education in the Methodist Churches of Karnataka. There appears to be misuse of Wesleyan legacy in order to survive as a denomination not as dynamic alternative to growing Christian sects and schisms. Many groups within the Methodism seem to have fallen prey to the so called 'holiness cult' subtly developed by western world. Therefore, Methodists in Karnataka have to go back to what Methodism stands for: Scriptural Christianity, personal theology, transformed living, tolerant churchmanship, warm-hearted worship, single faith, consecrated laymen and

---

739 Mullino Moore, *Teaching from the Heart: Theology and Educational Method*, p. 185.

740 *Ibid.*, p. 186.

devoted womanhood.[741] This in no doubt will help revitalize people of God, particularly Christian education ministry of the Churches in Karnataka.

Though Wesley did not discover/invent an educational theory like educational philosophers such as Paulo Freire, he synthesized available educational theories of his time and used them with necessary change based on his convictions and context.

The author being part of the academic world opines however, that neither the revivalist method of John Wesley nor the radical pedagogical approach of Paulo Freire will appeal to the learners of the twenty-first century; rather a balanced pedagogical approach may be more desired by learners and teachers of the post-modern world.

For both of them seem to take an extreme stand such as Freire who talks about, 'de-schooling' a radical shift from the conventional schooling system and Wesley talks about, 'formal schooling with properly framed curriculum and strict discipline.' However, an approach which takes into account the learners' past story, the present contextual experience and the future hope could form a model for the present day Christian education activities. In other words, the ideal approach to education should not be utilitarian in nature alone but it should provide the learners with both wisdom and insight, sense of what is right and fair and the direction that one can follow through their lives.[742]

The famous words of Wesley carved on a huge stone at the entrance of Kingswood school indicates the focus of his educational system – to do good to oneself and to others:

"Do all the good you can, by all the means you can, in all the ways you can, in all the places you can, at all the times you can, to all the people you can, as long you ever can."[743]

However, Wesley opined, 'we will effect change in the world best if we first transform ourselves and play our part to the best of our ability. It is far too easy to talk of transforming and liberating others without ever changing ourselves first.'[744] Similar thought is found in the quotation of the 13th Century Persian poet, Jalal ad-din Rumi. **Yesterday I was clever, so I wanted to change the world. Today I am wise, so I am changing myself.**[745]

---

[741] Frank Baker, *A Charge to Keep: An Introduction to People Called Methodists* (London: The Epworth Press, 1954, p. 40.

[742] Gary Best, *Transforming Lives: Christian Education in Multi-cultural Society*, p. 2.

[743] Mary Elizabeth Mullino Moore, *Teaching from the Heart: Theology and Educational Method*, p. 191.

[744] Gary Best, *Transforming Lives: Christian Education in Multi-cultural Society*, p. 17.

[745] David C. Scott, quoted in his correspondence with the author on 23.01.2016.

Conclusion

John Wesley was a multifaceted personality as is noted in chapters one and two. He showed interest in every subject matter that was known during his times such as science, mathematics, economy, philosophy, medicine, music, politics, theology etc. In other words, he was a theologian, an educator, a reformer and a politician in his own right. This work once again proves that Wesley made enormous contribution to education apart from many other services to the people of his country.

Wesley was raised in an orthodox Christian minister's family. His mother was an ardent Puritan in religious practice. She had a telling influence on the life and ministry of John Wesley. One of the chief sources of Wesley's detailed programme of training children was his mother. Therefore, he held his mother in high esteem for that indelible impression that she had on his life. Apart from his mother, Wesley came under several influences ranging from spiritual leaders to philosophical scholars such as Moravian brothers, educators like John Amos Comenius and John Locke among others.

The socio-political and religio-cultural conditions in Wesley's time were disdainful, moral and spiritual standards were at the lowest level. In fact, the eighteenth century England was characterized by a decay of religious licentiousness of morals, public corruption and profanity of language, while loose living, rioting and lawlessness were common and Christianity had no bearing on the people. Corrupt political and moral practices had caused increase in crimes, drinking, slavery, child labour, exploitation and oppression of the poor and marginalized people. In the light of such a scene, Wesley had declared, "our nation stands on the brink of destruction."

Educational conditions due to this were grim and gloomy, with a total lack of religion and religious motive. This pitiable situation stirred up John Wesley to save his people/country from decay and destruction. Like Paulo Freire, Wesley stood against the evil practices of the day saying religion and education must go together; people may be poor, they need not to be ignorant, but they deserve to know who they are, the world they live in and the oppressive forces that operate within that world. Thus, for him breaking down the barriers of privilege and making learning accessible to all, was important.

John Wesley's life had amazing and surprising antecedents which has been discussed in his brief biographical section. John Wesley seems to have had a premonition that he was destined to make a mark in God's ministry since his miraculous escape from the burning rectory in the month of February 1709. Wesley's Charterhouse schooling, Christ Church College education at Oxford, his involvement in parish work with his father, his election as a Fellow of Lincoln College Oxford, his fondness towards children, his adventurous missionary trip to Georgia, his famous Christian experience of "Warmth of Spiritual bliss" at Aldersgate, his involvement with so called 'holy club' at Oxford, etc., have had a lasting impact on his ministry and mission of the Church of Christ. All these above colourful experiences from childhood till Oxford days helped him to achieve positive results in educational front as well as with the Church of England are discussed in the second Chapter of this book. Chapter one is a brief summary of his background, his compelling concerns for the marginalized and the emergence of Methodist movement are its salient features.

Chapter two details the educational endeavour of John Wesley. The important personalities who helped Wesley in his thought formation are discussed in the first section of the chapter. His impulsive and elusive nature is noted in his reactions to educational theorists and general education of the eighteenth century. Some of his radical methods of teaching and fanatical approach to education with their implications to contemporary Christian education are discussed in this section too.

The second section of the chapter deals with his understanding of God, man, sin, salvation, humanity as a whole, Church and mission, family and education, etc., which were fundamentals to Wesley's thought formation and bases of his educational theory. His convictions in God and fallen nature of humanity compelled him to involve himself in the liberative and transformative educational programmes using all possible mediums and places, be it pulpit, street corners, convention platforms, house visits, Bible studies or journal writings, etc., to save and liberate every oppressed, exploited, marginalized people of the country and beyond. His concerns were simple and genuine yet he was considered a controversial figure by his own mother Church as well as the theological, political and social spectra. Some considered him a Quaker, a Papist, and a ranting enthusiast by many according to Richard Heitzenrater a well recognized author on Methodism.[746] These comments reveal though unwittingly that he was a powerful popular public figure. In the midst of these controversies and misperceptions, many have acknowledged that Wesley in most cases was trying to hold the middle ground, a stance that is characteristic of his theological and educational method.

[746] Richard P. Heitzenrater, *The Elusive Mr. Wesley*, 2nd edition (Nashville: Abingdon Press, 2003), p. 31.

Growing in maturity he went about his ministry, changing his stance and views at times, learning from his and other's mistakes, and developing his own theories of education to see that children are transformed into the likeness of Christ which he termed perfection.

The third section deals with the specific characteristics of John Wesley's educational theory and approach. He affirmed that the 'task of education is character building and guarding against indiscipline.' The grand objective of education is to cure the disease of human nature because the fallen nature of humanity has set the wrong way; education is designed to set it right.[747] In other words, the purpose of religious education is to instill in children true religion, holiness, the love of God and humankind. He felt that education as a means to character building would lead to transformation in one's life if the same is undergirded by a Christian perspective. Wesley had lofty conceptions of Christian education. His theory and methods were carefully crafted keeping this task in mind. He advised his teachers to adapt pedagogy of liberation so as to make education a process of humanization, liberation and justice. He believed this task cannot be achieved by teachers alone; it has to be a collective effort. Therefore, apart from teachers, he encouraged his preachers and parents to be participants in this liberative process of education. However, he had his limitations in the conception of his educational theory and method which the last section of the chapter points at. Some of his views (about children's play, rigid discipline, too much to learn at too early age, frightening methods of teaching religion etc.) today are considered rigid and anomalous, pointing to Wesley's confused 'intellectual' approach to education.

Chapter three analyses the empirical data. The empirical survey was limited to Methodist Churches in Karnataka covering nine district Central Churches and seven Bangalore city Churches were covered. 400 individuals were administered the questionnaire containing nearly 100 questions, out them only 210 responded; after scrutiny only 200 were selected for random sampling and analyses. 50 Individuals were interviewed over a period of 7 months.[748] Many have given conventional answers since the questionnaires were administered by senior pastors. If they had been done otherwise, it is assumed their answers could have been slightly different. On the other hand, many have sent their completed questionnaires directly to the researcher. Therefore, that assumption need not be true. Many have agreed with Wesleyan views and thoughts in principle but in reality the effect of his ideals are watered down. There is a considerable gap between Wesley's intended objectives of his theology and education compared to the present ministerial activities of the Methodists.

---

[747] John Wesley Prince, *Wesley on Religious Education*, p. 95.

[748] Interviewee names are not mentioned either in footnotes or in bibliographical entry for it was agreed by the interviewer not to publish their names. However, their names and other details are with the author.

The first section of the Chapter traces the theological foundation of educational ministry of the Methodists. Wesley's theological convictions and ground reality of the existing educational system of his country compelled him to embark on such a mission in establishing schools with a distinct curriculum based on his liberative praxis to showcase them as model schools to his known world. For Wesley, the ultimate purpose of education was to liberate people from their pitiable conditions and transform their lives as well as the society in which they lived, ushering in the just and egalitarian world.

The second section deals with the way the Wesleyan legacy of education is carried on by his followers called Methodists all over, particularly in India. This ministry of Christian Education is channelled through various wings of the Church Ministry like Sunday schools, Men's fellowships, Women's fellowships, Boarding schools etc.

The third section deals with the assessment and analyses of the empirical study.

Questionnaires are categorized and tabulated under different heading- the first one details the profile of the respondents, male-female ratio, their educational qualifications, whether they are from urban or rural congregation, their age group etc.

The second category of the questionnaire is aimed at probing into their Church and ministerial activities. Wesley, in a sense broke away from his mother Church for lack of spiritual mindedness and activities in the Church as well as among the ministers. In principle, Methodists consider themselves evangelical in faith and practice as compared to other mainline Churches. A majority of the respondents answered in line with this policy of the Church.

The third category questions were specific in nature intending to find out activities related to education, boarding schools, Sunday schools and the kind of materials used, kind of teachers involved in Sunday school ministry and the meaning of Christian education etc. Related to this aspect was to find out about youth fellowships, young men's fellowships and women's fellowships. Further, questions were intended to find out the objectives of their fellowships and how far they are able to achieve those set objectives. In the midst of all these informal questions was the fourth category which was the aim of this book, which is about John Wesley' educational thoughts and what they knew about it. Answers were encouraging as it is discussed in the chapter. The last category was about the general education system to find out their understanding and opinion about it. A majority of the respondents are well informed, as most of them are educated people. They know the value of education, particularly Christian education. While analysing their answers, it is found that there is no correlation between their theoretical knowledge of John Wesley and his actual educational thoughts. They have an idea of who John Wesley is but do have an idea of his educational contributions. There is no clarity as to the practical application of Wesleyan ideals in the Church and as well as in an individual's life. Though every respondent believed that Wesley's teachings are relevant today, they were seldom utilized in practice. In other words, the findings have revealed that there are gaps between the founder's intended purpose and the present practice and faith of the Church.

The fourth Chapter discusses Paulo Freire's brief life sketch and highlights his educational theory and approach to education which is used as a theoretical framework to analyse John Wesley's educational thoughts. Freire being the most modern theorist, his contribution to education is recognized worldwide as was Wesley in his century and thereafter. There are striking similarities between Wesley and Freire which are discussed in the second section of the chapter. What stands out among the two is that their ultimate objective was to liberate human beings from oppressive and exploitative forces and systems by restoring their lost human dignity to those victims of the system. They applied education as a method and means to conscientize the marginalized to recognise the exploitative world so that it will help them to liberate themselves by opposing such systemic forces.

The first section discusses briefly Freirean (main) educational conceptions such as conscientization, liberation, humanization, his problem posing and dialogical method to education etc. From his educational philosophy, insights are drawn and applied as a framework to analyse and re-read Wesley's educational thoughts on Christian Education. Though both the scholars belonged to two different epochs, and expressed their views in a language that was understandable by the intended people's group, their motives and concerns seem to have commonalities. There are a lot of insights from both the leaders that are relevant to reconstruct the present Christian education programmes particularly that of the Methodist Churches in Karnataka. However, there are certain inappropriate views and approaches that need to be deconstructed in order to make them relevant.

Basically, Wesley and Freire were reformers, educators and scholars in their own right, and no doubt history has acknowledged their contribution to the field of education.

The fifth and the final chapter highlights the theological resources and reflections which influenced Wesley to take a stand that was not in line with his mother Church and yet, how he was successful in his endeavours. His intent and sincerity in the service of humanity and children were unquestionable though certain of his methods and approaches to Christian education were harsh and primitive.

Wesley was a disciplinarian with a compassionate heart; our present Methodist leadership has lots to learn from the life and ministry of John Wesley. His leadership qualities of discipline and courage in the mission and evangelism of the Church are commendable. When the established Church remained hostile to his way of interpreting and preaching the Gospel, he was able to give an institutional form to his movement and thus start one of the most influential movements in Protestantism. His work and its effects on England and North America are a testimony for successfully resisting the monopolistic ambitions of a state Church (the Church of England).

The second section briefly mentions the relevance of Wesley's Christian educational thoughts for contemporary Christian education particularly the Methodist Churches in Karnataka.

The educational and evangelistic challenges implicit in the Christian education programmes of John Wesley should inspire and challenge the present Christian education and ministerial activities of the Methodists in Karnataka. His teachings and preaching were aimed at raising people's consciousness to value the importance of Christian Education to Methodists and there are some strategic ways in which his thoughts on Christian education should guide one to learn the theory and concept of education today. There is a definite need for more 'holiness'[749] among people who would understand and treasure the Wesleyan legacy. It is a challenge to own and incorporate it into the collective life of the Church, and allow it to guide and help shape the Methodists' unique identity afresh again.

Wesley believed in the union of education and religion, such was his method in promoting Christian education. The problems of today call for disciplined minds devoted to the pursuit of truth which no one will deny. But the ability to resolve them calls for something in addition to intellectual skills. It needs an honest approach to resolve the problems of life with a religious resolve. The drive that made John Wesley a great humanitarian was the result of a religious experience which caused him to love the Lord his God with all his mind and soul. However, this calls for an ontological education approach that is under-girded by a religious perspective, yet overriding it, to impart a liberative perspective in a pluralistic situation as in India. So, then the educational programmes or curriculum envisaged thus incorporates within itself to bring to the learner an outlook, openness to a secular and human approach, to move towards a transformative experience – that is liberative of the self, others and structures of governance so that its efforts are seen in the society to establish justice and peace. The most disturbing foe to ignorance, poverty and other elements which breed unrest, as John Wesley has shown, is an **educated Christian** ready to follow the implications of his Christian convictions.[750]

The most outstanding fact of Wesley is that being an ordained minister of the established Church of England,[751] he had the courage to support his conscience and convictions with action. He stood his ground despite severe opposition, from his own Church of England during the eighteenth century, and went ahead preaching 45,000 sermons moving on horseback with the message of liberation and transformation.

[749] People who are justified, sanctified and are faithful followers of Christ striving towards perfection in life and ministry of the Church of Christ.

[750] John Owen Gross, *John Wesley: Christian Educator*, p. 30.

[751] Wesley was disappointed with the ruling Anglicanism.

Finally one may conclude by saying that John Wesley was and is a rather elusive figure, as a person, as a leader, and as writer. Some of these are normal considerations that confront almost any attempt to reconstruct the life and thought of a historic person like Wesley.[752]

This research work has been a great learning process. It has helped the author to discover some of the important thoughts and convictions of John Wesley, the pioneer of Methodist movement which became a denomination later in the history during his time. It has proved beyond doubt that Methodism has a vibrant history and legacy which must be passed on to the next generation without diluting its founder's commitment and convictions to the cause of truth, justice and liberation.

In conclusion, the present research details the implications of reviving Wesley's reconstructed educational approach today and suggests proposals for a programme in that light, it calls for a fresh and a relevant model of Christian Education (programme) to be formed that is liberative and transformative in its aim and purpose. For there is no theory or approach to Christian education that can end its quest for a suitable model or approach, it is a continuous search for a relevant model and approach to liberative and transformative education in a rapidly changing world.

---

[752] Richard P. Heitzenrater, *The Elusive Mr. Wesley*, 2nd edition (Nashville: Abingdon Press, 2003), p. 26.

Bibliography

Primary Sources

Wesley, John. *A Plain Account of Christian Perfection*, London: The Epworth Press, 1990.

_________ . *A Short Account of the School in Kingswood, Near Bristol*, Bristol: Felix Farley, 1749.

_________ . *An Extract of the Life of Monsieur De Renty: A Late Nobleman of France*, 6th edition, London: G. Whitfield, 1796.

_________. *A Treatise on Christian Prudence*, extract from Mr. Norris, 2nd edition, London: W. Strahan, 1742.

_________ . *Collection of Hymns for Methodists*, London: Wesleyan Conference Office, 1877.

_________ . *Explanatory Notes upon the New Testament*, London: Epworth Press, 1950.

_________ . *Instructions for Children*, Wesley's Tract 2nd edition, London: Paternoster-Row; M. Cooper, 1745.

_________ . *John Wesley's New Testament*, London: Lutterwworth Press, 1938.

_________ . *John Wesley's Sermons: An Anthology*, edited by Albert C. Outler and Richard P. Heitzenrater, Nashville: Abingdon Press, 1991.

_________ . *John Wesley's Prayers*, edited by Frederick C. Gill, London: Epworth Press, 1951.

_________ . *Letters from a Parent on the Education of Children*, London: The Conference Office, 1800.

_________ . *Primitive Physick: An Easy and Natural Method of Curing Most Diseases*, London: R. Hawes, 1776.

_________ . *Reflections Upon the Conduct of Human Life: Learning and Knowledge*, 2nd edition, London: W. Strahan, 1741.

_________ . *Selected Prayers, Hymns, Journal Notes, Sermons, Letters and Treatises*, edited Frank Whaling, New York: Paulist Press, 1981.

_________ . *Sermons on Several Occasions*, London: The Epworth Press, 1950.

_________ . *The Character of a Methodist*, Wesley Tract 5th edition, London: W. Strahan and Henry Butler, 1745.

_________ . *The Complete Works of John Wesley*, 3rd edition, London: John Mason, 1829.

_________ . *The Enthusiasm of Methodist Compared*, part I, II & III, London: J & P Knapton in Ludgate Street, 1749.

_________ . *The John Wesley's Letters to a Roman Catholic*, Nashville: Abingdon Press, 1968.

_________ . *The Journal of the Rev. John Wesley, A.M. Vol. I-IV, From October 14th, 1735-October 24th,1790,* London: Wesleyan Conference Office, 1895.

_________ . *The Journal of the Rev. John Wesley, M.A.*, (8 vols.), London: The Epworth Press, n.d.

_________ . *The Works of John Wesley*, A bicentennial edition, edited by Reginald W. Ward and Richard P. Heitzenrater Nashville: Abingdon press, 1988.

_________ . *The Works of John Wesley,* 3rd edition, complete and unabridged, Vol.14, edited by Thomas Jackson, Grand Rapids: Michigan: Baker Books, 1998.

_________ . *Thoughts Upon Slavery*, First published in 1774, republished by the Racial Justice Office of the Methodist Church for the Bicentenary of Abolition of the Slave trade Act 1807, London: Methodist Church House, 2006.

_________ . *Treatise of the Imitation of Christ* by Thomas Kempis, Compared with Original and corrected throughout, London: C. Rivington, 1735.

_________ . *Wesley's Standard Sermons*, edited by Edward H. Sugden, London: Epworth Press, 1951.

_________ . *Wesley: The Man His Teaching and His Works*, London: Charles H. Kelly, 1891.

The Concise Evangelical Dictionary of Theology, 1991 edition, s.v. "Wesley John", by R. G. Tuttle Jr. (p. 549)

The Encyclopaedia of Protestantism Vol. 4, 2004 edition, s.v. "Wesley, John 1703-1791" by Richard P. Heitzenrater. (p. 1984)

_________ . s.v. "Wesleyanism" by Daniel L. Burnett (pp. 1992-97)

The Encyclopaedia of Religion and Ethics, Vol.12, s.v. "Wesley", by W. Bardsley Brash (pp. 724-727).

The Oxford Dictionary of the Christian Church, edited by F. L. Cross and E. A. Livingstone, 1998 edition, s.v. "Wesley, John, 1703-1791."

_________ . S.v. "Arminius, Jacobus 1560-1609" p.107; "Supralapsarianism" p.1552; "Sublapsarianism" p .1560.

Secondary Sources: Books on John Wesley

American Methodist Committee, *John Wesley's Room in Lincoln College Oxford*, Oxford: The University Press, 1929.

Ayling, Stanley E. *John Wesley*, Glasgow: William Collins Sons and Co. Ltd., 1979.

Baker, Frank. *A Charge to Keep: An Introduction to People Called Methodists*, London: The Epworth Press, 1954.

_________ . *John Wesley and the Church of England*, London: The Epworth Press, 2000.

_________ . (editor) *The Works of John Wesley*, 39 Vols, Nashville: Abingdon Press, 1984.

Best, G. M. *Continuity and Change: History of Kingswood School, 1748-1998*, Bath, Bristol: Published by Kingswood School, 1998.

_________ . *John Wesley: A Study of His Life to Commemorate the Tercentenary of His Birth,* Bath, Bristol: Published by Kingswood School, 2003.

_________ . *Wesley and Kingswood, 1738-1988 250th Conversion Anniversary*, Bath, Bristol: Published by Kingswood School, 1988.

Body, Alfred H. *John Wesley and Education*, London: The Epworth Press, 1936.

Bready, J. W. *This Freedom – Whence?, Faith and Freedom: The Roots of Democracy*, Indiana: Light and Life, 1952.

Brendlinger, Irv A. *Social Justice through the Eyes of Wesley*, Canada: Joshua Press Inc., 2006.

Burtner, Robert W. & Chiles Robert E. *A Compend of Wesley's Theology*, Nashville: Abingdon Press, 1954.

Burton, Vicki Tolar. *Spiritual Literature in John Wesley's Methodism: Reading, Writing and Speaking to Believe*, Taxes, Waco: Baylor University Press, 2008.

Butler, David. *Methodists and Papists: John Wesley and Catholic Church in the Eighteenth Century*, London: Darton, Longman and Todd Ltd., 1995.

Cadman, S. P. *The Three Religious Leaders of Oxford and their Movements*, New York: MacMillan,1916.

Cannon, William R. *Theology of John Wesley*, Nashville/New York: Abingdon Press, 1946.

Capon, John. *John and Charles Wesley: The Preacher and the Poet*, London: Hodder and Stoughton, 1988.

Carter, Henry. *The Methodist Heritage*, Nashville: Abingdon Press, 1951.

Carter, T. *John Wesley as a Philanthropist and the Social Mission of Methodism*, Nashville: Lambuth, 1905.

Cell, George Grant. *The Discovery of John Wesley*, New York: Holt Publishing House, 1935.

Cheetam, J. Keith. *On the Trail of John Wesley*, Glasgow, UK: Bell and Bains Ltd., 2003.

Chilcote, Paul Wesley. *John Wesley and Women Preachers of Early Methodism*, New Jersey: The American Theological Library Association and the ScarCrow Press Inc., 1991.

Clapper, Gregory S. *John Wesley on Religious Affections: His Views on Experience and Emotion and their Role in the Christian Life and Theology*, London: The ScarCrow Press, Inc., 1989.

Clarke, Adam. *Memoirs of the Wesley Family,* collected principally from original documents, London: Paternoster-Row, 1823.

Clarke, Elmer T. *The Warm Heart of Wesley*, New York: Association of Methodist Historical Societies, 1950.

_________ . *What Happened at Aldersgate*, Nashville: Methodist Publishing House, 1938.

Coke, Thomas and Henry Moore, *The Life of the Rev. John Wesley*, A.M, London: G. Paramore, 1792.

Coleman, Robert. *Nothing to Do But to Save Souls: John Wesley's Charge to His Preachers*, Wilmore, Kentucky: Wesley Heritage Press, 1990.

Collins, Kenneth J. *A Faithful Witness: John Wesley's Homiletical Theology*, Wilmore, Kentucky: Wesley Heritage Press, 1993.

_________ . *A Real Christian: The Life of John Wesley*, Nashville: Abingdon Press, 1999.

_________ . *The Scripture Way of Salvation: The Heart of John Wesley's Theology*, Nashville: Abingdon Press, 1997.

_________ . *The Theology of John Wesley: Holy Love and Shape of Grace*, Nashville: Abingdon Press, 2007.

Cox, Leo George. *John Wesley's Concept of Perfection*, Kansas, MO: Becon Hill Press, 1964.

Curnock, Nehemiah (ed). *The Journal of the Rev. John Wesley A.M., A Bicentenary Issue 1938*, Vols.1-8, London: The Epworth Press, 1938.

Davey, Cyril. *John Wesley and Methodism*, Nashville: Abingdon Press, 1985.

Davies, Rupert E. *A Christian Theology of Education*, Surrey, London: Denholm House Press, 1974.

________ . *Methodism*, London: The Epworth Press, 1985.

________ . *What Methodist Believe*, London: Mowbrays, 1976.

Davies, Rupert E., George A Raymond., and Rupp, E Gordon (eds). *A History the Methodist Church in Great Britain*, Vol. 2, London: The Epworth Press, 1978.

Dobree, Bonamy. *John Wesley*, London: Duckworth, 1933.

Doidge, R. *Wesley and Industrial Era*, London: The Epworth, 1938.

Doughty, W. L. *John Wesley: Preacher*, London: The Epworth Press, 1955.

Eayrs, George. *John Wesley, Christian Philosopher and Church Founder*, London: The Epworth Press, 1926.

Egermier. E. *John Wesley: The Christian Hero*, Anderson: Gospel Trumpet, 1923.

Ensley, F. G. *John Wesley , Evangelist*, Nashville: Tidings, 1955.

Everson, F. H. *This is Methodism*, London: The Epworth Press, 1957.

Faulkner, J. A. *Wesley as a Sociologist, Theologian, Churchman*, New York: Methodist Book Concern, 1918.

Fitchett, W. H. *Wesley and His Century*, Cincinnati, USA: Jennings and Graham, 1966.

Fitzgerald, W. B. *John Wesley on Horseback*, London: The Epworth Press, n.d.

Gill, Frederick C. *In the Steps of John Wesley*, London: Lutterworth, 1962.

Green, John Brazier. *John Wesley and William Law, London*: The Epworth Press, 1945.

Green, R. *John Wesley, Evangelist*, London: Religious Tract Society, 1905.

Green, Vivian Hubert Howard. *John Wesley*, London: Thomas Nelson and Sons Ltd, 1964.

_________ . John Wesley and Oxford, Oxford: Thomas –Photos, n.d.

_________ . *The Young Mr. Wesley*, London: Edward Arnold Ltd., 1961.

Gross, John Owen. *John Wesley: Christian Educator*, Nashville: Board of Education, the Methodist Church, 1954.

Haddal, I. *John Wesley*, London: The Epworth, 1961.

Harmon, R. L. *Susanna, Mother of Wesley's*, Nashville: Abingdon Press, 1968.

Harper, Steve. *John Wesley's Message for Today*, Grand Rapids, Michigan: Zondervan Publishing House, 1983.

Hattersley, Roy. *A Brand from the Burning: The Life of John Wesley*, London: Little Brown, 2002.

Heitzenrater, Richard P. *The Elusive Mr. Wesley*, 2nd edition, Nashville: Abingdon Press, 2003.

_________ . *Wesley and People Called Methodists*, Nashville: Kingswood Books & Abingdon Press, 1995.

Henderson, D. Michael. *A Model for Making Disciples: John Wesley's Class Meetings*, Nappanee, Indiana: Francis Asbury Press, 1997.

Hubery, D. The *Methodist Contribution to Education in England, 1938-1977*, London: Methodist Church Division of Education, 1977.

Ives, A. G. *Kingswood School in Wesley's Days and Since*, London: The Epworth Press, 1970.

Jackson, Thomas. (ed) *The Works of John Wesley*, 14 Vols., Grand Rapids, Michigan: Baker Book House, 1978.

Jennings, Theodore W. Jr. *Good News to the Poor: John Wesley's Evangelical Economics*, Nashville: Abingdon Press, 1990.

Kent, John. *Wesley and Wesleyan: Religion in Eighteenth-Century Britain*, Cambridge: Cambridge University Press, 2002.

Langford, Thomas A. *Wesleyan Theology : A Source Book*, Durham, North Carolina: The Labyrinth Press, 1984.

Lawson, Albert Brown. *John Wesley and The Anglican Evangelicals of the Eighteenth-Century*, Cambridge: The Pentland Press, 1994.

_________ . *John Wesley and The Christian Ministry: The Sources & Development of His Opinions and Practice*, London: SPCK, 1963.

Lean, G. *John Wesley , Anglican*, London: Blandforth, 1964.

Lecky, W. E. H. *A History of England in the Eighteenth Century* (8 vols.), New York: Appleton, 1891.

Lee, Umphrey. *John Wesley and Modern Religion*, Nashville: Cokesbury, 1936.

Lenton, John (ed.) *Vital Piety and Learning: Methodism and Education*, Oxford: Applied Theology Press, 2005.

Lunt, W. E. *History of England*, 3rd edition, London: Harper and Brothers, 1946.

Maddox, Randy L. *Responsible Grace: John Wesley's Practical Theology*, Nashville: Kingswood Books, 1994.

_________ . *Rethinking Wesley's Theology for Contemporary Methodism*, Nashville: Knigswood Books, 1998.

Marquardt, Manfred. *John Wesley's Social Ethics: Praxis and Principles*, Nashville: Abingdon Press, 1992.

Marshall, Dorothy. *John Wesley*, Oxford: Oxford University Press, 1965.

Martin, Hugh. *Selections from the Journal of John Wesley*, London: Student Christian Movement Press, 1955.

Maser, Frederick E. *Seven Sisters of John Wesley in Search of Love*, Vermont: Academy Books, 1988.

Mathew, H. F. *Methodism and the Education of the People, 1791-1851*, London: The Epworth Press, 1949.

Mavis, W. C. et. al. *Methodism's Aldersgate Heritage*, Nashville: Methodist Evangelistic Materials, 1964.

McConnell, F. J. *John Wesley*, New York: Abingdon Press, 1939.

McGonigle, Herbert Boyd. *Sufficient Saving Grace: John Wesley's Evangelical Arminianism*, Carlisle: Paternoster Press, 2001.

Meeks, M. Douglas (ed). *The Future of the Methodist Theological Traditions*, Nashville: Abingdon Press, 985.

Meredeth, William Henry. *John Wesley: His Courage and Ambition*, New York: Eaton and Mains, 1904.

Mickey, P. A. *Essentials of Wesleyan Theology: A Contemporary Affirmation*, Grand Rapids: Zondervan, 1980.

Miller, B.W. *John Wesley: The World His Parish*, Grand Rapids: Zondervan, 1943.

Monk, R.C. *John Wesley: His Puritan Heritage*, Nashville: Abingdon Press, 1966.

Moore, Henry. *The Life of The Rev. John Wesley M.A.: Fellow of Lincoln College Oxford*, Vol. 2, London: Paternoster-Row, 1825.

Muelder, Walter G. *Methodism and Society in the Twentieth Century*, Vol. II, New York: Abingdon Press, 1961.

Murray, Iain H. *Wesley and Men Who Followed*, Edinburgh: The Banner of Truth Trust, 2003.

Outler, Albert C. *John Wesley*, Oxford: Oxford University Press, 1964.

_________ . *John Wesley's Sermon: An Introduction*, Nashville: Abingdon Press, 1991.

_________ . (ed). *The Works of John Wesley: Volume I, Sermons I, 1-33*. Nashville: Abingdon Press, 1984.

Overton, J. H. *John Wesley*, London: Methuen and Co., 1905.

Parker, Percy Livingstone. *Spiritual Lives: John Wesley Journal*, abridged, edited by Robert Backhouse, London: Hodder and Stoughton, 1993.

_________ . (edited). *The Journal of John Wesley*, Chicago: Moody Press, 1962.

Parris, John R. *John Wesley's Doctrine of the Sacraments*, London: The Epworth Press, 1963.

Pellowe, W. C. S. *John Wesley: Master of Religions*, Nashville: Methodist Episcopal Church, South, 1939.

Piette, M. *John Wesley, in the Evolution of Protestantism*, New York: Sheed and Ward, 1937.

Pike, G. Holden. *John Wesley: The Man and His Mission*, London: The Religious Tract Society, n.d.

Pollock, John. *John Wesley, 1703-1791*, London: Hodder and Stoughton, 1989.

_________ . *Wesley the Preacher: A Biography*, Eastbourne, England: Kingsway Publication, 2000.

Prince, John Wesley. *John Wesley on Religious Education*, New York: Methodist Book Concern, 1926.

Pudney, John. *John Wesley and His World*, London: Thames and Hudson, 1978.

Rack, Henry D. *Reasonable Enthusiast: John Wesley and The Rise of Methodism*, London: The Epworth Press, 2002.

Rattenbury, J. Ernest. *The Conversion of the Wesley's: A Critical Study*, London: The Epworth Press, 1938.

_________ . *Wesley's legacy to the World*, Nashville: Cokebury, 1928.

Raynor, Frank C. *John Wesley: Fellow of Lincoln*, Leeds, UK: James Broadbent and Son Ltd., 1938.

Reddish, Robert O. Jr. *John Wesley His Way of Knowing God*, Evergreen, Colorado: The Roger Publishing Company, 1972.

Reynolds Joshua. *The True Likeness of John Wesley*, London: Privately Printed 1930.

Ride, Christopher. *The Journal of John Wesley*, England: Lion Books Publishing Plc., 1986.

Sangster, Paul. *Pity My Simplicity: The Evangelical Revival and Religious Education of Children, 1738-1800*, London: The Epworth Press, 1963.

Schmidt, Martin. *John Wesley: A Theological Biography*, Vol. I, Translated by Norman P. Goldhawk, London: The Epworth Press, 1962.

_________ . *John Wesley: A Theological Biography*, Vol. II, translated by Denis Inman, Nashville: Abingdon Press, 1973.

Sherwin, Oscar. *John Wesley , The Friend of the People*, NewYork: Twayne Publishers, 1961.

Shier-Jones, Angela and Reisman Kimberly D. (ed). *44 Sermons to Serve the Present Age*, Peterborough, UK: The Epworth Press, 2007.

Sigsworth, John Wilkins. *World – Changers : Karl Marx and John Wesley*, Ontario: Easingwold Publications, 1982.

Simon, J. S. *John Wesley and Methodist Societies, John Wesley the Master Builder*, London: The Epworth Press, 1923 and 1927, 2nd edition 1955.

Smith, John T. *Methodism and Education, 1849-1902: J. H. Rigg, Romanism, and Wesleyan Schools*, Oxford: Oxford University Press, 1998.

Smith, Warren. *John Wesley and Slavery*, Nashville: Abingdon Press, 1986.

Snell, F. J. *John Wesley and Methodism*, New York: Scribner's Sons, 1900.

Snyder, H. A. *The Radical Wesley*, London: InterVarsity Press, 1980.

Southey, R. *The Life of Wesley; and the Rise and Progress of Methodism*, 3rd edition, London: Longman and Others, 1846.

Stacey, John (ed). *John Wesley: Contemporary Perspective*, London: The Epworth Press, 1988.

Stanley, Sowton. *It Happened to John Wesley*, London: The Epworth Press, 1938.

Stevens, Abel. *The History of the Religious Movement of the Eighteenth Century Called Methodism*, Vol. III, London: Wesleyan Conference Office, Paternoster-Row, 1878.

Stone, Ronald H. *John Wesley's Life and Ethics*, Nashville: Abingdon Press, 2001.

Sugden, H. Edward (ed). *John Wesley's Fifty-Three Sermons*. Nashville: Abingdon Press, Second Printing, 1984.

Tabraham, Barrie W. *The Making of Methodism*, London: The Epworth Press, 1995.

Telford, John. *Popular Life of John Wesley*, London: Charles H. Kelly, 1900.

_________. *The Letters of the Rev. John Wesley, A.M., Vol. I, Nov. 3, 1721-Nov. 14, 1741*, London: The Epworth Press, 1931.

_________. *The Letters of the Rev. John Wesley, A.M., Vol. II, May 17, 1742-January 4, 1749,*

_________. *The Letters of the Rev. John Wesley, A.M., Vol. III, March 28, 1749-Jan.10,1758,*

_________. *The Letters of the Rev. John Wesley, A.M., Vol. IV, Jan.16, 1758-Feb.28,1766,*

_________. *The Letters of the Rev. John Wesley, A.M., Vol., V, Feb.28, 1766-December 9, 1772,*

_________. *The Letters of the Rev. John Wesley, A.M., Vol, VI, Dec.11, 1772-March 12, 1780,*

_________. *The Letters of the Rev. John Wesley, A.M., Vol, VII, March 23, 1780-July 24,1787,*

_________. *The Letters of the Rev. John Wesley, A.M., Vol, VIII, July 24, 1787-Feb. 24, 1791*, London: The Epworth Press, 1931.

_________. *The Life of John Wesley*, London: Hodder and Stoughton, 1886.

The Editors. *The Book of Discipline of the Methodist Church in India*, Lucknow: Published by the Methodist Church in India, 2004.

Todd, J. M. *John Wesley and Catholic Church*, London: Catholic Book Club, 1958.

Tomkins, Stephen. *John Wesley: A Biography*, England: Lion Books Publishing Plc., 2003.

Towns Elmer L. "John Wesley" in *A History of Religious Educators*, edited by Elmer L. Towns, Grand Rapids: Baker Book House, 1975.

Turner, John Munsey. *John Wesley: The Evangelical Revival and the Rise of Methodism in England*, London: The Epworth Press, 2002.

Tuttle, R. G. *John Wesley: His Life and Theology*, Grand Rapids: Zondervan, 1978.

Tyerman, L. *The Life and Times of the Rev. John Wesley, M.A., the Founder of the Methodists* (Vol. I, 1880; Vol. II, 1872; Vol. III, 1875), London: Hodder and Stoughton, 1872-1880.

Vickers, John A. *A Dictionary of Methodism in Britain and Ireland*, London: The Epworth Press, 2000.

Vulliamy, Colwyn Edward. *John Wesley*, 3rd edition, London: The Epworth Press, 1954.

Waller, Ralph. *John Wesley: A Personal Portrait*, London: SPCK, 2003.

Walter, Arthur. *John Wesley*, London: S.W. Partridge and Co., n.d.

Walters, Helen. *When John Wesley was a Boy*, Grand Rapids: Baker Book House, 1961.

Warner, W. J. *The Wesleyan Movement in the Industrial Revolution*, London: Longman's Green and Co., 1930.

Watson, David Lowes. *The Early Methodist Class Meeting*, Nashville: Discipleship Resources, 1995.

Watson, Richard. *The Life of The Rev. John Wesley, M.A.*, New York: Hunt & Eaton, 1831.

__________ . *The Life of The Rev. John Wesley A.M., 10th edition,* London: Published by John Mason, City Road, 1861.

Wearmouth, R. F. *Methodism and the Working Class Movements of England, 1800-1850, Methodism and the Common People of the Eighteenth Century*, London: The Epworth Press, 1937 and 1945.

Weber, Theodore R. *Politics in the order of Salvation: New Directions in Wesleyan Political Ethics*, Nashville: Kingwood Books, 2001.

Whitehead, J. *The Life of The John Wesley M.A.*, (2 vols.), London: Stephen Couchman, 1793.

Whitelock, Dorothy. *The Beginnings of English Society*, Harmondsworth, Middlesex: Penguin Books Ltd., 1952.

Williams, Collin W. *John Wesley's Theology Today*, New York: Abingdon Press, 1970.

Wilson W. *John Wesley's Place in History*, New York: Abingdon Press, 1903.

Wynkoop, Mildred Bangs. *John Wesley: Christian Revolutionary*, Kansas City MO: Beacon Hill Press, 1970.

Secondary Source: General Books on Christian Education

A. Anza. *Pedagogical and Theological Presuppositions of Education*, Hong Kong: Lutheran Southeast Asia Christian Education Curriculum Committee, 1977.

Anthony, Michael J. (ed). *Introducing Christian Education: Foundations for the Twenty-First Century*, Grand Rapids: Baker Academic, 2001.

Antone, Hope S. *Religious Education in Context*, Quezon: New Day Publishers, 2003.

Arles, Siga & Wintle, Brian (ed). *Striving for Excellence: Educational Ministry in the Church*, Bangalore: Asia Theological Association, 2007.

Ashton, T. S. *The Industrial Revolution, 1760-1830*, New York: Oxford University Press, 1964.

Astley, Jeff. *The Philosophy of Christian Religious Education,* Birmingham: Religious Education Press, 1994.

Astley, Jeff. Francis, Leslie J. & Crowder, Colin. *Theological Perspectives on Christian Formation: A Reader on Theological and Christian Education*, Grand Rapids: W. B. Eerdmans Publishing Company,1996.

Barber, Lucie W. *Teaching Christian Values,* Alabama: Religious Education Press, 1984.

Best, Gary. *Transforming Lives: Christian Education in a Multi-Cultural Society*, Peterborough, London: Epworth, 2008.

Boston, Bruce O. "Paulo Freire." In *Paulo Freire*. Stanley Grabowski, ed. Syracuse University Publications in Continuing Education, 1972

Bowers, C. A. *Educating for an Ecologically Sustainable Culture: Rethinking Moral Education, Creativity, Intelligence, and Other Modern Orthodoxies*, New York: State University of New York Press, 1995.

Boys, Mary C. *Educating in Faith: Maps and Visions*, San Francisco: Harper & Row, 1989.

Brezinka, Wolfgang. *Beliefs, Morals and Education*, Aldershot: Avebury, 1994.

Bruner, Jerome. *The Process of Education*, Cambridge: Harvard University Press, 1960.

Bugge, K. E., et. al. *A Survey of Moral Instruction and Religious Education in Bangalore*, Bangalore: United Theological College, 1973.

Burgess, Harold W. *An Invitation to Religious Education*, Mishawaka, Indiana: Religious Education Press, 1975.

__________ . *Models of Religious Education,* Wheaton: Victor Books SP Publications, 1996.

Bushnell, Horace. *Christian Nurture*, London: Yale University Press, 1953.

Butler, Donald J. *Religious Education: The Foundations and Practices of Nurture*, New York: Harper & Row Publishers, 1962.

Byrne, H. W. *A Christian Approach to Education*, Grand Rapids: Zondervan Publishing House, 1961.

________. *Christian Education for the Local Church: An Evangelical and Functional Approach*, Grand Rapids: Zondervan Publishing House, 1963.

________ . *Improving Church Education*, Birmingham, Alabama: Religious Education Press, Inc., 1979.

Carter, Robert E. *Dimensions of Moral Education*, Toronto: University of Toronto Press, 1984.

Chamberlin, J. Gordon. *Parents and Religion: A Preface to Christian Education*, Philadelphia: The Westminster Press, 1971.

Collins, Denis E. *Paulo Freire: His Life, Works and Thought*, New York: Paulist Press, 1971.

Conover, Charles Eugene., *Moral Education in Family, School, and Church*, Philadelphia: The Westminster Press, 1962.

Cove, Mary K. & Mary L. Mueller. *Regarding Religious Education*, Mishawaka: Religious Education Press, 1977.

Cragg, G. R. *The Church in the Age of Reason (1648-1789)*, New York: Penguin books, 1970.

Cully, Iris V. *The Bible in Christian Education*, Minneapolis: Fortress Press, 1995.

________ . *The Dynamics of Christian Education*, Philadelphia: The Westminster Press, 1958.

Cully, Kending Brubaker. *The Search for a Christian Education Since 1940*, Philadelphia: The Westminster press, 1965.

Dewey, John. *Democracy and Education: An Introduction to the Philosophy of Education*, New York: Free Press 1966.

Durkheim, Emile. *Moral Education*, London: The Free Press, 1973.

Eavey, C. B. *History of Christian Education*, Chicago: Moody Press, 1964.

Elwell, Walter A. (ed). *The Concise Evangelical Dictionary of Theology*, (Grand Rapids, Michigan: Baker Book House, 1991.

Evenson, C. Richard. *Foundation for Educational Ministry: Year Books in Christian Education*, Vol. III, US: Fortress Press, 1971.

Foster, Charles R. *The Future of Christian Education: Educating Congregations*, Nashville: Abingdon Press, 1994.

Foster, Virgil E. *Christian Education - Where the Learning Is*, New Jersey: Prentice-Hall Inc., 1968.

Fowler, James W. *Becoming Adult, Becoming Christian*, San Francisco: Harper & Row, 1984.

________ . *Stages of Faith*, New York: Harper & Row, 1981.

Freire, Paulo. *Cultural Action for Freedom*, Cambridge, Mass: Harvard Education Review, 1970

________. *Education for Liberation*, Bangalore, Whitefield: Ecumenical Christian Centre, 1975.

________ . *Education for Critical Consciousness*, New York, Seabury Press, 1973.

________ . *Education: The Practice of Freedom*, London: Writers and Readers, 1976.

________ . *Learning to Question : A Pedagogy of Liberation*, Geneva: WCC Publications, 1989.

________ . *Letters to Cristina: Reflections on My Life and Work*, translated from the Portuguese by Donaldo Macedo, New York: Routledge, 1996.

________ . *Pedagogy in Progress: The Letters to Guinea-Bissau*, translated by Carman St. John Hunter, New York: WCC-The Seabury Press, 1978.

________ . *Pedagogy of the Oppressed*, New York: Herder and Herder, 1972.

________ . *The Politics of Education: Culture, Power, and Liberation*, South Hadley, MA: Bergin & Garvey Publishers, 1985.

Freire, Paulo. and Ira, Shor., *A Pedagogy for Liberation: Dialogues on Transformative Education,* Amherst, Massachusetts: Bergin & Garvey, 1987.

Gadotti, Moacir. *Reading Paulo Freire: His Life and Work*, translated by John Milton, New York: State University of New York Press, 1994.

Gandhi, P. Jegadish and George Cheriyan (eds)., *Globalization: A Challenge to the Church,* Bangalore: Association of Christian Institutes for social Concern in Asia & National Council of Churches in India-Urban Rural Mission, 1998.

Gaebelein, Frank E., *Christian Education in a Democracy*, New York: Oxford Press, 1951.

George, M. K. "Paulo Freire's Concept of Education", in *Changing Perspectives in Education*, edited by Denis Coelho, New Delhi: Indian Social Institute, 1995.

Gibbs, Eugene S. (ed). *A Reader in Christian Education: Foundations and Basic Perspectives,* Grand Rapids: Baker Book House, 1992.

Giroux, Henry. *Schooling and Struggle for Public Life: Critical Pedagogy in the Modern Age*, Minneapolis: University of Minnesota Press, 1988.

________ . *Teachers as Intellectuals*, Minneapolis: University of Minnesota Press, 1988.

Giroux, Henry A. & Mclaren, Peter L. (eds). *Paulo Freire on Higher Education: A Dialogue at the National University of Mexico,* New York: State University of New York Press, 1994.

Giroux, Henry A. Lankshear, Colin., Maclaren, Peter and Peters, Michael. *Counter Narratives: Cultural Studies and Critical Pedagogies in Post-modern Spaces,* London: Routledge, 1996.

Grimmitt, Michael. *Religious Education and Human Development*, England: McCrimmon Limited, 1987.

Groome, Thomas H. *Christian Religious Education: Sharing our Story and Vision*, San Francisco: Harper and Row, Publishers, 1980.

________ . *Educating for Life – A Spiritual Vision for Every Teacher and Parent,* New York: The Crossroad Publishing Company, 2001.

________ . *Sharing Faith: A Comprehensive Approach to Religious Education & Pastoral Ministry: A Way of Shared Praxis,* New York: Harper San Francisco, 1991.

Habermas, J. *Moral Consciousness and Communicative Action*, London: Polity, 1990.

Harris, Maria. *Teaching and Religious Imagination*, New York: Harper Collins Publishers, 1991.

Harris, Maria and Gabriel, Moran. *Reshaping Religious Education: Conversation on Contemporary Practice,* Kentucky: Westminster John Knox Press, 1998.

Hofinger, Johannes. *The Art of Teaching Christian Doctrine*, Notre Dame, Indiana: University of Notre Dame Press, 1962.

Hooks, Bell. *Teaching to Transgress: Education as the Practice of Freedom*, London: Routledge, 1994.

Hull, E. R. *The Formation of Character*, Bombay: St. Paul Publication, n.d.

Hull, John (ed). *New Directions in Religious Education*, Sussex: The Falmer Press, 1982.

Hurlock, Elizabeth B. *Developmental Psychology: A Life-span Approach*, New Delhi:Tata McGraw-Hill Publishing Co. Ltd., 1999.

Johnson, Paul E. *Personality and Religion*, New York: Abingdon Press, 1957.

________ . *Psychology of Religion*, Nashville: Abingdon Press, 1959, 1997.

Jungmann, Josef Andreas. Handing on the Faith: A Manual of Catechetics, New York: Herder and Herder, 1962.

Kalathuveetill, Thomas. *Shared–Praxis as Christian Religious Education*, Bangalore: Kristu Jytoti Publications, 1992.

Kohlberg, Lawrence. *Essays on Moral Development: The Philosophy of Moral Development,* Vol. I, New York: Harper & Row, 1981.

________ . "Stages of Moral Development as a Basis for Moral Education", in *Moral Development, Moral Education, and Kohlberg,* edited by Brenda Munsey, Birmingham: Religious Education Press, 1980.

________ . et.al. *Moral Education, Justice and Community: A Study of Three Democratic High Schools*, New York: Columbia University Press, 1988.

________ . *The Psychology of Moral Development*, New York: Harper Religious Books, 1983.

Law, William. *A Serious call to a Devout and Holy Life,* London: Hodder and Stoughton 1987.

________ . *Spirit of Prayers; or the Soul Rising Out of the Vanity of Times into the Riches of Eternity*, Part I, 2nd edition, London: W. Innys, in Pater-noster Row, 1750.

LeBar, Lois E. *Children in Bible School*, Westwood, New Jersey: Fleming H. Revell, 1952.

_______ . "Christ The Centre", in *The Search for a Christian Education Since 1940* by Kending Brubaker Cully, Philadelphia: The Westminster Press, 1965.

________ . *Education that is Christian*, Old Tappan, New Jersey: Fleming H. Revell Company, 1958.

________ . *Focus on People in Christian Education*, New Jersey: Fleming H. Revell, 1968.

Lee, James Michael. *The Content of Religious Instruction: A Social Science Approach*, Birmingham: Religious Education Press, 1985.

Lewalski, Barbara K. *The Life of John Milton: A Critical Biography*, revised edition Oxford: Blackwell Publishing, 2007.

Locke, John. *Some Thoughts Concerning Education*, edited by John W. and Jean S. Yolton, Oxford: Clarendon Press, 1989.

Lord Eric & C. Bailey. *A Reader in Religious and Moral Education*, London: SCM, 1973.

Lossky, Nicholas, et. al. (ed). *Dictionary of the Ecumenical Movement,* 2nd edition, Geneva: World Council of Churches, Publication 2002.

Mabry, Hunter P. *A Manual for Researchers and Writers*, 2nd edition, Bangalore: The Board of Theological Education Senate of Serampore College, 2004.

Mackie, R. (ed). *Literacy and Revolution: The Pedagogy of Paulo Freire*, London: Pluto Press, 1980.

Mary, Marlene (ed). *Modern Masters of Religious Education*, Birmingham: Religious Education Press, 1983.

Mason, Harold Carlton. *Abiding values in Christian Education*, Westwood, New Jersey: Fleming H. Revell, 1955.

________ . "The History of Christian Education", in *An Introduction to Evangelical Christian Education,* edited by J. Edward Hakes, Chicago: Moody Press, 1964.

________ . *The Teaching Task of the Local Church*, Winona Lake, Indiana: Light and Life, 1960.

Mathew, George (ed). *A Day with Paulo Freire,* Delhi: ISPCK, 1980.

McLaren, Peter & Leonard Peter., *Paulo Freire: A Critical Encounter*, London: Routledge, 1993.

________ . *Life in Schools: An Introduction to Critical Pedagogy in the Foundations of Education*, New York: Longmans, 1989.

________ . *Revolutionary Multiculturalism: Pedagogies of Dissent for the New Millennium,* Oxford: West View Press, 1997.

Miller, Randolph C. *Biblical Theology and Christian Education*, New York: Charles Scribner's Sons, 1956.

________ . "Christian Education as a Theological discipline and Method," in *Who Are We? The Quest for a Religious Education*, edited by John Westerhoff, Alabama: Religious Education Press, 1978.

________ . *Christian Nurture and The Church,* New York: Charles Scribner's Sons, 1961.

________ . *Education for Christian Living*, New Jersey: EagleWood Cliffs, 1956.

________. *The Clue to Christian Education*, New York: Charles Scribner's Sons, 1950.

________. *The Theory of Christian Education Practice: How Theology Affects Christian Education*, Alabama: Religious Education Press, 1980.

Moberg, D., *The Church as a Social Institute*, New York: Prentice-Hall, 1962.

Moore, Allen J. *Religious Education as Social Transformation*, Birmingham, Alabama: Religious Education Press, 1998.

Moore, Mary Elizabeth Mullino. *Teaching from the Heart: Theology and Educational Method*, Minneapolis: Fortress Press, 1991.

Moran, Gabriel. *Religious Education Development: Images for the Future*, Minneapolis: Winston Press Inc. 1983.

More, Mary Elizabeth. *Education for Continuity: A New Model for Christian Religious Education*, Nashville: Abingdon Press, 1983.

Morris, Edward E. *Milton's Tractate of Education*, London: Macmillan and Co., 1895.

Munsey, Brenda (ed). *Moral Development, Moral Education, and Kohlberg*, Birmingham: Religious Education Press, 1980.

Murray, A. Victor. *Education into Religion*, New York: Harper and Row, 1953.

Niblett, W. R. *Christian Education in a Secular Society*, London: Oxford University Press, 1960.

Oliver, Donald W. *Education, Modernity, and Fractured Meaning: Toward a Process Theory of Teaching and Learning*, New York: State University of New York Press, 1989.

Paulus, Vimala. *Introducing Christian Education*, Madras: The Christian Literature Society, 1986.

Pazmino, Robert W. *Foundational Issues in Christian Education: An Introduction in Evangelical Perspective*, Grand Rapids: A Division of Baker Book House Co., 1999.

Peatling, John H. *Religious Education: In a Psychological Key*, Alabama: Religious Education Press, 1981.

Plumb, J. H. *England in the Eighteenth Century*, Maryland: Penguin Books, 1969.

Power, F. Clark. Ann Higgins & Lawrence Kohlberg, *Moral Education Though Democratic Communities, Lawrence Kohlberg's Approach to Moral Education*, New York: Columbia University Press, 1989.

Prabhakar, Samson. *Essays on Christian Education and Liturgy*, Bangalore: South Asia Theological Research Institute, 2003.

Price, J. M. "Philosophy of Religious Education", in *A Survey of Religious Education*, New York: Ronald Press Company, 1959.

Rao, V. K., & Reddy R. S. Parent Education, New Delhi: Commonwealth Publishers, 1997.

Reed, J. E. and R. Prevost. *A History of Christian Education*, Nashville: Broadman and Holman, 1993.

Richards, Lawrence O. *A Theology of Christian Education*, Grand Rapids: Zondervan Publishing House, 1975.

Rogers, Carl. *Freedom to Learn for the 80s*, London: Charles E. Merril Publishing Company- A Bell & Howell Company, 1983.

Rood, Wayne R. *Understanding Christian Education*, Nashville: Abingdon Press, 1970.

Samuel, Monica Aruna. *A Brief History of Methodism in India*, Lucknow: Published by the Methodist Church in India, 2006.

Seymour Jack L (ed). *Mapping Christian Education: Approaches to Congregational Learning*, Nashville: Abingdon Press, 1997.

________ . *Theological Approaches to Christian Education*, Nashville: Abingdon Press, 1990.

Seymour, Jack L. and Donald E. Miller, *Contemporary Approaches to Christian Education,* Nashville: Abingdon Press, 1984.

Shor, Ira., and Freire Paulo. *A Pedagogy for Liberation*, Westport, Connecticut: Bergin & Garvey, 1987.

Shotton, John Robert. *Learning and Freedom: Policy, Pedagogy and Paradigm in Indian Education and Schooling*, New Delhi: Sage Publications, 1998

Smith J. W. D. *Religious Education in Secular Setting*, London: SCM, 1969.

Spellman, W. M. *John Locke*, London: Macmillan Press Ltd., 1997.

Stanislaus, L. SVD. *Education as Mission*, New Delhi: Ishvani Kendra/ISPCK, 2004.

Sumi, Akheto. *Understanding the Nature and Purpose of Christian Religious Education*, Assam, Jorhat: Barkataki and Company Pvt. Ltd., 2005.

Tarcov, Nathan. *Locke's Education for Liberty*, London: The University of Chicago Ltd., 1984.

Taylor, Marvin J. "A Historical Introduction to Religious Education", in *Religious Education: A Comprehensive Survey*, Nashville: Abingdon Press, 1960.

________ . *An Introduction to Christian Education*, Nashville: Abingdon Press, 1966.

________ . *Foundations for Christian Education in an Era of Change*, Nashville: Abingdon press, 1976.

________ . (ed). *Religious education: A Comprehensive Survey*, New York: Abingdon Press, 1960.

"The Objectives of Christian Education: A Study Document", New York: National Council of Churches 1958.

Tipton, I. C. (ed) *Locke on Human Understanding : Selected Essays*, Oxford: Oxford University Press, 1977.

Thomas, M. M. *Salvation and Humanization: Some Crucial Issues of the Theology of Mission in Contemporary India*, Madras: Christian Institute for the Study of Religion and Society/Christian Literature Service, 1971.

Torres, Carlos Alberto. "The Political Pedagogy of Paulo Freire", in *Paulo Freire: A Critical Encounter*, edited by Peter McLaren & Peter Leonard, New York: Routledge, 1993.

Towns, Elmer L.(ed). *A History of Religious Educators*, Grand Rapids: Baker Book House, 1975.

Trifonas, Peter Pericles (ed). *Revolutionary Pedagogies: Cultural Politics, Instituting Education, and the Discourse of Theory*, London: Routledge Falmer, 2000.

Turbain, Kate L. *A Manual for Writers of Term Papers, Theses, and Dissertations*, 4th edition, Chicago: University of Chicago Press, 1973.

Ulich, Robert. *A History of Religious Education: Documents and Interpretaions from the Judeo - Christian Tradition*, London: University of London Press Ltd, 1968.

Vella, Jane. *Learning to Listen Learning to Teach: Power of Dialogue in Educating Adults*, San Francisco: Jossey-Bass Publishers, 1997.

Verstraeten, A. S. J. *Ideas about Christian Education in India*, Bangalore: Theological Publication in India, 1973.

Vieth, Paul H. *The Church and Christian Education*, St. Louis: The Bethany Press, 1960.

Vidales, Raul. "Methodological issues in liberation theology" in Rosino Gibellim (ed) *Frontiers of Theology in Latin America*, London: SCM Press, 1980.

Vijaykumar, David. *23rd Session of the South India Regional Conference and Deaconesses Conferences of the Methodist Church in India 13th-15th May 2005*, Bangalore: Methodist Church, Bangalore Regional Conference, 2006.

Ward, T. W. *Values begin at Home*, (revised) Wheaton, Illinois: Scripture, 1989.

Watson, Brenda and Elizabeth Ashton. *Education, Assumption and Values*, London: David Fulton, 1995.

Westerhoff III, John. *Who are We? The Quest for a Religious Education*, Birmingham: Religious Education Press, 1978.

________ . *Living the Faith Community*, Minneapolis: Winston Press, Inc. 1985.

Whitehead, Alfred North. *The Aims of Education and Other Essays*, New York: The Free Press, 1929.

Wickett, R.E.Y. *Models for adult Religious Education Practice*, Birmingham: Religious Education Press, 1991.

Wiencke, Gustav K. (ed). *Christian Education in a Secular Society*, Philadelphia: Fortress Press, 1970.

Wilhot, Jim. *Christian Education and the Search for Meaning*, Grand Rapids: Baker Book House, 1993.

Wilkerson, Barbara (ed). *Multicultural Religious Education*, Birmingham, Alabama: Religious Education Press, 1997.

Woltersdorff, Nicholas. *Educating for Responsible Action*, Grand Rapids: Eerdmans, 1980.

Wyckoff, D. Campbell. "Religious Education as a Discipline" in *Who Are we?* Edited by John Westerhoff, Alabama: Religious Education Press, 1978.

________ . *The Church and Christian Education: A Theory of Christian Education for Our Times*, Philadelphia: The Westminster Press, 1959.

________ . *The Task of Christian Education*, Philadelphia: The Westminster Press, 1955.

Wynn, J. C. *Christian Education for Liberation: And Other Upsetting Ideas*, Nashville: Abingdon Press, 1977.

Yolton, John W. *Locke: An Introduction*, Oxford: Basil Blackwell Ltd., 1985.

Articles about John Wesley

Baker, Frank. "The Birth of John Wesley's Journal", *Methodist History*, Vol. VIII, No. 2, 1970.

________ . "The Origins, character, and influence of John Wesley's thoughts upon Slavery", *Methodist History*, Vol. XXII, No. 2, January 1984.

________ . " The Oxford edition of Wesley's Works", *Methodist History*, Vol.VIII, No.4, July 1970.

________ . "The Shaping of Wesley's *Calm address*", *Methodist History*, Vol. XIV, No.1, October 1975.

Beals, J. Duane. "Doing Christian Education in the Wesleyan Mode: A Response to Wesley Tracy", in *Wesleyan Theological Journal*, Vol.17, No.1, Spring 1982.

Bishop, Michael. "Wesley's Four Schools in Kingswood," in *Issues in Education Some Methodist Perspectives, Westminster Wesley Series* No.4, Spring 1996.

Brown, Kenneth O. "John Wesley – Post or Premillennialist?" *Methodist History*, Vol. XXVIII, No. 1, October 1989.

Campbell, Ted A. "John Wesley and The legacy of Methodist Theology," in *Bulletin of The John Ryland's University Library* Manchester, Vol. 85, Number 2 and 3, Summer and Autumn 2003. (pp. 405-420)

________ . "The Wesleyan Quadrilateral: The Story of Modern Methodist Myth," *Methodist History*, Vol. XXIX, No. 2, January 1991.

Cannon, William R. "Salvation in theology of John Wesley", *Methodist History*, Vol. IX, No.1, October 1970.

________ . "The Meaning of the Ministry in Methodism", *Methodist History*, Vol.VIII, No. 1, October 1969.

Carey, Brycchan. "John Wesley's Thoughts upon Slavery and the language of the heart," in *Bulletin of The John Ryland's University Library* Manchester, Vol. 85, Number 2 and 3, Summer and Autumn 2003. (pp. 269-284)

Chilcote, Paul Wesley. "John Wesley as revealed by the Journal of Hester Ann Rogers, July 1775-Octber 1984", *Methodist History*, Vol. XX, No. 3, April 1982.

Collins, Kenneth J. "John Wesley's Correspondence with His father", *Methodist History*, XXVI, No.1, October 1987.

________ . "Rethinking the systematic nature of John Wesley's Theology," in *Bulletin of The John Ryland's University Library* Manchester, Vol. 85, Number 2 and 3, Summer and Autumn 2003. (pp. 309-330)

Durbin, Linda M. "The Nature of Ordination in Wesley's View of the Ministry," *Methodist History*, Vol. IX, No. 3, April 1971.

English, J. C., "John Wesley's Indebtedness to John Norris," *Church History*, March 1991.

________ . "John Wesley's Scientific Education," in *Methodist History*, Vol. XXX, No.1, October 1991.

Estep, James Riley Jr. "John Wesley's Philosophy of Formal Childhood Education," in *Christian Education Journal*, Vol. INS, No. 2, Fall 1997.

Felton, Gayle Carlton. "John Wesley and the teaching ministry: Ramifications for education in the church today", in *Religious Education*, Vol. 92, Issue 1, Winter 1997.

Ferguson, Duncan S. "John Wesley on Scripture: The Hermeneutics of Pietism," *Methodist History*, Vol. XX, No. 4, July 1984.

Gibbs, John. "Methodist Influence on National Education Policy," in *Issues in Education Some Methodist Perspectives, Westminster Wesley Series* No. 4, Spring 1996.

Gregory, Jeremy. "Wesley' tercentenary and the state of Wesley Studies," in *Bulletin of The John Ryland's University Library* Manchester, Vol. 85, Number 2 and 3, Summer and Autumn 2003. (pp. 17-30)

Harper, Steve. "Wesley's sermons as Spiritual formation documents", in *Methodist History*, Vol. XXVI, No. 3, April 1988.

Hempton, David. "John Wesley and Rise of Methodism," in *Bulletin of The John Ryland's University Library* Manchester, Vol. 85, Number 2 and 3, Summer and Autumn 2003. (pp. 31-56)

Henderson, Bernard W. "John Wesley's last University Sermon," in *The Cornhill Magazine*, January 1925. (pp. 93-100)

Hunt, Thomas C. "Methodism, Moral Education and Public schools: A Look into the Past", *Methodist History*, Vol. XIX, No. 2, January 1981.

Hynson, Leon O. "John Wesley and Political Reality", *Methodist History*, Vol.XII, No.1, October 1973.

Jacob, W. M. "John Wesley and the Church of England, 1736-1740," in *Bulletin of The John Ryland's University Library* Manchester, Vol. 85, Number 2 and 3, Summer and Autumn 2003. (pp. 57-72)

Jagessar, Michael N. "Interrogating John Wesley's *Thoughts Upon Slavery*: A Black British and Caribbean Theological perspective," *Bangalore Theological Forum*, Vol. XL, No. 1, June 2008.

Jennings, Theodore Wesley Jr., "John Wesley on the Origin of Methodism," in *Methodist History*, Vol. XXIX, No. 2, January 1991.

Keefer, Luke L. "Presidential address: John Wesley, Methodists and social reform in England," In *Wesleyan Theological Journal*, Vol. 25, No. 1, Spring 1990.

Kirkham, Donald H. "John Wesley's *Calm Address*: The Response of the Critics," *Methodist History*, Vol. XIV, No.1, October 1975.

Lenton, John. "John Wesley and the travelling preachers," in *Bulletin of The John Ryland's University Library* Manchester, Vol. 85, Number 2 and 3, Summer and Autumn 2003. (pp. 99-110)

Lynch, Elizabeth Kurtz. "John Wesley's editorial hand in Susanna Annesley Wesley's 1732 'education' letter," in *Bulletin of The John Ryland's University Library* Manchester, Vol. 85, Number 2 and 3, Summer and Autumn 2003.

Maser, Federick E. "John Wesley's Only Marriage", *Methodist History*, Vol. XVI, No.1, October 1977.

McEllhenney, John G. "John Wesley and Samuel Johnson: A tale of three Coincidences," *Methodist History*, Vol. XXI, No. 3, April 1983.

Mealy, Mark T. "Tilting at Windmills: John Wesley's reading of John Locke's epistemology," in *Bulletin of The John Ryland's University Library* Manchester, Vol. 85, Number 2 and 3, Summer and Autumn 2003. (pp. 331-346)

Noble, Thomas A. " East and West in the Theology of John Wesley," in *Bulletin of The John Ryland's University Library* Manchester, Vol. 85, Number 2 and 3, Summer and Autumn 2003. (pp. 359-372)

Norwood, Frederick E. "Wesleyan and Methodist Historical Studies," 1960-70, A Bibliographical Article", *Methodist History*, Vol. X, No. 2, January 1972.

Nygren, E. Herbert. "John Wesley's Concept of the Ministry," *Religion in Life*, Vol. XXXI, No.2, Spring 1962.

Outler, Albert C. "The Place of Wesley in the Christian Tradition," in *The Wesleyan Theological Heritage*, edited by Thomas C. Oden and Leicester R. Longden, Grand Rapids: Zondervan Publishing House, 1991. (pp. 75-95)

Ott, Philip W. "John Wesley on Health: A Word for Sensible Regimen", *Methodist History*, Vol. XVIII, No. 3, April 1980.

________ . "John Wesley on Mind and Body: Towards an Understanding of Health and Wholeness", *Methodist History*, Vol. XXVII, No. 2, January 1989.

Rogal, Samuel J. "John Wesley and Mary Queen of Scots: A Love affair with History", *Methodist History*, Vol. XXIV, No.4, July 1986.

________ . "John Wesley's Daily Routine", *Methodist History*, Vol. XIII, No. 1, October 1974.

________ . "John Wesley Takes a Wife", *Methodist History*, Vol. XXVII, No.1, October 1988.

Smith, Warren Thomas. "Eighteenth Century Encounters: Methodist-Moravians," *Methodist History*, Vol. XXIV, No. 3, April 1986.

Stoeffler, F. Ernest. "Religious roots of Moravians and Methodist Movements," *Methodist History*, Vol. XXIV, No. 3, April 1986.

Thomas, Howe Octavius Jr. "John Wesley's Awareness and Application of the Method of distinguishing between Theological Essentials and Theological Opinions", *Methodist History*, Vol. XXVI, No. 2, January 1988.

Tracy, Wesley. "Christian Education in the Wesleyan Mode", in *Wesleyan Theological Journal*, Vol. 17, No.1, Spring 1982.

Tranter, Donald. "John Wesley and The Education of Children," in *Issues in Education some Methodist Perspectives, Westminster Wesley Series* No. 4, Spring 1996.

Wallace, Charles Jr. "Susanna Wesley's Spirituality: The Freedom of a Woman," *Methodist History*, Vol. XX, No. 2, April 1984.

Walls, Jerry L. "John Wesley's Critique of Martin Luther", *Methodist History*, Vol. XXX, No.1, October 1981.

Walters, Orville S. "John Wesley's Footnotes to Christian Perfection", *Methodist History*, Vol. XII, No. 1, October 1973.

________ . "The Concept of Attainment in John Wesley's Christian Perfection," *Methodist History*, Vol. X, No. 3, April 1972.

Webb, James R Jr. "The Young John Wesley – A New Monument," *Methodist History*, Vol.VIII, No. 2, January 1970.

White, Charles Edward. "John Wesley's Use of Church Discipline," *Methodist History*, Vol. XXIX, No. 2, January 1991.

Wood, Laurence W. John Fletcher's influence on John Wesley's Theology," in *Bulletin of The John Ryland's University Library* Manchester, Vol. 85, Number 2 and 3, Summer and Autumn 2003. (pp. 387-404)

General Articles on Christian Education

Antone, Hope S. "Shifts In Education Theory," *NCC Review*, Vol. cxxiii, No.10, November 2003.

Bailey, John. "Religious Education in Lincolnshire Secondary School," *British Journal of Religious Education*, Vol.1, No. 3, Spring 1979.

Bellett, Eileen. "Religious Education for Liberation: A Perspective from Paulo Freire," *British Journal of Religious Education*, Vol. 20, No.3, summer, 1998.

Berthoff, Ann E. "Paulo Freire's Liberation Pedagogy, in *Language Arts*, Vol. 67, No. 4, 1990.

Botton, Ken. Chuck King, Junias Venugopal, "Educating for Spirituality," *Christian Education Journa*l, Vol. LIV, 3rd quarter, September 1975.

Buss, Eileen and Others (editors). *Christian Education*, Vol. LVI, 1-4 Quarters, Jabalpore: Published by the Council of Christian Education of the Methodist Church in Southern Asia, 1977.

Charter, Mark. "A Healing Model of Religious Education," *British Journal of Religious Education*, Vol. 17, No. 2, Spring 1995.

Conway, Ruth. "The Influence of Beliefs and Values on Technological activities – a challenge to Religious Education," *British Journal of Religious Education*, Vol.13, No.1, Autumn 1990.

Cooling, Trevor. "Science and Religious Education – conflict or Cooperation?" *British Journal of Religious Education*, Vol. 13, No. 1, Autumn 1990.

Crawford and Graham Rossiter. "The Secular Spirituality of Youth: Implications for Religious Education," *British Journal of Religious Education*, Vol. 18, No. 3, summer 1996.

Elias, John L. "Paulo Freire: Religious Educator," *Religious Education*, Vol. LXXI, No.1, Jan-Feb, 1976.

Gearon, Liam. "Human Rights and Religious Education: Some Postcolonial Perspectives," *British Journal of Religious Education*, Vol. 24, No. 2, Spring 2002.

________ . "The Imagined Other: Postcolonial theory and Religious Education," *British Journal of Religious Education*, Vol. 23, No. 2, Spring 2001.

Geaves, Ron. "The Borders between religions: A Challenge to the World Religions A approach to Religious education," *British Journal of Religious Education*, Vol. 21, No.1, Autumn 1998.

Hammersley, Peter. "Development in Faith Development Theory: Review Article," *British Journal of Religious Education*, Vol. 11, No. 3, summer 1989.

Hanford, Jack T. "The relationship between Faith Development of James Fowler and Moral Development of Lawrence Kohlberg: A Theoretical Review," in *Journal of Psychology and Christianity*, Vol. 10, No. 4, 1991.

Heywood, David. "Christian Education as Enculturation," *British Journal of Religious Education*, Vol. 10, No. 2, Spring 1988.

Joshua, Paul (ed). "Christ and the Child," *Dharma Deepika: A South Asian Journal of Missiological Research,* Issue 28, Vol. 12, No. 2 July-December 2008.

Kapolo, Matthew T. "Contemporary Understanding of Christian Education Curriculum Development in the Church," *Educator Magazine*, December, 1994.

Kerry, Trevor. "Evaluating Learning in Religious Education; Some Possible Approaches," *British Journal of Religious Education*, Vol. 2, No. 2, Winter 1979.

Leaby, Michael. "Indoctrination, Evangelism, Catechisis and Religious Education," *British Journal of Religious Education*, Vol. 12, No. 3, summer 1990.

Lovat, Terence J. "Action Research and the Praxis Model of Religious Education: A Critique," *British Journal of Religious Education*, Vol. 11, No. 1, Autumn 1988.

Martin, Robert K. "Congregational Studies and Critical Pedagogy in Theological Perspective," *Theological Education*, Vol. 33, No.2, (1997) pp. 121-146.

Mason, Marilyn. "Religion and Schools: A human rights based approach," *British Journal of Religious Education*, Vol. 25, No. 2, Spring 2003.

Meakin, Derek C. "Personal, Social and Moral Education and Religious Education: The need for conceptual clarity," *British Journal of Religious Education*, Vol. 11, No.1, Autumn 1988.

Miller, Joyce. "Using the Visual Arts in Religious Education: An Analysis and Critical Evaluation," *British Journal of Religious Education*, Vol. 25, No. 3, Summer 2003.

Murray, Eileen. "Religious Education: Theological or Social science," *Bangalore Theolgical Forum*, Vol.XIX, No.1, April 1987.

Parmar, S. K. (Editor) *Christian Education*, Vol. LVII, 1-4 Quarters, Jabalpore, Madhya Pradesh: Published by the Council of Christian Education of the Methodist Church in Southern Asia, 1978.

Pearce, Robin T. "Religious Education and emotion," *British Journal of Religious Education*, Vol.1, No.4, Summer 1979.

Proffitt, Anabel. "A Liberating Education?" *Religious Education*, Vol. 88, no1, winter 1993.

Radford, Mike. Religious Education, Spiritual Experience and Truth," *British Journal of Religious Education*, Vol.21, No.3, Summer, 1999.

Reddie, Anthony G. "African- Centred Approaches to Education as a Resource for Christian Education", *British Journal of Religious Education*, Vol.25, No.1, Autumn 2002.

"Religious and Moral Instruction in Educational Institutions," Editorial, *NCC Review*, Vol. LXXX, No. 4, April 1960.

Riggs, Anne. "Biotechnology and religious Education," *British Journal of Religious Education*, Vol.13, No.1, Autumn 1990.

Samuel, Kariappa Editor. *Christian Education*, Vol. LVIII, 1-4 Quarters, Jabalpore, Madhya Pradesh: Published by the Council of Christian Education of the Methodist Church in Southern Asia, 1979.

________ . *Christian Education*, Vol. LXII, 1-4 Quarters, Jabalpore, Madhya Pradesh: Published by the Council of Christian Education of the Methodist Church in Southern Asia, 1980.

Shaw, A. J. Editor. *Christian Education*, Vol. XIV, 1-4 Quarters, Jabalpore, Madhya Pradesh: Published by the Council of Christian Education of the Methodist Church in Southern Asia, 1964.

Siejk, Kate. "Towards a Holistic Religious Education: Reflection and pedagogical Possiblities," in *Religious Education*, Vol. 89, No. 2, Spring 1994.

Sikes, Pat & Judith Everington. "Becoming a Religious Education Teacher: A Life History Approach," British Journal of Religious Education, Vol. 24, No.1, Autumn 2001.

Startin, R. J. and D.H. Webster. "Religious Education in Secondary School: The Initial year of Teaching," *British Journal of Religious Education*, Vol. 18, No. 2, Spring 1996.

Stonehouse, Catherine. "Child Theology Matters: Offering Guidance for Practice of Christian Nurture," *Dharma Deepika: A South Asian Journal of Missiological Research*, Issue 28, Vol. 12, No. 2 July-December 2008.

Streak, Danilo. "The Quest for People Oriented Christian Education," *Educator*, Vol.1, 1994.

Thomas, Theo. "Education for Community – a Christian Perspective," *Christian Education Journal* Vol. LIV, 3rd quarter, September 1975.

Thornton, Kevin Mott. "Language, dualism, and experiential Religious Education: A critical appraisal of the debate between Adrian Thatcher and the authors of new Methods in Religious Education teaching," *British Journal of Religious Education*, Vol.18, No.3, Summer 1996.

Watson, Jacqueline. "Educating for Citizenship – Emerging Relationship between Religious Education and Citizenship Education," *British Journal of Religious Education*, Vol. 26, No. 3, September 2004.

Westerhoff, John. 'Formation, Education, Instruction," in *Religious Education*, Vol. 82, No. 4, Fall 1987.

White, Keith J. "Insights into Child Theology through the life and work of Pandita Ramabai," *Dharma Deepika: A South Asian Journal of Missiological Research*, Issue 28, Vol.12, No.2 July-December 2008.

Willmer, Haddon. "Child Theology and Christology in Matthew 18:1-5," *Dharma Deepika: A South Asian Journal of Missiological Research*, Issue 28, Vol.12, No. 2 July-December 2008.

World Council of Churches, "Education for Liberation and Community," *Christian Education Journal*, Vol. LIV, 3rd quarter, September 1975.

Wright, Andrew., "The Contours of Critical Religious Education: Knowledge, Wisdom, Truth," *British Journal of Religious Education*, Vol. 25, No. 4, Autumn 2003.

Zinger, Ronald Lee. "The Formation and Transformation of Moral impulse," *Journal of Moral Education*, Vol. 28. No. 4, December 1999.

Unpublished articles

Best, G.M. "John Wesley and A Christian Education", An unpublished paper, 2003. (7 pages)

_________ . "Susanna Wesley's Views on Education", An unpublished paper, 2003. (3 pages)

_________ . "Wesley and Education", A paper presented at Lincoln College, Oxford, 4 May 2003. (18 pages)

_________ . Wesley, John. " Original hand written Letter to Mr. Joseph Benson, Headmaster of Kingsowood 1768 -1770 from Wycombe, London" received personally on the researchers visit on 11th May 2009 from the archivists of Present Kingswood School Bath near Bristol UK. See Appendix 'F'

Correspondence

Scott, David C., This quotation is taken from Dr. David Scott's correspondence with the author on 23.01.2016.

Webliography

http://www.amazon.com/***John- Wesley***-Library-Protestant-Thought/dp/0195028104

http://www.amazon.co.uk/***John- Wesley***-Burning-Roy-Hattersley/dp/0349116571

http://www.amazon.com/Pedagogy-Oppressed-***Paulo- Freire***/dp/0826412769

http://www.britannica.com/EBchecked/topic/639945/***John-Wesley***
http://www.brycchancarey.com/abolition/***wesley***.htm
http://www.education.miami.edu/ep/contemporaryed/***Paulo_Freire***/***paulo_freire***.html
http://www.godrules.net/library/***wesley***/***wesley***.htm
http://www.infed.org/thinkers/et-freir.htm
http://www.library.manchester.ac.uk/specialcollections/exhibitions/web/***johnwesley***
www.marxists.org/subject/education/***freire***/pedagogy/ch02.htm
http://*www.naic.edu/~pfreire*
http://www.***paulofreire***institute.org
http://www.***paulofreire***school.org
*http://*www.raptureme.com/resource/***wesley***/***john_wesley***.html
http://www.spartacus.schoolnet.co.uk/RE***wesley***.htm
*http://*www.***wesley***2003.org.uk
http//www.theopedia.com/***Wesleyan_Quadrilateral*** - 21k
http//www.wesley.nnu.edu/***wesleyan***_theology/theojrnl/16-20/20-01.htm - 59k

Appendix A

Susanna Wesley's Views on Education

[This is a part of paper written by Mr. Gary M. Best, the former Principal of Kingswood School at Bath, UK. He has authored quite a few articles and books on Wesleys in relation to wide range of issues/topics to encourage Wesleyans all over]

Susanna Wesley devised a system of religious training for all her children and her faith undoubtedly the biggest single influence on John Wesley. She had read the works of Richard Baxter, who stated: "Especially you, mothers, remember this; you are more with your children while they are little than their fathers, be you therefore still teaching them as soon as they are ever capable of learning.... What a deal of pains you are at with the bodies of children more than the fathers, and what do you suffer to bring them into the world; and will you not be with much pains for the saving of their souls?....Teach them, admonish them, watch over them, and give them no rest till you have brought them over to Christ." The following principles lay behind Susanna's upbringing of her children:

1. She recognized that humans are creatures of habit and so she wanted to get her children used to "a regular method of living" from babyhood.
2. She believed that humans were innately predisposed towards sinfulness so it was essential for her children to conquer and control their passions. Any wilful behaviour or childish tantrums had to be sternly dealt with. Children had to eat what they were given (and the family had to sit down together for meals so proper table manners were learnt) and learn never to shout for what they wanted (but make whispered requests instead). They had to be courteous to others, including servants. They had to play quietly so as not to disturb others. They had to seek permission before doing anything, even leaving the room.
3. Children respond best to praise. Every act of obedience "should be always commended, and frequently rewarded." If a child did something

wrong but the intention was good, that should be recognized "and the child with sweetness directed how to do better for the future." Charles Wesley reflected her views:

"We would persuade their hearts to obey;
With mildest zeal proceed;
And never take the harsher way
When love will do the deed."

4. There is nothing worse than a spoiled child. Parents should avoid the "foolish fondness" of not correcting their children. Though the world might judge them to be "kind and indulgent," they were "cruel parents" to allow their children to develop bad habits. Again, Charles Wesley reflected this in his hymns:

   "To time our every smile or frown
   To mark the bounds of good and ill:
   And beat the pride of nature down,
   And bend or break his rising will."

5. No sinful action "should ever pass unpunished." By physically punishing the child when very small, he or she child learnt to obey and then such physical punishment became quickly unnecessary. Just to raise the voice or an admonishing finger was sufficient. "By neglecting timely correction, they will contract a stubbornness and obstinancy which are hardly ever after conquered." She also warned: "Never correct your children to satisfy your passions, but out of sense of duty to reclaim them from their errors and to preserve your authority.... Be exceeding careful to let the measure of correction be proportionable to fault."
6. Once a parent had the right kind of relationship with his or her child and had the respect a parent deserved, then physical punishment became unnecessary and "a great many childish follies and inadvertencies may be passed by."
7. Forgiveness was essential and, once corrected, no child should again face words or further punishment for the offence they had committed. "If they amended, they should never again be upbraided with it afterwards." A parent should "make allowances for the weakness of their reason, and immaturity of their judgements."
8. Children should be encouraged to keep their promises, be honest in all they say, and admit any mistakes. If her children confessed "and promised to amend" they were not then punished for any offence.
9. Children should be encouraged to respect other people's property and "none suffered to invade the property of another in the smallest matter, whether it were but the value of a farthing or a pin." No one should borrow anything without the full consent of its owner.

10. It was essential to monitor with whom your children mixed. Bad habits, such as "a clownish accent and many rude ways" were easily transferred between children if left unobserved.
11. Home tuition offered a good means of educating children providing it was carefully structured. Her children were taught the Lord's Prayer "as soon as they could speak" and "to be still at family prayers". Once they were five years old, she taught her children six hours a day. The aim was to "prepare their minds (by accustoming them to think and learn) for further instruction". Moral and spiritual education was as important as reading, writing and arithmetic. Singing psalms and saying prayers were a regular feature of every day.
12. The personal example you set to your children was essential. Actions speak louder than words.

Susannah produced her own version of the Creed sometime shortly after the Epworth fire of 1709. It shows the nature of her own faith and the beliefs she shared with her children.

"**I believe in God**, one supreme, independent power, who is a Spirit infinitely wise, hold, good, just, true, unchangeable...**the Father**...of all things.... **Almighty**...boundless, incomprehensible, and eternal...the **Maker of Heaven and Earth**, of all things visible.... Not the least spire of grass, or most despicable insect, but bears the Divine signature.... **I believe in Jesus**...the promised Messiah, who was so long the hope and expectation of the Jews, the **Christ** or Anointed....[who revealed] the will of God of our salvation ... [and who was] in a state of equality with the Father being **His only Son...our Lord**...co-equal and co-essential with the Father.... **He was conceived by the Holy Ghost**...[making Him] infinitely pure and holy**.... Born of the Virgin Mary**, whose spotless purity no age of the Catholic Church hath presumed to question.... It was only as a man that He **suffered** those infirmities and calamities incident to human nature.... Indeed His whole life was one continual scene of misery. No sooner was He born, than He was persecuted by Herod, and forced to flee into Egypt, in the arms of a weak virgin, under the protection of a foster-father. And when He returned into His own country, He for thirty years lived in a low condition, probably employed in the mean trade of a carpenter, which made Him in the eyes of the world despicable, of no reputation....[As a preacher] He was hungry and athirst, often wearied with travelling from place to place. And though He went about doing good, and never sent anyone away from Him who needed relief without healing their diseases and casting out those evil spirits which afflicted them; yet He was despised, and rejected of men!... All His life he was a man of sorrow, and acquainted with grief; yet His greatest sufferings were **under Pontius Pilate**.... His soul was pressed with fear, horror and dejection.... He knew...inexpressible misery man had brought upon himself.... [He sustained in the Garden of Gethsemane] the whole weight of that grief and sorrow...for the sins of the whole world.... He must be betrayed by one disciple, denied by another, and forsaken by all.... He had to suffer in His body...[all that] the malice and rage of His enemies could inflict upon it.... Nor would they be satisfied till **He was crucified**...and that crown of thorns, which they platted and put on His head, ...expressed the scorn of His tormentors.... That blessed face, which angels rejoice to behold, they buffeted and spat upon... till wearied with their own barbarity, they...led Him away to crucifixion.... See with what cruel pleasure they nail His hands and feet to the infamous wood.... [Upon the cross] the measure of His sufferings is completed; and He... gave up His pure and spotless Soul into the hands of His Almighty Father.... He was truly **dead...and buried**... [and they] rolled a stone at the door of the sepulchre, and departed. **He descended into Hell...**[thus undergoing] the condition of a sinner of this world...not to suffer, but to triumph over principalities and powers, over the rulers of the kingdom of darkness.... **The third day He rose again from the dead**....[and therefore] Christians have ever since observed the Sabbath.... [on a Sunday to mark] His finishing the great work of man's [sic] redemption.... **He ascended into Heaven**...[after forty days] during which time He frequently appeared to His disciples, ate and drank with them, showed them His hands and His feet, which visibly retained the marks of His crucifixion, to convince them it was the same body which was nailed to the cross.... And when He had spoken to His disciples and blessed them, He parted from them and ascended into highest heaven, where He still remains, **and sitteth on the right hand of God, the Father Almighty**.... [which] signifies His exceeding great and infinite power and glory.... **From thence He shall come to judge the quick and dead.** All ... [will] be by Him judged according to what they have done on earth.... Those that have done well shall....remain forever with Him in eternal blessedness; and those that have done evil He shall condemn them to the kingdom of darkness, there to remain in insupportable misery for ever, with the Devil and His angels.... And so we must every one truly and heartily say **I believe in the Holy Ghost**...sanctifying our natures, illuminating our minds, rectifying our wills and affections...conveying grace into the soul... **the Holy Catholic Church**... [which] is composed of all congregations...who hold the faith of Jesus Christ and are obedient to His laws... **and the communion of saints**...who not only join in devotion with the Church triumphant above, but are...sent forth to minister... [to those still remaining] in this world.... Having the same promises and hopes of the forgiveness of sins through Jesus Christ...our bodies may rest in hopes of **the resurrection of the body**.... [But the resurrected body] shall differ greatly in its qualities... [and be] raised a spiritual body....to enjoy **the life everlasting**.... Here we see as in a glass – have dark and imperfect perceptions of God; but there we shall behold Him as He is, shall know as we are known...those dark and mysterious methods of Providence which here puzzle and confound the wisest heads...shall there be unriddled in a moment.... Our wills shall be no longer averse from God's.... [and] no pain or misery shall ever find admittance into that Heavenly Kingdom...."

Appendix B

John Wesley's Time-Table for Kingswood

Hour	Class 1	Class 2	Class 3	Class 4	Class 5	Class 6	Class 7	Class 8
7:00 AM		Manners of the Ancient Christians	Primitive Christianity	Pilgrim's Progress	Life of Mr. Haliburton	Life of Mr. De Renty	Law's Christian Perfection	Law's Serious Call
8:00 AM	Reading	English or Latin Grammar	English or Latin Grammar	Latin Grammar	Latin Grammar	Latin Grammar	Greek Grammar or Tully	Latin/Greek
9:00 AM	Reading	Do	Corderius or Historiae Select	Kempis or Cornelius Nepos	Erasmus Phaedrus or Sallust	Caesar Terence or Vell. Paterc.	Virgil alternate later. Greek test	Hebrew alternate
10:00 AM	Writing	Writing	Writing	Writing & Arithmetic	Arithmetic	Geography	Chronology	Rhetoric
1:00 & 2:00 PM	Reading	Construe & Parse	Corderius or History select	Kempis or Nepos	Erasmus & c	Caesar & c	Greek Grammar or Tully & Virgil	Latin Greek & Hebrew
3:00 PM	Do	Praelect Pueriles	Do	Do	Do	Roman Antiques	Greek Antiques	Hebrew Antiques
4:00 PM	Writing	Translation into English/Latin	Translation	Translation	Translation	Translation	Translation & Verses	Translation & Verses

Appendix C

John Wesley's picture on the side, Upper one is new Kingswood School in Bath
Below is original school in Kingswood village near Bristol

This is a Lincoln college where Wesley taught after M.A.

Appendix D

John Wesley's Original letter written to Mr. Joseph Benson Headmaster of Kingswood, 1768-1770 from Wycombe London on 7th November 1768. Importance of this letter lies in the statement that Wesley made to the Headmaster about Education: "But beware you be not swallowed up in books. An ounce of **love** is worth a pound of Knowledge." This letter was made available to the author while visiting the present Kingswood School by the archivists. (Only of its kind, established by John Wesley remains today), on 11th May 2009, Bath near Bristol UK.

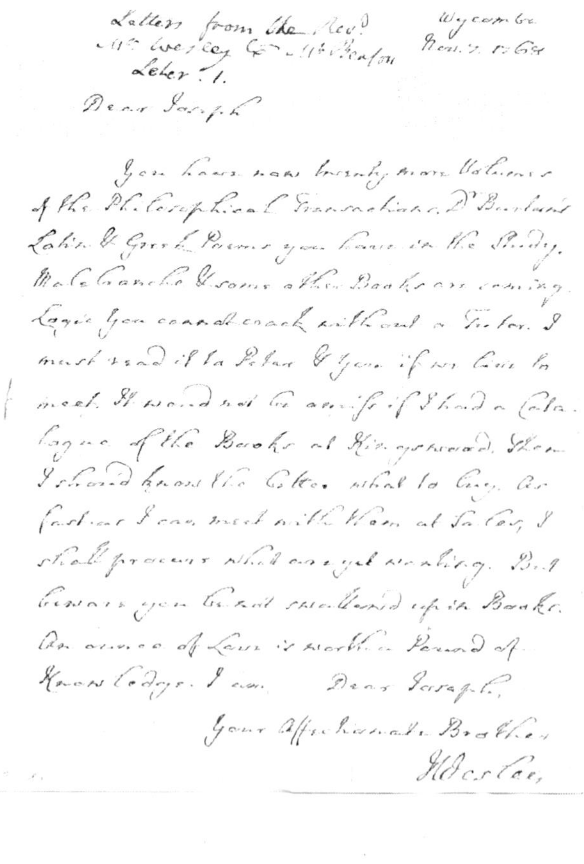

Letters from the Revd Mr Wesley to Mr Benson
Letter 1.

Wycombe
Nov. 7. 1768

Dear Joseph

You have now twenty more Volumes of the Philosophical Transactions. Dr Burton's Latin & Greek Poems you have in the Study. Malebranche & some other Books are coming. Logic you cannot crack without a Tutor. I must read it to Peter & you if we live to meet. It would not be amiss if I had a Catalogue of the Books at Kingswood. Then I should know the better what to buy. As fast as I can meet with them at Sales, I shall procure what are yet wanting. But beware you be not swallowed up in Books. An ounce of Love is worth a Pound of Knowledge. I am Dear Joseph,

Your Affectionate Brother
J Wesley

Typescript of the Hand Written Letter of John Wesley

Letter to Joseph Benson (HeadMaster of Kingswood, 1768-1770)

Wycombe
Nov. 7, 1768

Dear Joseph,

You have now twenty more volumes of the philosophical transactions. Dr. Burton's Latin and Greek Poems you have in the study. Malebranche and some other books are coming. Logic you cannot crack without a Tutor.... It would not be amiss if I had a catalogue of the books at Kingswood. Then I should know the better what to buy. As fast as I can meet with themat sales, I shall procure what are yet wanting. But beware you be not swolled up in books. An ounce of love is worth a pound of knowledge. I am Dear Joseph,

Your affectionately Brother
Sd/ John Wesley